Learning Ray
Flexible Distributed Python
for Machine Learning

Max Pumperla, Edward Oakes, and Richard Liaw

Beijing · Boston · Farnham · Sebastopol · Tokyo

Learning Ray

by Max Pumperla, Edward Oakes, and Richard Liaw

Copyright © 2023 Max Pumperla and O'Reilly Media, Inc. All rights reserved.

Published by O'Reilly Media, Inc., 1005 Gravenstein Highway North, Sebastopol, CA 95472.

O'Reilly books may be purchased for educational, business, or sales promotional use. Online editions are also available for most titles (*http://oreilly.com*). For more information, contact our corporate/institutional sales department: 800-998-9938 or *corporate@oreilly.com*.

Acquisitions Editor: Jessica Haberman	**Indexer:** Ellen Troutman-Zaig
Development Editor: Jeff Bleiel	**Interior Designer:** David Futato
Production Editor: Katherine Tozer	**Cover Designer:** Karen Montgomery
Copyeditor: Piper Editorial Consulting, LLC	**Illustrator:** Kate Dullea
Proofreader: Kim Wimpsett	

February 2023:   First Edition

Revision History for the First Edition

2023-02-13:   First Release

See *http://oreilly.com/catalog/errata.csp?isbn=9781098117221* for release details.

978-1-098-11722-1

[LSI]

Für Alma

Table of Contents

Foreword. xi

Preface. xiii

1. An Overview of Ray. 1
   What Is Ray?   2
      What Led to Ray?   2
      Ray's Design Principles   4
      Three Layers: Core, Libraries, and Ecosystem   5
   A Distributed Computing Framework   6
   A Suite of Data Science Libraries   8
      Ray AIR and the Data Science Workflow   8
      Data Processing with Ray Datasets   10
      Model Training   12
      Hyperparameter Tuning   16
      Model Serving   18
   A Growing Ecosystem   20
   Summary   21

2. Getting Started with Ray Core. 23
   An Introduction to Ray Core   24
      A First Example Using the Ray API   25
      An Overview of the Ray Core API   35
   Understanding Ray System Components   36
      Scheduling and Executing Work on a Node   36
      The Head Node   39
      Distributed Scheduling and Execution   39

A Simple MapReduce Example with Ray   41
   Mapping and Shuffling Document Data   43
   Reducing Word Counts   45
Summary   47

3. Building Your First Distributed Application. 49
Introducing Reinforcement Learning   49
Setting Up a Simple Maze Problem   50
Building a Simulation   55
Training a Reinforcement Learning Model   59
Building a Distributed Ray App   62
Recapping RL Terminology   66
Summary   67

4. Reinforcement Learning with Ray RLlib. 69
An Overview of RLlib   70
Getting Started with RLlib   71
   Building a Gym Environment   71
   Running the RLlib CLI   73
   Using the RLlib Python API   75
Configuring RLlib Experiments   82
   Resource Configuration   83
   Rollout Worker Configuration   83
   Environment Configuration   84
Working with RLlib Environments   85
   An Overview of RLlib Environments   85
   Working with Multiple Agents   86
   Working with Policy Servers and Clients   90
Advanced Concepts   93
   Building an Advanced Environment   94
   Applying Curriculum Learning   95
   Working with Offline Data   97
   Other Advanced Topics   98
Summary   99

5. Hyperparameter Optimization with Ray Tune. 101
Tuning Hyperparameters   102
   Building a Random Search Example with Ray   102
   Why Is HPO Hard?   104
An Introduction to Tune   105
   How Does Tune Work?   106

    Configuring and Running Tune   110
   Machine Learning with Tune   115
    Using RLlib with Tune   115
    Tuning Keras Models   116
   Summary   119

6. Data Processing with Ray.. 121
   Ray Datasets   122
    Ray Datasets Basics   123
    Computing Over Ray Datasets   126
    Dataset Pipelines   127
    Example: Training Copies of a Classifier in Parallel   130
   External Library Integrations   134
   Building an ML Pipeline   136
   Summary   138

7. Distributed Training with Ray Train...................................... 139
   The Basics of Distributed Model Training   139
   Introduction to Ray Train by Example   141
    Predicting Big Tips in NYC Taxi Rides   141
    Loading, Preprocessing, and Featurization   142
    Defining a Deep Learning Model   143
    Distributed Training with Ray Train   144
    Distributed Batch Inference   147
   More on Trainers in Ray Train   148
    Migrating to Ray Train with Minimal Code Changes   150
    Scaling Out Trainers   152
    Preprocessing with Ray Train   153
    Integrating Trainers with Ray Tune   154
    Using Callbacks to Monitor Training   156
   Summary   156

8. Online Inference with Ray Serve.. 157
   Key Characteristics of Online Inference   158
    ML Models Are Compute Intensive   158
    ML Models Aren't Useful in Isolation   159
   An Introduction to Ray Serve   160
    Architectural Overview   160
    Defining a Basic HTTP Endpoint   161
    Scaling and Resource Allocation   163
    Request Batching   165

      Multimodel Inference Graphs   166
    End-to-End Example: Building an NLP-Powered API   170
      Fetching Content and Preprocessing   172
      NLP Models   172
      HTTP Handling and Driver Logic   173
      Putting It All Together   175
    Summary   176

9. Ray Clusters. **179**
    Manually Creating a Ray Cluster   180
    Deployment on Kubernetes   182
      Setting Up Your First KubeRay Cluster   183
      Interacting with the KubeRay Cluster   184
      Exposing KubeRay   186
      Configuring KubeRay   187
      Configuring Logging for KubeRay   189
    Using the Ray Cluster Launcher   190
      Configuring Your Ray Cluster   190
      Using the Cluster Launcher CLI   191
      Interacting with a Ray Cluster   191
    Working with Cloud Clusters   192
      AWS   192
      Using Other Cloud Providers   193
    Autoscaling   194
    Summary   194

10. Getting Started with the Ray AI Runtime. **195**
    Why Use AIR?   195
    Key AIR Concepts by Example   197
      Ray Datasets and Preprocessors   198
      Trainers   199
      Tuners and Checkpoints   201
      Batch Predictors   203
      Deployments   204
    Workloads That Are Suited for AIR   207
      AIR Workload Execution   209
      AIR Memory Management   211
      AIR Failure Model   212
      Autoscaling AIR Workloads   213
    Summary   213

11. Ray's Ecosystem and Beyond. 215
    A Growing Ecosystem   216
        Data Loading and Processing   216
        Model Training   218
        Model Serving   222
        Building Custom Integrations   225
        An Overview of Ray's Integrations   226
    Ray and Other Systems   227
        Distributed Python Frameworks   227
        Ray AIR and the Broader ML Ecosystem   228
        How to Integrate AIR into Your ML Platform   230
    Where to Go from Here?   231
    Summary   232

Index. 235

Foreword

For the past decade, the computation demands of machine learning and data applications have vastly outgrown the capabilities of a single server or a single processor, including hardware accelerators such as GPUs and TPUs. This trend leaves us no choice but to distribute these applications. Unfortunately, building such distributed applications is notoriously difficult.

Over the past few years, Ray has emerged as the framework of choice to simplify the development of such applications. Ray includes a flexible core and a set of powerful libraries that enable the developers to easily scale a variety of workloads, including training, hyperparameter tuning, reinforcement learning, model serving, and batch processing of unstructured data. Ray is one of the most popular open source projects and has been used by thousands of companies to implement everything from machine learning platforms to recommendation systems, fraud detection, and training some of the largest models, including Open AI's ChatGPT.

In this book, Max Pumperla, Edward Oakes, and Richard Liaw have done an outstanding job in providing a gentle and comprehensive introduction to Ray and its libraries using easy to follow examples. At the end of this book, you will master the key concepts and abstractions in Ray and be able to develop and quickly scale end-to-end machine learning applications from your laptop to large on-premise clusters or to the cloud.

— Ion Stoica
Cofounder of Anyscale and Databricks, and
Professor, UC Berkeley Berkeley, California
January 2023

Preface

Distributed computing is a fascinating topic. Looking back at the early days of computing, one can't help but be impressed by the fact that so many companies today distribute their workloads across clusters of computers. It's impressive that we have figured out efficient ways to do so, but scaling out is also becoming more and more of a necessity. Individual computers keep getting faster, and yet our need for large-scale computing keeps exceeding what single machines can do.

Recognizing that scaling is both a necessity and a challenge, Ray aims to make distributed computing simple for developers. It makes distributed computing accessible to nonexperts and makes it possible to scale your Python scripts across multiple nodes fairly easily. Ray is good at scaling both *data- and compute-heavy workloads*, such as data preprocessing and model training—and it explicitly targets machine learning (ML) workloads with the need to scale. While it is possible today to scale these two types of workloads without Ray, you would likely have to use different APIs and distributed systems for each. And managing several distributed systems can be messy and inefficient in many ways.

The addition of the Ray AI Runtime (AIR) with the release of Ray 2.0 in August 2022 increased the support for complex ML workloads in Ray even further. AIR is a collection of libraries and tools that make it easy to build and deploy end-to-end ML applications in a single distributed system. With AIR, even the most complex workflows can usually be expressed as a *single Python script*. That means you can run your programs locally first, which can make a big difference in terms of debugging and development speed.

Data scientists benefit from Ray because they can rely on a growing ecosystem of Ray ML libraries and third-party integrations. Ray AIR helps you to quickly prototype ideas and go more easily from development to production. Unlike many other distributed systems, Ray has native support for GPUs as well, which can be particularly important to roles like ML engineers. To support data engineers, Ray also has tight integrations with tools like Kubernetes and can be deployed in multicloud setups.

And you can use it as a unified compute layer to provide scaling, fault tolerance, scheduling, and orchestration of your workloads. In other words, it's well worth investing in *learning Ray* for a variety of roles.

Who Should Read This Book

It's likely that you picked up this book because you're interested in some aspects of Ray. Maybe you're a distributed systems engineer who wants to know how Ray's engine works. You might also be a software developer interested in picking up a new technology. Or you could be a data engineer who wants to evaluate how Ray compares to similar tools. You could also be a machine learning practitioner or data scientist who needs to find ways to scale experiments.

No matter your concrete role, the common denominator to get the most out of this book is to feel comfortable programming in Python. This book's examples are written in Python, and an intermediate knowledge of the language is a requirement. Explicit is better than implicit, as you know full well as a Pythonista. So, let us be explicit by saying that knowing Python implies to me that you know how to use the command line on your system, how to get help when stuck, and how to set up a programming environment on your own.

If you've never worked with distributed systems before, that's OK. We cover all the basics you need to get started with that in the book. On top of that, you can run most code examples presented here on your laptop. Covering the basics means that we can't go into too much detail about distributed systems. This book is ultimately focused on application developers using Ray, specifically for data science and ML.

For the later chapters of this book, you'll need some familiarity with ML, but we don't expect you to have worked in the field. In particular, you should have a basic understanding of the ML paradigm and how it differs from traditional programming. You should also know the basics of using NumPy and Pandas. Also, you should at least feel comfortable *reading* examples using the popular TensorFlow and PyTorch libraries. It's enough to follow the flow of the code, on the API level, but you don't need to know how to write your own models. We cover examples using both dominant deep learning libraries (TensorFlow and PyTorch) to illustrate how you can use Ray for ML workloads, regardless of your preferred framework.

We cover a lot of ground in advanced ML topics, but the main focus is on Ray as a technology and how to use it. The ML examples we discuss might be new to you and could require a second reading, but you can still focus on Ray's API and how to use it in practice. Knowing the requirements, here's what you might get out of this book:

- If you are a data scientist, Ray will open up new ways for you to think about and build distributed ML applications. You will know how to do hyperparameter selection for your experiments at scale, gain practical knowledge on large-scale model training, and get to know a state-of-the-art reinforcement learning library.
- If you are a data engineer, you will learn to use Ray Datasets for large-scale data ingesting, how to improve your pipelines by leveraging tools such as Dask on Ray, and how to effectively deploy models at scale.
- If you are an engineer, you will understand how Ray works under the hood, how to run and scale Ray Clusters in the cloud, and how Ray can be used to build applications that integrate with projects you know.

You can learn all of these topics regardless of your role, of course. Our hope is that by the end of this book, you will have learned to appreciate Ray for all its strengths.

Goals of This Book

This book was written primarily for readers who are new to Ray and want to get the most out of it quickly. We chose the material in such a way that you will understand the core ideas behind Ray and learn to use its main building blocks. Having read it, you will feel comfortable navigating more complex topics on your own that go beyond this introduction.

We should also be clear about what this book is not. It's not built to give you the most information possible, like API references or definitive guides. It's also not crafted to help you tackle concrete tasks, like how-to guides or cookbooks do. This book is focused on learning and understanding Ray and giving you interesting examples to start with.

Software develops and deprecates quickly, but the fundamental concepts underlying software often remain stable even across major release cycles. We're trying to strike a balance here between conveying ideas and providing you with concrete code examples. The ideas you find in this book will ideally remain useful even when the code eventually needs updating.

While Ray's documentation keeps getting better, we do believe that books can offer qualities that are difficult to match in a project's documentation. Since you're reading these lines, we realize we might be knocking down open doors with this statement. But some of the best tech books we know spark interest in a project and make you want to dig through terse API references that you'd never have touched otherwise. We hope this is one of those books.

Navigating This Book

We organized this book to guide you naturally from core concepts to more sophisticated topics of Ray. Many of the ideas explained come with example code that you can find in the book's GitHub repo (*https://oreil.ly/learning_ray_repo*).

In a nutshell, the first three chapters of the book teach the basics of Ray as a distributed Python framework with practical examples. Chapters 4 to 10 introduce Ray's high-level libraries and show how to build applications with them. The last chapter gives you a conclusive overview of Ray's ecosystem and shows you where to go next. Here's what you can expect from each chapter:

Chapter 1, *"An Overview of Ray"*
> Introduces you to Ray as a system composed of three layers: its core, its ML libraries, and its ecosystem. You'll run your first examples with Ray's libraries in this chapter to give you a glimpse of what you can do with Ray.

Chapter 2, *"Getting Started with Ray Core"*
> Walks you through the foundations of the Ray project, namely, its core API. It also discusses how Ray tasks and actors naturally extend from Python functions and classes. You will also learn about Ray's system components and how they work together.

Chapter 3, *"Building Your First Distributed Application"*
> Guides you through implementing a distributed reinforcement learning application with Ray Core. You will implement this app from scratch and see Ray's flexibility in distributing your Python code in action.

Chapter 4, *"Reinforcement Learning with Ray RLlib"*
> Gives you a quick introduction to reinforcement learning and shows how Ray implements important concepts in RLlib. After building some examples together, we'll also dive into more advanced topics like curriculum learning or working with offline data.

Chapter 5, *"Hyperparameter Optimization with Ray Tune"*
> Covers why efficiently tuning hyperparameters is hard, how Ray Tune works conceptually, and how you can use it in practice for your machine learning projects.

Chapter 6, *"Data Processing with Ray"*
> Introduces you to the Ray Datasets abstraction of Ray and how it fits into the landscape of other data processing systems. You will also learn how to work with third-party integrations such as Dask on Ray.

Chapter 7, "Distributed Training with Ray Train"
Provides you with the basics of distributed model training and shows you how to use Ray Train with ML frameworks like PyTorch. We also show you how to add custom preprocessors to your models, how to monitor training with callbacks, and how to tune the hyperparameters of your models with Tune.

Chapter 8, "Online Inference with Ray Serve"
Teaches you the basics of exposing your trained ML models as API endpoints that can be queried from anywhere. We discuss how Ray Serve addresses the challenges of online inference, cover its architecture, and show you how to use it in practice.

Chapter 9, "Ray Clusters"
Discusses how you configure, launch, and scale Ray Clusters for your applications. You'll learn about Ray's Cluster launcher CLI and autoscaler, as well as how to set up clusters in the cloud. We'll also show you how to deploy Ray on Kubernetes and with other cluster managers.

Chapter 10, "Getting Started with the Ray AI Runtime"
Introduces you to Ray AIR, a unified toolkit for your ML workloads that offers many third-party integrations for model training or accessing custom data sources.

Chapter 11, "Ray's Ecosystem and Beyond"
Gives you an overview of the many interesting extensions and integrations that Ray has attracted over the years.

How to Use the Code Examples

You can find all the code for this book in its GitHub repository (*https://oreil.ly/learn ing_ray_repo*). In the GitHub repo you'll find a *notebook* folder with notebooks for each chapter. We built the examples in such a way that you can either type along as you read or follow the main text and run the code from GitHub at another time. The choice is yours.

For the examples we assume that you have Python 3.7 or later installed. At the time of this writing, support for Python 3.10 for Ray is experimental, so we can currently only recommend a Python version no later than 3.9. All code examples assume that you have Ray installed, and each chapter adds its own specific requirements. The examples have been tested on Ray version 2.2.0, and we recommend that you stick to this version for the whole book.

Conventions Used in This Book

The following typographical conventions are used in this book:

Italic

 Indicates new terms, URLs, email addresses, filenames, and file extensions.

`Constant width`

 Used for program listings, as well as within paragraphs to refer to program elements such as variable or function names, databases, data types, environment variables, statements, and keywords.

`Constant width bold`

 Shows commands or other text that should be typed literally by the user.

<Text in angle brackets>

 Should be replaced with user-supplied values or by values determined by context.

 This element signifies a general note.

 This element indicates a warning or caution.

Using Code Examples

Supplemental material (code examples, exercises, etc.) is available for download at *https://oreil.ly/learning_ray_repo*.

If you have a technical question or a problem using the code examples, please send email to *bookquestions@oreilly.com*.

This book is here to help you get your job done. In general, if example code is offered with this book, you may use it in your programs and documentation. You do not need to contact us for permission unless you're reproducing a significant portion of the code. For example, writing a program that uses several chunks of code from this book does not require permission. Selling or distributing examples from O'Reilly books does require permission. Answering a question by citing this book and quoting example code does not require permission. Incorporating a significant amount of example code from this book into your product's documentation does require permission.

We appreciate, but generally do not require, attribution. An attribution usually includes the title, author, publisher, and ISBN. For example: "*Learning Ray* by Max Pumperla, Edward Oakes, and Richard Liaw (O'Reilly). Copyright 2023 Max Pumperla and O'Reilly Media, Inc., 978-1-098-11722-1."

If you feel your use of code examples falls outside fair use or the permission given above, feel free to contact us at *permissions@oreilly.com*.

O'Reilly Online Learning

 For more than 40 years, *O'Reilly Media* has provided technology and business training, knowledge, and insight to help companies succeed.

Our unique network of experts and innovators share their knowledge and expertise through books, articles, and our online learning platform. O'Reilly's online learning platform gives you on-demand access to live training courses, in-depth learning paths, interactive coding environments, and a vast collection of text and video from O'Reilly and 200+ other publishers. For more information, visit *http://oreilly.com*.

How to Contact Us

Please address comments and questions concerning this book to the publisher:

O'Reilly Media, Inc.
1005 Gravenstein Highway North
Sebastopol, CA 95472
800-998-9938 (in the United States or Canada)
707-829-0515 (international or local)
707-829-0104 (fax)

We have a web page for this book, where we list errata, examples, and any additional information. You can access this page at *https://oreil.ly/learning-ray*.

Email *bookquestions@oreilly.com* to comment or ask technical questions about this book.

For news and information about our books and courses, visit *https://oreilly.com*.

Find us on LinkedIn: *https://linkedin.com/company/oreilly-media*.

Follow us on Twitter: *https://twitter.com/oreillymedia*.

Watch us on YouTube: *https://youtube.com/oreillymedia*.

Acknowledgments

We'd like to acknowledge the whole team at O'Reilly for helping us make this book possible. In particular, we'd like to thank our tireless editor, Jeff Bleiel, for invaluable input and feedback. Many thanks to Jess Haberman for many fruitful discussions and having an open mind in the early stages of the process. We'd also like to thank Katherine Tozer, Chelsea Foster, and Cassandra Furtado, among many others at O'Reilly.

Many thanks to all the reviewers for their valuable feedback and suggestions: Mark Saroufim, Kevin Ferguson, Adam Breindel, and Jorge Davila-Chacon. We'd also like to thank the many colleagues at Anyscale who helped us with the book in any capacity, including Sven Mika, Stephanie Wang, Antoni Baum, Christy Bergman, Dmitri Gekhtman, Zhe Zhang, and many others.

On top of that, we'd like to wholeheartedly thank the Ray contributors team and the community for their support and feedback, as well as many key stakeholders at Anyscale supporting this project.

I (Max) would also like to thank the team at Pathmind for their support in the early phases of the project, especially Chris Nicholson, who has been more helpful over the years than I could describe here. Special thanks go out to the Espresso Society in Winterhude for helping me turn coffee into books, and an increasing array of GPT-3-based tools for helping me finish half-sentences when the caffeine wore off. I would also like to express my gratitude to my family for their encouragement and patience. As always, none of this would have been possible without Anne, who always supports me when it counts—even if I take on one-too-many projects such as this one.

## CHAPTER 1

An Overview of Ray

One of the reasons we need efficient distributed computing is that we're collecting ever more data with great variety at increasing speeds. The storage systems, data processing, and analytics engines that have emerged in the past decade are crucial to the success of many companies. Interestingly, most "big data" technologies are built for and operated by (data) engineers who are in charge of data collection and processing tasks. The rationale is to free up data scientists to do what they're best at. As a data science practitioner, you might want to focus on training complex machine learning models, running efficient hyperparameter selection, building entirely new and custom models or simulations, or serving your models to showcase them.

At the same time, it might be *inevitable* to scale these workloads to a compute cluster. To do that, the distributed system of your choice needs to support all of these fine-grained "big compute" tasks, potentially on specialized hardware. Ideally, it also fits into the big data tool chain you're using and is fast enough to meet your latency requirements. In other words, distributed computing has to be powerful and flexible enough for complex data science workloads—and Ray can help you with that.

Python is likely the most popular language for data science today; it's certainly the one we find the most useful for our daily work. Python is now more than 30 years old, but it still has a growing and active community. The rich PyData ecosystem (*https://pydata.org*) is an essential part of a data scientist's toolbox. How can you make sure to scale out your workloads while still leveraging the tools you need? That's a difficult problem, especially since communities can't be forced to just toss their toolbox or programming language. That means distributed computing tools for data science have to be built for their existing community.

What Is Ray?

What we like about Ray is that it checks all these boxes. It's a flexible distributed computing framework built for the Python data science community.

Ray is easy to get started and keeps simple things simple. Its core API is as lean as it gets and helps you reason effectively about the distributed programs you want to write. You can efficiently parallelize Python programs on your laptop and run the code you tested locally on a cluster practically without any changes. Its high-level libraries are easy to configure and can seamlessly be used together. Some of them, like Ray's reinforcement learning library, would likely have a bright future as standalone projects, distributed or not. While Ray's core is built in C++, it's been a Python-first framework since day one,[1] integrates with many important data science tools, and can count on a growing ecosystem.

Distributed Python is not new, and Ray is not the first framework in this space (nor will it be the last), but it is special in what it has to offer. Ray is particularly strong when you combine several of its modules and have custom, machine learning–heavy workloads that would be difficult to implement otherwise. It makes distributed computing easy enough to run your complex workloads flexibly by leveraging the Python tools you know and want to use. In other words, by *learning Ray* you get to know *flexible distributed Python for machine learning*. And showing you how is what this book is all about.

In this chapter you'll get a first glimpse of what Ray can do for you. We will discuss the three layers that make up Ray: its core engine, high-level libraries, and ecosystem. Throughout the chapter we'll first show you code examples to give you a feel for Ray. You can view this chapter as a quick preview of the book; we defer any in-depth treatment of Ray's APIs and components to later chapters.

What Led to Ray?

Programming distributed systems is hard. It requires specific knowledge and experience you might not have. Ideally, such systems get out of your way and provide abstractions to let you focus on your job. But in practice, as Joel Spolsky notes (*https://oreil.ly/mpzSe*), "all nontrivial abstractions, to some degree, are leaky," and getting clusters of computers to do what you want is undoubtedly difficult. Many software systems require resources that far exceed what single servers can do. Even if one server were enough, modern systems need to be failsafe and provide features

---

1 By "Python-first" we mean that all higher-level libraries are written in Python and that the development of new features is driven by the needs of the Python community. Having said this, Ray has been designed to support multiple language bindings and, for example, comes with a Java API. So, it's not out of the question that Ray might support other languages that are important to the data science ecosystem.

like high availability. That means your applications might have to run on multiple machines, or even datacenters, just to make sure they're running reliably.

Even if you're not too familiar with machine learning (ML) or artificial intelligence (AI) more generally, you must have heard of recent breakthroughs in the field. To name just two, systems like Deepmind's AlphaFold (*https://oreil.ly/RFaMa*) for solving the protein folding problem and OpenAI's Codex (*https://oreil.ly/vGnyh*) for helping software developers with the tedium of their jobs, have made the news lately. You might also have heard that ML systems generally require large amounts of data to be trained, and that ML models tend to get larger. OpenAI has shown exponential growth in compute needed to train AI models in their paper "AI and Compute" (*https://oreil.ly/7huR_*). The number of operations needed for AI systems in their study is measured in petaflops (thousands of trillions of operations per second) and has been *doubling every 3.4 months* since 2012.

Compare this to Moore's law,[2] which states that the number of transistors in computers would double every two years. Even if you're bullish on Moore's law, you can see how there's a clear need for distributed computing in ML. You should also understand that many tasks in ML can be naturally decomposed to run in parallel. So, why not speed things up if you can?[3]

Distributed computing is generally perceived as hard. But why is that? Shouldn't it be realistic to find good abstractions to run your code on clusters without having to constantly think about individual machines and how they interoperate? What if we specifically focused on AI workloads?

Researchers at RISELab (*https://oreil.ly/1zsMj*) at UC Berkeley created Ray to address these questions. They were looking for efficient ways to speed up their workloads by distributing them. The workloads they had in mind were quite flexible in nature and didn't fit into the frameworks available at the time. RISELab also wanted to build a system that took care of how the work was distributed. With reasonable default behaviors in place, researchers should be able to focus on their work, regardless of the specifics of their compute cluster. And ideally they should have access to all their favorite tools in Python. For this reason, Ray was built with an emphasis on high-performance and heterogeneous workloads.[4] To understand these points better, let's have a closer look at Ray's design philosophy.

---

2 Moore's law held for a long time, but there might be signs that it's slowing down. Some even say it's dead (*https://oreil.ly/fhPg-*). We're not here to argue these points. What's important is not that our computers generally keep getting faster, but the relation to the amount of compute we need.

3 There are many ways to speed up ML training, from basic to sophisticated. For instance, we'll spend a considerable amount of time elaborating on distributed data processing in Chapter 6 and distributed model training in Chapter 7.

4 Anyscale (*https://www.anyscale.com*), the company behind Ray, is building a managed Ray platform and offers hosted solutions for your Ray applications.

Ray's Design Principles

Ray is built with several design principles in mind. Its API is designed for simplicity and generality, and its compute model aims for flexibility. Its system architecture is designed for performance and scalability. Let's look at each of these in more detail.

Simplicity and abstraction

Ray's API not only banks on simplicity, it's also intuitive to pick up (as you'll see in Chapter 2). It doesn't matter whether you want to use all the CPU cores on your laptop or leverage all the machines in your cluster. You might have to change a line of code or two, but the Ray code you use stays essentially the same. And as with any good distributed system, Ray manages task distribution and coordination under the hood. That's great, because you're not bogged down by reasoning about the mechanics of distributed computing. A good abstraction layer allows you to focus on your work, and we think Ray has done a great job of giving you one.

Since Ray's API is so generally applicable and *pythonic*, it's easy to integrate with other tools. For instance, Ray actors can call into or be called by existing distributed Python workloads. In that sense, Ray makes for good "glue code" for distributed workloads, too, as it's performant and flexible enough to communicate between different systems and frameworks.

Flexibility and heterogeneity

For AI workloads, in particular when dealing with paradigms like reinforcement learning, you need a flexible programming model. Ray's API is designed to make it easy to write flexible and composable code. Simply put, if you can express your workload in Python, you can distribute it with Ray. Of course, you still need to make sure you have enough resources available and be mindful of what you want to distribute. But Ray doesn't limit what you can do with it.

Ray is also flexible when it comes to *heterogeneity* of computations. For instance, let's say you work on a complex simulation. Simulations can usually be decomposed into several tasks or steps. Some of these steps might take hours to run, others just a few milliseconds, but they always need to be scheduled and executed quickly. Sometimes a single task in a simulation can take a long time, but other, smaller tasks should be able to run in parallel without blocking it. Also, subsequent tasks may depend on the outcome of an upstream task, so you need a framework to allow for *dynamic execution* that deals well with task dependencies. Ray gives you full flexibility when running heterogeneous workflows like that.

You also need to ensure you are flexible in your resource usage, and Ray supports heterogeneous hardware. For instance, some tasks might have to run on a GPU, while others run best on a couple of CPU cores. Ray provides you with that flexibility.

Speed and scalability

Another of Ray's design principles is the speed at which Ray executes its tasks. It can handle millions of tasks per second, and you incur very low latencies with it. Ray is built to execute its tasks with just milliseconds of latency.

For a distributed system to be fast, it also needs to scale well. Ray is efficient at distributing and scheduling your tasks across your compute cluster. And it does so in a fault-tolerant way, too. As you'll learn in detail in Chapter 9, Ray Clusters support *autoscaling* to support highly elastic workloads. Ray's autoscaler tries to launch or stop machines in your cluster to match the current demand. This helps both to minimize costs and to ensure that your cluster has enough resources to run your workload.

In distributed systems, it's not a question of if, but when, things will go wrong. A machine might have an outage, abort a task, or simply go up in flames.[5] In any case, Ray is built to recover quickly from failures, which contributes to its overall speed.

As we haven't talked about Ray's architecture (Chapter 2 will introduce you to it), we can't tell you how these design principles are realized just yet. Let's instead shift our attention to what Ray can do for you in practice.

Three Layers: Core, Libraries, and Ecosystem

Now that you know why Ray was built and what its creators had in mind, let's look at the three layers of Ray. This presentation is not the only way to slice it, but it's the way that makes most sense for this book:

- A low-level, distributed computing framework for Python with a concise core API and tooling for cluster deployment called Ray Core.[6]
- A set of high-level libraries built and maintained by the creators of Ray. This includes the so-called Ray AIR to use these libraries with a unified API in common machine learning workloads.
- A growing ecosystem of integrations and partnerships with other notable projects that span many aspects of the first two layers.

There's a lot to unpack here, and we'll look into each of these layers individually in the remainder of this chapter.

---

5 This might sound drastic, but it's not a joke. To name just one example, in March 2021 a French datacenter powering millions of websites burned down completely (*https://oreil.ly/Nl9_o*). If your whole cluster burns down, we're afraid Ray can't help you.

6 This is a Python book, so we'll exclusively focus on Python, but you should know that Ray also has a Java API, which is less mature than its Python equivalent at this point.

You can imagine Ray's core engine with its API at the center of things, on which everything else builds. Ray's data science libraries build on top of Ray Core and provide a domain-specific abstraction layer.[7] In practice, many data scientists will use these libraries directly, while ML or platform engineers might rely heavily on building their tools as extensions of the Ray Core API. Ray AIR can be seen as an umbrella that links Ray libraries and offers a consistent framework for dealing with common AI workloads. And the growing number of third-party integrations for Ray is another great entry point for experienced practitioners. Let's look into each one of the layers one by one.

A Distributed Computing Framework

At its core, Ray is a distributed computing framework. We'll provide you with just the basic terminology here and talk about Ray's architecture in depth in Chapter 2. In short, Ray sets up and manages clusters of computers so that you can run distributed tasks on them. A Ray Cluster consists of nodes that are connected to each other via a network. You program against the so-called *driver*, the program root, which lives on the *head node*. The driver can run *jobs*, a collection of tasks, that are run on the nodes in the cluster. Specifically, the individual tasks of a job are run on *worker* processes on *worker nodes*. Figure 1-1 illustrates the basic structure of a Ray Cluster. Note that we're not concerned with communication between nodes just yet; this diagram merely shows the layout of a Ray Cluster.

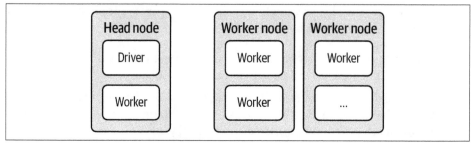

Figure 1-1. The basic components of a Ray Cluster

What's interesting is that a Ray Cluster can also be a *local cluster*, a cluster consisting of just your own computer. In this case, there's just one node, namely, the head node, which has the driver process and some worker processes. The default number of worker processes is the number of CPUs available on your machine.

---

7 One of the reasons so many libraries are built on top of Ray Core is that it's so lean and straightforward to reason about. One of the goals of this book is to inspire you to write your own applications, or even libraries, with Ray.

With that knowledge at hand, it's time to get your hands dirty and run your first local Ray Cluster. Installing Ray on any of the major operating systems should work seamlessly using pip:

```
pip install "ray[rllib, serve, tune]==2.2.0"
```

With a simple pip install ray, you will install just the basics of Ray. Since we want to explore some advanced features, we installed the "extras" rllib, serve, and tune, which we'll discuss in a bit.[8] Depending on your system configuration, you may not need the quotation marks in this installation command.

Next, go ahead and start a Python session. You could, for instance, use the ipython interpreter, which is often suitable for following simple examples. In your Python session you can now easily import and initialize Ray:

```
import ray
ray.init()
```

 If you don't feel like typing in the commands yourself, you can also jump into the Jupyter notebook for this chapter (*https://oreil.ly/j9ccz*) and run the code there. The choice is up to you, but in any case please remember to use Python version 3.7 or later.[9]

With those two lines of code, you've started a Ray Cluster on your local machine. This cluster can utilize all the cores available on your computer as workers. Right now your Ray Cluster doesn't do much, but that's about to change.

The init function you use to start the cluster is one of the six fundamental API calls that you will learn about in depth in Chapter 2. Overall, the *Ray Core API* is very accessible and easy to use. But since it is also a rather low-level interface, it takes time to build interesting examples with it. Chapter 2 has an extensive first example to get you started with the Ray Core API, and in Chapter 3 you'll see how to build a more interesting Ray application for reinforcement learning.

In the preceding code you didn't provide any arguments to the ray.init(...) function. If you wanted to run Ray on a "real" cluster, you'd have to pass more arguments to init. This init call is often called the *Ray Client*, and it is used to interactively connect to an existing Ray Cluster.[10] You can read more about using

---

8 We generally introduce dependencies in this book only when we need them, which should make it easier to follow along. In contrast, the notebooks on GitHub (*https://oreil.ly/j9ccz*) give you the option to install all dependencies up front so that you can focus on running the code instead.

9 At the time of this writing, there's no Python 3.10 support for Ray, so sticking to a version between 3.7 and 3.9 should work best to follow this book.

10 There are other means of interacting with Ray Clusters, such as the Ray Jobs CLI (*https://oreil.ly/XXnlW*).

the Ray Client to connect to your production clusters in the Ray documentation (*https://oreil.ly/nNhMt*).

Of course, if you've ever worked with compute clusters, you know there are many pitfalls and intricacies. For instance, you can deploy Ray applications on clusters hosted by cloud providers such as Amazon Web Services (AWS), Google Cloud Platform (GCP), or Microsoft Azure—and each choice needs good tooling for deployment and maintenance. You can also spin up a cluster on your own hardware or use tools such as Kubernetes to deploy your Ray Clusters. In Chapter 9 (following chapters with concrete Ray applications), we'll come back to the topic of scaling workloads with Ray Clusters.

Before moving on to Ray's higher-level libraries, let's briefly summarize the two foundational components of Ray as a distributed computation framework:

Ray Clusters
This component is in charge of allocating resources, creating nodes, and ensuring they are healthy. A good way to get started with Ray Clusters is its dedicated quick start guide (*https://oreil.ly/rBUil*).

Ray Core
Once your cluster is up and running, you use the Ray Core API to program against it. You can get started with Ray Core by following the official walkthrough (*https://oreil.ly/7r0Lv*) for this component.

A Suite of Data Science Libraries

Moving on to the second layer of Ray, in this section we'll briefly introduce all the data science libraries that Ray comes with. To do so, let's first take a bird's-eye view of what it means to do data science. Once you understand this context, it's much easier to review Ray's higher-level libraries and see how they can be useful to you.

Ray AIR and the Data Science Workflow

The somewhat elusive term "data science" (DS) has evolved quite a bit in recent years, and you can find many definitions of varying usefulness online.[11] To us, it's *the practice of gaining insights and building real-world applications by leveraging data.* That's quite a broad definition of an inherently practical and applied field that centers around building and understanding things. In that sense, describing practitioners of

---

11 We never liked the categorization of data science as an intersection of disciplines, like math, coding, and business. Ultimately, that doesn't tell you what practitioners *do*.

this field as "data scientists" is about as bad a misnomer as describing hackers as "computer scientists."[12]

In broad strokes, doing data science is an iterative process that entails requirements engineering, data collection and processing, building models and evaluating them, and deploying solutions. Machine learning is not necessarily part of this process but often is. If ML is involved, you can further specify some steps:

Data processing
> To train ML models, you need data in a format that your ML model understands. The process of transforming and selecting what data should be fed into your model is often called *feature engineering*. This step can be messy. You'll benefit a lot if you can rely on common tools to do the job.

Model training
> In ML you need to train your algorithms on data that got processed in the previous step. This includes selecting the right algorithm for the job, and it helps if you can choose from a wide variety.

Hyperparameter tuning
> Machine learning models have parameters that are tuned in the model training step. Most ML models also have another set of parameters called *hyperparameters* that can be modified prior to training. These parameters can heavily influence the performance of your resulting ML model and need to be tuned properly. There are good tools to help automate that process.

Model serving
> Trained models need to be deployed. To serve a model means to make it available to whomever needs access by whatever means necessary. In prototypes, you often use simple HTTP servers, but there are many specialized software packages for ML model serving.

This list is by no means exhaustive, and there's a lot more to be said about building ML applications.[13] However, it is true that these four steps are crucial for the success of a data science project using ML.

Ray has dedicated libraries for each of the four ML-specific steps we just listed. Specifically, you can take care of your data processing needs with *Ray Datasets*, run distributed model training with *Ray Train*, run your reinforcement learning

---

12 As a fun exercise, we recommend reading Paul Graham's famous "Hackers and Painters" essay (*https://oreil.ly/ZEDtU*) on this topic and replace "computer science" with "data science." What would hacking 2.0 be?

13 If you want to understand more about the holistic view of the data science process when building ML applications, *Building Machine Learning Powered Applications* by Emmanuel Ameisen (O'Reilly) is entirely dedicated to it.

workloads with *Ray RLlib*, tune your hyperparameters efficiently with *Ray Tune*, and serve your models with *Ray Serve*. And the way Ray is built, all these libraries are *distributed by design*, a point we can't stress enough.

What's more is that all of these steps are part of a process and are rarely tackled in isolation. Not only do you want all the libraries involved to seamlessly interoperate, it can also be a decisive advantage if you can work with a consistent API throughout the whole data science process. This is exactly what Ray AIR was built for: having a common runtime and API for your experiments and the ability to scale your workloads when you're ready. Figure 1-2 shows a quick overview of all the components of AIR.

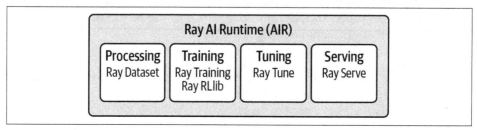

Figure 1-2. Ray AIR as an umbrella of all current data science libraries of Ray

While introducing the Ray AI Runtime API would be too much for this chapter (you can jump ahead to Chapter 10 for that), we'll introduce you to all the building blocks that feed into it. Let's go through each of Ray's DS libraries one by one.

Data Processing with Ray Datasets

The first high-level library of Ray we'll talk about is Ray Datasets. This library contains a data structure aptly called `Dataset`, a multitude of connectors for loading data from various formats and systems, an API for transforming such datasets, a way to build data processing pipelines with them, and many integrations with other data processing frameworks. The `Dataset` abstraction builds on the powerful Arrow framework (*https://arrow.apache.org*).[14]

To use Ray Datasets, you need to install Arrow for Python, for instance by running `pip install pyarrow`. The following simple example creates a distributed `Dataset` on your local Ray Cluster from a Python data structure. Specifically, you'll create a dataset from a Python dictionary containing a string `name` and an integer-valued `data` for 10,000 entries:

```
import ray
```

---

14 In Chapter 6 we will introduce you to the fundamentals of what makes Ray Datasets work, including its use of Arrow. For now, we want to focus on its API and concrete usage patterns.

```
items = [{"name": str(i), "data": i} for i in range(10000)]
ds = ray.data.from_items(items)   ❶
ds.show(5)   ❷
```

❶ Creating a Dataset by using from_items from the ray.data module.

❷ Printing the first five items of the Dataset.

To show a Dataset means to print some of its values. You should see precisely five elements on your command line, like this:

```
{'name': '0', 'data': 0}
{'name': '1', 'data': 1}
{'name': '2', 'data': 2}
{'name': '3', 'data': 3}
{'name': '4', 'data': 4}
```

Great, now you have some rows, but what can you do with that data? The Dataset API bets heavily on functional programming, as this paradigm is well suited for data transformations.

Even though Python 3 made a point of hiding some of its functional programming capabilities, you're probably familiar with functionality such as map, filter, flat_map, and others. If not, it's easy enough to pick up: map takes each element of your dataset and transforms it into something else, in parallel; filter removes data points according to a Boolean filter function; and the slightly more elaborate flat_map first maps values similarly to map, but then it also "flattens" the result. For instance, if map produced a list of lists, flat_map would flatten out the nested lists and give you just a list. Equipped with these three functional API calls,[15] let's see how easily you can transform your dataset ds:

```
squares = ds.map(lambda x: x["data"] ** 2)   ❶

evens = squares.filter(lambda x: x % 2 == 0)   ❷
evens.count()

cubes = evens.flat_map(lambda x: [x, x**3])   ❸
sample = cubes.take(10)   ❹
print(sample)
```

❶ We map each row of ds to only keep the square value of its data entry.

---

15 We'll elaborate more on this in later chapters, specifically in Chapter 6, but note that Ray Datasets is not meant as a general-purpose data processing library. Tools such as Spark have more mature and optimized support for large-scale data processing.

❷ Then we `filter` the `squares` to keep only even numbers (a total of five thousand elements).

❸ We then use `flat_map` to augment the remaining values with their respective cubes.

❹ To `take` a total of 10 values means to leave Ray and return a Python list with these values that we can print.

The drawback of `Dataset` transformations is that each step gets executed synchronously. In this example that is a nonissue, but for complex tasks that, for example, mix reading files and processing data, you would want an execution that can overlap individual tasks. `DatasetPipeline` does exactly that. Let's rewrite the previous example into a pipeline:

```
pipe = ds.window()  ❶
result = pipe\
    .map(lambda x: x["data"] ** 2)\
    .filter(lambda x: x % 2 == 0)\
    .flat_map(lambda x: [x, x**3])  ❷
result.show(10)
```

❶ You can turn a `Dataset` into a pipeline by calling `.window()` on it.

❷ Pipeline steps can be chained to yield the same result as before.

There's a lot more to be said about Ray Datasets, especially its integration with notable data processing systems, but we'll defer an in-depth discussion until Chapter 6.

Model Training

Moving on to the next set of libraries, let's look at the distributed training capabilities of Ray. For that, you have access to two libraries. One is dedicated to reinforcement learning specifically; the other one has a different scope and is aimed primarily at supervised learning tasks.

Reinforcement learning with Ray RLlib

Let's start with *Ray RLlib* for reinforcement learning (RL). This library is powered by the modern ML frameworks TensorFlow and PyTorch, and you can choose which one to use. Both frameworks seem to converge more and more conceptually, so you can pick the one you like most without losing much in the process. Throughout the book we use both TensorFlow and PyTorch examples so you can get a feel for both frameworks when using Ray.

For this section, go ahead and install TensorFlow with `pip install tensorflow` right now.[16] To run the code example, you also need to install the `gym` library with `pip install "gym==0.25.0"`.

One of the easiest ways to run examples with RLlib is to use the command-line tool `rllib`, which we already installed implicitly when we ran `pip install "ray[rllib]"`. Once you run more complex examples in Chapter 4, you will mostly rely on its Python API, but for now we want to get a first taste of running RL experiments with RLlib.

We'll look at a fairly classic control problem of balancing a pole on a cart. Imagine you have a pole like the one in Figure 1-3, fixed at a joint of a cart, and subject to gravity. The cart is free to move along a frictionless track, and you can manipulate the cart by giving it a push from the left or the right with a fixed force. If you do this well enough, the pole will remain in an upright position. For each time step the pole didn't fall over, we get a reward of 1. Collecting a high reward is our goal, and the question is whether we can teach a reinforcement learning algorithm to do this for us.

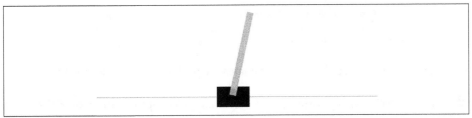

Figure 1-3. Controlling a pole attached to a cart by asserting force to the left or the right

Specifically, we want to train a reinforcement learning agent that can carry out two actions, namely, push to the left or to the right, observe what happens when interacting with the environment in that way, and learn from the experience by maximizing the reward.

To tackle this problem with Ray RLlib, we can use a so-called *tuned* example, which is a preconfigured algorithm that runs well for a given problem. You can run a tuned example with a single command. RLlib comes with many such examples, and you can list them all with `rllib example list`.

One of the available examples is `cartpole-ppo`, a tuned example that uses the PPO algorithm to solve the cart–pole problem, specifically, the `CartPole-v1` environment (*https://oreil.ly/YNxoz*) from OpenAI Gym. You can take a look at the configuration

---

16 If you're on a Mac, you'll have to install `tensorflow-macos`. In general, if you encounter any issues installing Ray or its dependencies on your system, please refer to the installation guide (*https://docs.ray.io/en/latest/ray-overview/installation.html*).

of this example by typing `rllib example get cartpole-ppo`, which will first download the example file from GitHub and then print its configuration. This configuration is encoded in YAML file format and reads as follows:

```
cartpole-ppo:
    env: CartPole-v1  ❶
    run: PPO  ❷
    stop:
        episode_reward_mean: 150  ❸
        timesteps_total: 100000
    config:  ❹
        framework: tf
        gamma: 0.99
        lr: 0.0003
        num_workers: 1
        observation_filter: MeanStdFilter
        num_sgd_iter: 6
        vf_loss_coeff: 0.01
        model:
            fcnet_hiddens: [32]
            fcnet_activation: linear
            vf_share_layers: true
        enable_connectors: True
```

❶ The `CartPole-v1` environment simulates the problem we just described.

❷ Use a powerful RL algorithm called Proximal Policy Optimization, or PPO.

❸ Once we reach a reward of 150, stop the experiment.

❹ PPO needs some RL-specific configuration to make it work for this problem.

The details of this configuration file don't matter much at this point, so don't get distracted by them. The important part is that you specify the `Cartpole-v1` environment and sufficient RL-specific configuration to ensure the training procedure works. Running this configuration doesn't require any special hardware and finishes in a matter of minutes. To train this example, you'll have to install the PyGame dependency with `pip install pygame` and then simply run:

```
rllib example run cartpole-ppo
```

If you run this, RLlib creates a named experiment and logs important metrics such as the `reward` or the `episode_reward_mean` for you. In the output of the training run, you should also see information about the machine (`loc`, meaning hostname and port), as well as the status of your training runs. If your run is `TERMINATED` but you've never seen a successfully `RUNNING` experiment in the log, something must have gone wrong. Here's a sample snippet of a training run:

```
+--------------------------------+----------+----------------+
| Trial name                     | status   | loc            |
|--------------------------------+----------+----------------|
| PPO_CartPole-v0_9931e_00000    | RUNNING  | 127.0.0.1:8683 |
+--------------------------------+----------+----------------+
```

When the training run finishes and things went well, you should see the following output:

```
Your training finished.
Best available checkpoint for each trial:
  <checkpoint-path>/checkpoint_<number>
```

You can now evaluate your trained algorithm from any checkpoint, for example, by running:

```
rllib evaluate <checkpoint-path>/checkpoint_<number> --algo PPO
```

Your local Ray checkpoint folder is *~/ray-results* by default. For the training configuration we used, your *<checkpoint-path>* should be of the form *~/ray_results/ cartpole-ppo/PPO_CartPole-v1_<experiment_id>*. During the training procedure, your intermediate and final model checkpoints get generated into this folder.

To evaluate the performance of your trained RL algorithm, you can now evaluate it *from checkpoint* by copying the command the previous example training run printed:

```
rllib evaluate <checkpoint-path>/checkpoint_<number> --algo PPO
```

Running this command will print evaluation results, namely, the rewards achieved by your trained RL algorithm on the CartPole-v1 environment.

There's much more that you can do with RLlib, and we'll cover more of it in Chapter 4. The point of this example was to show you how easily you can get started with RLlib and the rllib command-line tool, just by leveraging the example and evaluate commands.

Distributed training with Ray Train

Ray RLlib is dedicated to reinforcement learning, but what do you do if you need to train models for other types of machine learning, like supervised learning? You can use another Ray library for distributed training in this case: *Ray Train*. At this point, we don't have enough knowledge of frameworks such as TensorFlow to give you a concise and informative example for Ray Train. If you're interested in distributed training, you can jump ahead to Chapter 6.

Hyperparameter Tuning

Naming things is hard, but *Ray Tune*, which you can use to tune all sorts of parameters, hits the spot. It was built specifically to find good hyperparameters for machine learning models. The typical setup is as follows:

- You want to run an extremely computationally expensive training function. In ML, it's not uncommon to run training procedures that take days, if not weeks, but let's say you're dealing with just a couple of minutes.

- As a result of training, you compute a so-called objective function. Usually you want to either maximize your gains or minimize your losses in terms of performance of your experiment.

- The tricky bit is that your training function might depend on certain parameters, called hyperparameters, that influence the value of your objective function.

- You may have a hunch what individual hyperparameters should be, but tuning them all can be difficult. Even if you can restrict these parameters to a sensible range, it's usually prohibitive to test a wide range of combinations. Your training function is simply too expensive.

What can you do to efficiently sample hyperparameters and get "good enough" results on your objective? The field concerned with solving this problem is called *hyperparameter optimization* (HPO), and Ray Tune has an enormous suite of algorithms for tackling it. Let's look an example of Ray Tune used for the situation we just explained. The focus is yet again on Ray and its API, not on a specific ML task (which we simply simulate for now):

```python
from ray import tune
import math
import time


def training_function(config):         ❶
    x, y = config["x"], config["y"]
    time.sleep(10)
    score = objective(x, y)
    tune.report(score=score)           ❷


def objective(x, y):
    return math.sqrt((x**2 + y**2)/2)  ❸


result = tune.run(                     ❹
    training_function,
    config={
        "x": tune.grid_search([-1, -.5, 0, .5, 1]),   ❺
```

```
        "y": tune.grid_search([-1, -.5, 0, .5, 1])
    })

print(result.get_best_config(metric="score", mode="min"))
```

❶ Simulate an expensive training function that depends on two hyperparameters, x and y, read from a config.

❷ After sleeping for 10 seconds to simulate training and computing the objective, the score is reported to tune.

❸ The objective computes the mean of the squares of x and y and returns the square root of this term. This type of objective is fairly common in ML.

❹ Use tune.run to initialize hyperparameter optimization on our training_function.

❺ A key part is to provide a parameter space for x and y for tune to search over.

Notice how the output of this run is structurally similar to what you saw in the RLlib example. That's no coincidence, as RLlib (like many other Ray libraries) uses Ray Tune under the hood. If you look closely, you will see PENDING runs that wait for execution, as well as RUNNING and TERMINATED runs. Tune takes care of selecting, scheduling, and executing your training runs automatically.

Specifically, this Tune example finds the best possible choices of parameters x and y for a training_function with a given objective we want to minimize. Even though the objective function might look a little intimidating at first, since we compute the sum of squares of x and y, all values will be non-negative. That means the smallest value is obtained at x=0 and y=0, which evaluates the objective function to 0.

We do a so-called *grid search* over all possible parameter combinations. As we explicitly pass in 5 possible values for both x and y, that's a total of 25 combinations that get fed into the training function. Since we instruct training_function to sleep for 10 seconds, testing all combinations of hyperparameters sequentially would take more than 4 minutes total. Since Ray is smart about parallelizing this workload, this whole experiment took only about 35 seconds for us, but it might take much longer, depending on where you run it.

Now, imagine each training run would have taken several hours, and we'd have 20 instead of 2 hyperparameters. That makes grid search infeasible, especially if you don't have educated guesses on the parameter range. In such situations you'll have to use more elaborate HPO methods from Ray Tune, as discussed in Chapter 5.

Model Serving

The last of Ray's high-level libraries we'll discuss specializes in model serving and is simply called *Ray Serve*. To see an example of it in action, you need a trained ML model to serve. Luckily, nowadays, you can find many interesting models on the internet that have already been trained for you. For instance, Hugging Face has a variety of models available for you to download directly in Python. The model we'll use is a language model called *GPT-2* that takes text as input and produces text to continue or complete the input. For example, you can prompt a question and GPT-2 will try to complete it.

Serving such a model is a good way to make it accessible. You may not know how to load and run a TensorFlow model on your computer, but you do know how to ask a question in plain English. Model serving hides the implementation details of a solution and lets users focus on providing inputs and understanding outputs of a model.

To proceed, make sure to run `pip install transformers` to install the Hugging Face library that has the model we want to use.[17] With that we can now import and start an instance of Ray's `serve` library, load and deploy a GPT-2 model, and ask it for the meaning of life, like so:

```python
from ray import serve
from transformers import pipeline
import requests

serve.start()  ❶


@serve.deployment  ❷
def model(request):
    language_model = pipeline("text-generation", model="gpt2")  ❸
    query = request.query_params["query"]
    return language_model(query, max_length=100)  ❹


model.deploy()  ❺

query = "What's the meaning of life?"
response = requests.get(f"http://localhost:8000/model?query={query}")  ❻
print(response.text)
```

---

17 Depending on the operating system you're using, you may need to install the Rust compiler first to make this work. For instance, on a Mac, you can install it with `brew install rust`.

❶ Start serve locally.

❷ The @serve.deployment decorator turns a function with a request parameter into a serve deployment.

❸ Loading language_model inside the model function for every request is inefficient, but it's the quickest way to show you a deployment.

❹ Ask the model to give us at most 100 characters to continue our query.

❺ Formally deploy the model so that it can start receiving requests over HTTP.

❻ Use the indispensable *requests* library to get a response for any question you might have.

In Chapter 9 you will learn how to properly deploy models in various scenarios, but for now we encourage you to play around with this example and test different queries. Running the last two lines of code repeatedly will give you different answers practically every time. Here's a darkly poetic gem, raising more questions, from one query that we've slightly censored for underaged readers:

```
[{
    "generated_text": "What's the meaning of life?\n\n
    Is there one way or another of living?\n\n
    How does it feel to be trapped in a relationship?\n\n
    How can it be changed before it's too late?
    What did we call it in our time?\n\n
    Where do we fit within this world and what are we going to live for?\n\n
    My life as a person has been shaped by the love I've received from others."
}]
```

This concludes our whirlwind tour of Ray's data science libraries, the second of Ray's layers. Ultimately, all high-level Ray libraries presented in this chapter are extensions of the Ray Core API. Ray makes it relatively easy to build new extensions, and there are a few more that we can't discuss in full in this book. For instance, there is the relatively recent addition of Ray Workflows (*https://oreil.ly/XUT7y*), which allows you to define and run long-running applications with Ray.

Before we wrap up this chapter, let's have a very brief look at the third layer, the growing ecosystem around Ray.

A Growing Ecosystem

Ray's high-level libraries are powerful and deserve a much deeper treatment throughout the book. While their usefulness for the data science experimentation lifecycle is undeniable, we also don't want to give the impression that Ray is all you need from now on. No surprise, the best and most successful frameworks are the ones that integrate well with existing solutions and ideas. It's better to focus on your core strengths and leverage other tools for what's missing in your solution, and Ray does this quite well.

Throughout the book, and in Chapter 11 in particular, we will discuss many useful third-party libraries built on top of Ray. The Ray ecosystem also has a lot of integrations with existing tools. To give you an example of that, recall that Ray Datasets is Ray's data loading and compute library. If you happen to have an existing project that already uses data processing engines like Spark or Dask,[18] you can use those tools together with Ray. Specifically, you can run the entire Dask ecosystem on top of a Ray Cluster using the Dask-on-Ray scheduler, or you can use the Spark on Ray project (*https://oreil.ly/J1D5I*) to integrate your Spark workloads with Ray. Likewise, the Modin project (*https://oreil.ly/brGPJ*) is a distributed drop-in replacement for Pandas DataFrames that uses Ray (or Dask) as a distributed execution engine ("Pandas on Ray").

The common theme here is that Ray doesn't try to replace all these tools, but rather integrates with them while still giving you access to its native Ray Datasets library. We'll go into much more detail about the relationship of Ray with other tools in the broader ecosystem in Chapter 11.

One important aspect of many Ray libraries is that they seamlessly integrate common tools as *backends*. Ray often creates common interfaces, instead of trying to create new standards.[19] These interfaces allow you to run tasks in a distributed fashion, a property most of the respective backends don't have, or not to the same extent. For instance, Ray RLlib and Train are backed by the full power of TensorFlow and PyTorch. And Ray Tune supports algorithms from practically every notable HPO tool available, including Hyperopt, Optuna, Nevergrad, Ax, SigOpt, and many others. None of these tools is distributed by default, but Tune unifies them in a *common interface for distributed workloads*.

---

18 Spark was created by another lab in Berkeley, AMPLab. The internet is full of blog posts claiming that Ray should therefore be seen as a replacement of Spark. It's better to think of them as tools with different strengths that are both likely here to stay.

19 Before the deep learning framework Keras (*https://keras.io*) became an official part of TensorFlow, it started out as a convenient API specification for various lower-level frameworks such as Theano or CNTK. In that sense, Ray RLlib has the chance to become "Keras for RL," and Ray Tune might just be "Keras for HPO." The missing piece for more adoption might just be a more elegant API for both.

Summary

Figure 1-4 gives you an overview of the three layers of Ray as we laid them out. Ray's core distributed execution engine sits at the center of the framework. The Ray Core API is a versatile library for distributed computing, and Ray Clusters allow you to deploy your workloads in a variety of ways.

For practical data science workflows you can use Ray Datasets for data processing, Ray RLlib for reinforcement learning, Ray Train for distributed model training, Ray Tune for hyperparameter tuning, and Ray Serve for model serving. You've seen examples for each of these libraries and have an idea of what their APIs entail. Ray AIR provides a unified API for all other Ray ML libraries and was built with the needs of data scientists in mind.

On top of that, Ray's ecosystem has many extensions, integrations, and backends that we'll look more into later. Maybe you can already spot a few tools you know and like in Figure 1-4?

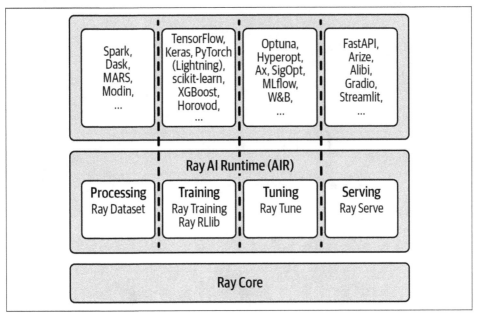

Figure 1-4. Ray in three layers

The Ray Core API sits at the center of Figure 1-4, surrounded by the libraries RLlib, Ray Tune, Ray Train, Ray Serve, Ray Datasets, and the many third-party integrations that are too many to list here.

## CHAPTER 2

Getting Started with Ray Core

For a book on distributed Python, it's not without a certain irony that Python on its own is largely ineffective for distributed computing. Its interpreter is effectively single threaded. For instance, this makes it difficult to leverage multiple CPUs on the same machine, let alone a whole cluster of machines, using plain Python. That means you need extra tooling, and luckily the Python ecosystem has some options for you. Libraries like `multiprocessing` can help you distribute work on a single machine,[1] but not beyond.

Seen as a Python library, the Ray Core API is powerful enough to make general distributed programming more accessible to the Python community as a whole. By way of analogy, some companies get by with deploying pretrained ML models for their use cases, but that strategy is not always effective. It's often inevitable to need to train custom models to be successful. In the same way, your distributed workloads *might* just fit into the (potentially limiting) programming model of existing frameworks, but Ray Core can unlock the full spectrum of building distributed applications, due to its generality.[2] As it is so fundamental, we dedicate this whole chapter to the basics of Ray Core and spend all of Chapter 3 on building an interesting application with the Core API. This way you're equipped with practical knowledge about Ray Core and can use it in later chapters and your own projects.

In this chapter you'll understand how Ray Core handles distributed computing by spinning up a local cluster, and you'll learn how to use Ray's lean and powerful API to parallelize some interesting computations. For instance, you'll build an example that

---

1 Note that Ray comes with a drop-in replacement for `multiprocessing` (*https://oreil.ly/UMg73*) that you might find useful for certain workloads.

2 This represents a trade-off in terms of generality versus specialization. By also providing specialized yet interoperable libraries on top of the Core API, Ray provides tooling at various levels of abstraction.

runs a data-parallel task efficiently and asynchronously on Ray, in a convenient way that's not easily replicable with other tooling. We discuss how *tasks* and *actors* work as distributed versions of functions and classes in Python. You'll also learn how to put *objects* in Ray's object store and how to retrieve them. We give you concrete examples for these three fundamental concepts (tasks, actors, and objects), using just six basic API calls of the Ray Core API. Lastly, we'll discuss the system components underlying Ray and what its architecture looks like. In other words, in this chapter we'll give you a look under the hood of Ray's engine.

An Introduction to Ray Core

The bulk of this chapter is an extended Ray Core example that we'll build together. Many of Ray's concepts can be explained with a good example, so that's exactly what we'll do.

 As before, you can follow this example by typing the code yourself (which is highly recommended) or by following the notebook for this chapter (*https://oreil.ly/lMmfp*). In any case, make sure you have Ray installed, for instance with `pip install ray`.

In Chapter 1 we showed you how start a local cluster simply by calling `import ray` and then initializing it with `ray.init()`. After running this code you will see output of the following form. We omit a lot of information in this example output, as that would require you to understand more of Ray's internals first:

```
... INFO services.py:1263 -- View the Ray dashboard at http://127.0.0.1:8265
{'node_ip_address': '192.168.1.41',
 ...
 'node_id': '...'}
```

This output indicates that your Ray Cluster is up and running. As you can see from the first line of the output, Ray comes with its own, prepackaged dashboard.[3] You can check it out at *http://127.0.0.1:8265*, unless your output shows a different port. You can take your time if you want to explore the dashboard. For instance, you should see all your CPU cores listed and the total utilization of your (trivial) Ray application. To see the resource utilization of your Ray Cluster in Python, you can simply call `ray.cluster_resources()`. The output should look something like this:

```
{'CPU': 12.0,
 'memory': 14203886388.0,
```

---

3 The dashboard is being redesigned as we write these lines. As much as we'd like to show you screenshots of it and walk you through it, you'll have to discover it for yourself (*https://oreil.ly/c6vtM*) for now.

```
'node:127.0.0.1': 1.0,
'object_store_memory': 2147483648.0}
```

You'll need a running Ray Cluster to run the examples in this chapter, so make sure you've started one before continuing. The goal of this section is to give you a quick introduction to the Ray Core API, which we'll simply refer to as the Ray API from now on.

For Python programmers, the great thing about the Ray API is that it hits so close to home. It uses familiar concepts such as decorators, functions, and classes to provide you with a fast learning experience. The Ray API aims to provide a universal programming interface for distributed computing. That's certainly no easy feat, but we think Ray succeeds in this respect, as it provides you with good abstractions that are intuitive to learn and use. Ray's engine does all the heavy lifting for you in the background. This design philosophy is what enables Ray to be used with existing Python libraries and systems.

Note that the reason we start out with Ray Core in this book is that we believe it has massive potential to make distributed computing more accessible. In essence, this chapter is all about getting a peek behind the curtains of what makes Ray work so well and how you can pick up its fundamentals. If you're a less experienced Python programmer or just want to focus on higher-level tasks, Ray Core might take some getting used to.[4] Having said that, we emphatically recommend learning the Ray Core API, as it's a great way to get into distributed computing with Python.

A First Example Using the Ray API

To give you an example, take the following function that retrieves and processes data from a database. Our sample database is a plain Python list containing the words of the title of this book. We act as if retrieving an individual `item` from this database and further processing it is expensive by letting Python `sleep`:

```
import time

database = [  ❶
    "Learning", "Ray",
    "Flexible", "Distributed", "Python", "for", "Machine", "Learning"
]


def retrieve(item):
    time.sleep(item / 10.)  ❷
    return item, database[item]
```

---

4 In case you fall into these categories, it might be comforting to hear that many data scientists rarely use Ray Core directly. Instead, they work directly with Ray's higher-level libraries like Datasets, Train, or Tune.

❶ A sample database containing string data with the title of this book.

❷ Emulate a data-crunching operation that takes a long time.

Our database has eight items in total. If we were to retrieve all items sequentially, how long would that take? For the item with index 5, we wait for half a second (5 / 10) and so on. In total, we can expect a runtime of around (0 + 1 + 2 + 3 + 4 + 5 + 6 + 7) / 10 = 2.8 seconds. Let's see if that's what we actually get:

```
def print_runtime(input_data, start_time):
    print(f'Runtime: {time.time() - start_time:.2f} seconds, data:')
    print(*input_data, sep="\n")


start = time.time()
data = [retrieve(item) for item in range(8)]  ❶
print_runtime(data, start)  ❷
```

❶ Uses a list comprehension to retrieve all eight items.

❷ Unpacks the data to print each item on its own line.

If you run this code, you should see the following output:

```
Runtime: 2.82 seconds, data:
(0, 'Learning')
(1, 'Ray')
(2, 'Flexible')
(3, 'Distributed')
(4, 'Python')
(5, 'for')
(6, 'Machine')
(7, 'Learning')
```

There's a little overhead that brings the total runtime to 2.82 seconds. On your end this might be slightly less, or much more, depending on your computer. The important takeaway is that our naive Python implementation is not able to run this function in parallel.

This may not come as a surprise to you, but you could at least have suspected that Python list comprehensions are more efficient in that regard. The runtime we got is pretty much the worst-case scenario, namely, the 2.8 seconds we calculated prior to running the code. If you think about it, it might even be a bit frustrating to see that a program that essentially sleeps most of its runtime is that slow overall. Ultimately you can blame the *Global Interpreter Lock* (GIL) for that, but it gets enough of the blame already.

Python's Global Interpreter Lock

The GIL is undoubtedly one of the most infamous features of the Python language. In a nutshell, it's a lock that makes sure only one thread on your computer can ever execute your Python code at a time. If you use multithreading, the threads need to take turns controlling the Python interpreter.

The GIL has been implemented for good reasons. For one, it makes memory management that much easier in Python. Another key advantage is that it makes single-threaded programs quite fast. Programs that primarily use lots of system input and output (we say they are I/O-bound), like reading files or databases, benefit as well. One of the major downsides is that CPU-bound programs are essentially single-threaded. In fact, CPU-bound tasks might even run *faster* when not using multithreading, as the latter incurs write-lock overheads on top of the GIL.

Given all that, the GIL might somewhat paradoxically be one of the reasons for Python's popularity, if you believe Larry Hastings (*https://oreil.ly/UShnM*). Interestingly, Hastings also led (unsuccessful) efforts to remove it in a project called *GILectomy*, which is exactly the kind of complicated surgery that it sounds like. The jury is still out, but Sam Gross (*https://oreil.ly/J4I-q*) might just have found a way to remove the GIL in his nogil branch of Python 3.9. For now, if you absolutely have to work around the GIL, consider using an implementation different from CPython. CPython is Python's standard implementation, and if you don't know that you're using it, you're definitely using it. Implementations like Jython, IronPython, or PyPy don't have a GIL, but they come with their own drawbacks.

Functions and remote Ray tasks

It's reasonable to assume that such a task can benefit from parallelization. Perfectly distributed, the runtime should not take much longer than the longest subtask, namely, 7/ 10 = 0.7 seconds. So, let's see how you can extend this example to run on Ray. To do so, start by using the @ray.remote decorator as follows:

```
@ray.remote  ❶
def retrieve_task(item):
    return retrieve(item)  ❷
```

❶ Make any Python function a Ray task with just this decorator.

❷ All else remains unchanged. retrieve_task just passes through to retrieve.

In this way, the function retrieve_task becomes a so-called Ray task. In essence, a Ray task is a function that gets executed on a different process than it was called from, potentially on a different machine.

That's an extremely convenient design choice, as you can focus on your Python code first and don't have to completely change your mindset or programming paradigm to use Ray. Note that in practice you would have simply added the `@ray.remote` decorator to your original `retrieve` function (after all, that's the intended use of decorators), but to keep things as clear as possible, we didn't want to touch previous code.

Easy enough, so what do you have to change in the code that retrieves the database entries and measures performance? It turns out, not much. Example 2-1 shows how you would do that.[5]

Example 2-1. Measuring performance of your Ray task

```
start = time.time()
object_references = [    ❶
    retrieve_task.remote(item) for item in range(8)
]
data = ray.get(object_references)    ❷
print_runtime(data, start)
```

❶   To run `retrieve_task` on your local Ray Cluster, you use `.remote()` and pass in your items as before. Each task returns an object.

❷   To get back actual data, and not just Ray object references, you use `ray.get`.

Did you spot the differences? You have to execute your Ray task remotely using a `.remote()` call.[6] When Ray executes tasks remotely, even on your local cluster, it does so *asynchronously*. The list items in `object_references` in the last code snippet do not contain the results directly. In fact, if you check the Python type of the first item with `type(object_references[0])`, you'll see that it's in fact an `ObjectRef`. These object references correspond to *futures*, which you need to ask the result of. This is what the call to `ray.get(...)` is for. Whenever you call `remote` on a Ray task, it will immediately return one or more object references. You should consider Ray tasks the primary method of creating objects. In the next section we'll show you an example that chains multiple tasks together and lets Ray take care of passing and resolving the objects between them.

---

5 Strictly speaking, this first example is a bit of an anti-pattern (*https://oreil.ly/OuOWC*), as you should not normally share mutable state across Ray tasks through global variables. Having said that, for this toy data example you shouldn't overthink this part. Rest assured that we'll show you a better way of doing things in the next section.

6 This book is geared to data science practitioners, so we won't discuss the conceptual details of Ray's architecture here. If you're curious and want to learn more about how Ray tasks are executed, check out the Ray architecture whitepaper (*https://oreil.ly/Pe-hT*).

We still want to work more on this example,[7] but let's take a step back here and recap what we did so far. You started with a Python function and decorated it with @ray.remote. This made your function a Ray task. Then, instead of calling the original function in your code, you called .remote(...) on the Ray task. The last step was to use .get(...) to get the results from your Ray Cluster. This procedure is so intuitive that you might be able to create your own Ray task from another function without having to look back at this example. Why don't you give it a try right now?

Coming back to our example: by using Ray tasks, what did we gain in terms of performance? The runtime clocks in at 0.71 seconds for us, which is just slightly more than the longest subtask, which comes in at 0.7 seconds. That's great and much better than before, but we can further improve our program by leveraging more of Ray's API.

Using the object store with put and get

One thing you might have noticed is that in the definition of retrieve we *directly* accessed items from our database. When working on a local Ray Cluster, this is fine, but imagine you're running on an actual cluster that includes several computers. How would all those computers access the same data? Remember from Chapter 1 that in a Ray Cluster there is one head node with a driver process (running ray.init()) and many worker nodes with worker processes executing your tasks. By default, Ray will create as many worker processes as there are CPU cores on your machine. Our database is currently defined on the driver only, but the workers running your tasks need to have access to it to run the retrieve task. Luckily, Ray provides an easy way to share *objects* between the driver and workers (or between workers). You can simply use put to place your data into Ray's *distributed object store*. In our definition of retrieve_task we explicitly pass in a db argument, to which we later will pass our db_object_ref object:

```
db_object_ref = ray.put(database)  ❶
```

```
@ray.remote
def retrieve_task(item, db):  ❷
    time.sleep(item / 10.)
    return item, db[item]
```

❶ put your database into the object store and receive a reference to it. This way we can explicitly pass this reference to our Ray task later.

❷ The Ray task retrieve_task takes the object reference as an argument.

---

7 This example has been adapted from Dean Wampler's fantastic report "What Is Ray?" (*https://oreil.ly/8Hc9y*).

By using the object store this way, you can let Ray handle data access across the whole cluster. We'll talk about how exactly values are passed between nodes and within workers when talking about Ray's infrastructure. While the interaction with the object store requires some overhead, it gives you performance gains when working with larger, more realistic datasets. For now, the important part is that this step is essential in a truly distributed setting. If you like, try to rerun Example 2-1 with this new retrieve_task function and confirm that it still runs as expected.

Using Ray's wait function for nonblocking calls

Note how in Example 2-1 we used ray.get(object_references) to access results. This call is *blocking*, which means that our driver has to wait for all the results to be available. That's not a big deal in our case; the program now finishes in under a second. But imagine that the processing of each database item would take several minutes. In that case, you would want to free up the driver process for other tasks, instead of sitting idly by. Also, it would be great to process results as they come in (some finish much quicker than others), rather than waiting for all items to be processed. One more question to keep in mind is, what happens if one of the database items can't be retrieved as expected? Let's say there's a deadlock somewhere in the database connection. The driver would simply hang and never retrieve all items. For that reason it's a good idea to work with reasonable timeouts. Let's say we don't want to wait longer than 10 times the longest data retrieval task before stopping the task. Here's how you can do that with Ray by using wait:

```
start = time.time()
object_references = [
    retrieve_task.remote(item, db_object_ref) for item in range(8)   ❶
]
all_data = []

while len(object_references) > 0:   ❷
    finished, object_references = ray.wait(   ❸
        object_references, num_returns=2, timeout=7.0
    )
    data = ray.get(finished)
    print_runtime(data, start)   ❹
    all_data.extend(data)   ❺
```

❶ Run remote on our retrieve_task and pass the respective item we want to retrieve and the object reference to our database.

❷ Instead of blocking, loop through unfinished object_references.

❸ We asynchronously wait for finished data with a reasonable timeout. object_references gets overridden here, to prevent an infinite loop.

❹ Print results as they come in, namely in blocks of two.

❺ append new `data` to the `all_data` until finished.

As you can see, `ray.wait` returns two arguments: finished values and futures that still need to be processed. We use the `num_returns` argument, which defaults to 1, to let `wait` return whenever a new pair of database items is available. This results in the following output for us:

```
Runtime: 0.11 seconds, data:
(0, 'Learning')
(1, 'Ray')
Runtime: 0.31 seconds, data:
(2, 'Flexible')
(3, 'Distributed')
Runtime: 0.51 seconds, data:
(4, 'Python')
(5, 'for')
Runtime: 0.71 seconds, data:
(6, 'Machine')
(7, 'Learning')
```

Note how in the `while` loop, instead of just printing results, we could have done many other things, like starting entirely new tasks on other workers with the values already retrieved up to this point.

Handling task dependencies

So far our example program has been fairly easy on a conceptual level. It consists of a single step: retrieving a bunch of database items. Now, imagine that once your data is loaded you want to run a follow-up processing task. To be more concrete, let's say we want to use the result of our first retrieve task to query other, related data (pretend that you're querying data from a different table in the same database). Example 2-2 sets up such a task and runs both our `retrieve_task` and `follow_up_task` consecutively.

Example 2-2. Running a follow-up task that depends on another Ray task

```
@ray.remote
def follow_up_task(retrieve_result):    ❶
    original_item, _ = retrieve_result
    follow_up_result = retrieve(original_item + 1)    ❷
    return retrieve_result, follow_up_result    ❸


retrieve_refs = [retrieve_task.remote(item, db_object_ref) for item in [0, 2, 4, 6]]
follow_up_refs = [follow_up_task.remote(ref) for ref in retrieve_refs]    ❹
```

```
result = [print(data) for data in ray.get(follow_up_refs)]
```

❶ Using the result of `retrieve_task`, compute another Ray task on top of it.

❷ Leveraging the `original_item` from the first task, `retrieve` more data.

❸ Return both the original and the follow-up data.

❹ Pass the object references from the first task to the second task.

Running this code results in the following output:

```
((0, 'Learning'), (1, 'Ray'))
((2, 'Flexible'), (3, 'Distributed'))
((4, 'Python'), (5, 'for'))
((6, 'Machine'), (7, 'Learning'))
```

If you don't have a lot of experience with asynchronous programming, you might not be impressed by Example 2-2. But we hope to convince you that it's at least a bit surprising that this code snippet runs at all.[8] So, what's the big deal? After all, the code reads like regular Python: a function definition and a few list comprehensions. The point is that the function body of `follow_up_task` expects a Python `tuple` for its input argument `retrieve_result`, which we unpack in the first line of the function definition.

But by invoking `[follow_up_task.remote(ref) for ref in retrieve_refs]` we do *not* pass in tuples to the follow-up task at all. Instead, we pass in Ray *object references* with `retrieve_refs`. What happens under the hood is that Ray knows that `follow_up_task` requires actual values, so internally in this task it will call `ray.get` to resolve the futures.[9] Ray builds a dependency graph for all tasks and executes them in an order that respects the dependencies. You do not have to tell Ray explicitly when to wait for a previous task to finish; it will infer that information for you. This also shows you a powerful feature of the Ray object store: if intermediate values are large, you can avoid copying them back to the driver. You can just pass your object references to the next task and let Ray handle the rest.

The follow-up tasks will be scheduled only once the individual retrieve tasks have finished. If you ask us, that's an incredible feature. In fact, if we had called

---

8 According to Clarke's third law (*https://oreil.ly/VHJ_o*), any sufficiently advanced technology is indistinguishable from magic. For me, this example has a bit of magic to it.

9 The same thing happened earlier, when we passed an object reference to the remote call of `retrieve_task` and then directly accessed the respective items of the database db there. We didn't want to distract you too much from the main point of that example.

`retrieve_refs` something like `retrieve_result`, you may not have even noticed this important detail. That's by design. Ray wants you to focus on your work, not on the details of cluster computing. In Figure 2-1 you can see the dependency graph for the two tasks visualized.

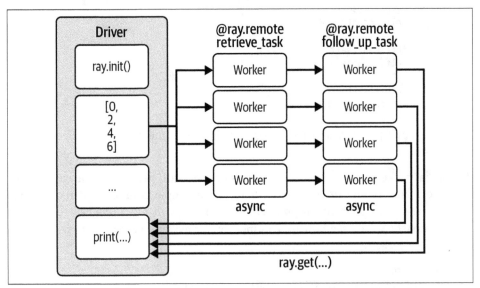

Figure 2-1. Running two dependent tasks asynchronously and in parallel with Ray

If you feel like it, try to rewrite Example 2-2 so that it explicitly uses `get` on the first task before passing values into the follow-up task. Not only does this introduce more boilerplate code, it's also a bit less intuitive to write and understand.

From classes to actors

Before wrapping up this example, let's discuss one more important concept of Ray Core. Notice how everything is essentially a function in our example. We just used the `ray.remote` decorator to make some of them remote functions, and other than that we used plain Python.

Let's say we wanted to track how often our database has been queried. Sure, we could simply count the results of our retrieve tasks, but is there a better way to do this? We want to track this in a "distributed" way that will scale. For that, Ray has the concept of *actors*. Actors allow you to run *stateful* computations on your cluster. They can also communicate between each other.[10] Much like Ray tasks were simply decorated

---

10 The actor model is an established concept in computer science, which you can find implemented, e.g., in Akka or Erlang. However, the history and specifics of actors are not relevant to our discussion.

functions, Ray actors are decorated Python classes. Let's write a simple counter to track our database calls:

```python
@ray.remote  ❶
class DataTracker:
    def __init__(self):
        self._counts = 0

    def increment(self):
        self._counts += 1

    def counts(self):
        return self._counts
```

❶ Make any Python class a Ray actor by using the same ray.remote decorator as before.

This DataTracker class is already an actor, since we equipped it with the ray.remote decorator. This actor can track state, here just a simple counter, and its methods are Ray tasks that get invoked precisely like we did with functions before, namely, using .remote(). Let's see how we can modify our existing retrieve_task to incorporate this new actor:

```python
@ray.remote
def retrieve_tracker_task(item, tracker, db):  ❶
    time.sleep(item / 10.)
    tracker.increment.remote()  ❷
    return item, db[item]


tracker = DataTracker.remote()  ❸

object_references = [  ❹
    retrieve_tracker_task.remote(item, tracker, db_object_ref)
    for item in range(8)
]
data = ray.get(object_references)

print(data)
print(ray.get(tracker.counts.remote()))  ❺
```

❶ Passes in the tracker actor into this task.

❷ The tracker receives an increment for each call.

❸ Instantiates our DataTracker actor by calling .remote() on the class.

❹ The actor gets passed into the retrieve task.

⑤ Aftwerward, we can get the `counts` state from our `tracker` from another remote invocation.

Not surprisingly, the result of this computation is in fact 8. We didn't need actors to compute this, but it can be useful to have a mechanism to track state across the cluster, potentially spanning multiple tasks. In fact, we could pass our actor into any dependent task, or even into the constructor of yet another actor. There is no limitation to what you can do, and it's this flexibility that makes the Ray API so powerful. It's not very common for distributed Python tools to allow for stateful computations like this. This feature can come in handy, especially when running complex distributed algorithms, for instance when using reinforcement learning.

This completes our extensive first Ray API example. We'll concisely summarize the Ray API next.

 In this introduction by example we focused a lot on Ray tasks and actors as distributed versions of Python functions and classes. But *objects* are also first-class citizens in Ray Core and should be seen as equal in status to tasks and actors. The object store is a central component of Ray.

An Overview of the Ray Core API

If you recall what we did in the previous example, you'll notice that we used a total of just six API methods.[11] We used `ray.init()` to start the cluster and `@ray.remote` to turn functions and classes into tasks and actors. Then we used `ray.put()` to pass values into Ray's object store and `ray.get()` to retrieve objects from the cluster. Finally, we used `.remote()` on actor methods or tasks to run code on our cluster, and `ray.wait` to avoid blocking calls.

While six API methods might not seem like much, those are the only ones you'll likely ever care about when using the Ray API.[12] We briefly summarize them in Table 2-1 so you can easily reference them in the future.

---

11 To paraphrase Alan Kay (*https://oreil.ly/lNdxi*), to get simplicity, you need to find slightly more sophisticated building blocks. The Ray API does just that for distributed Python.

12 Check out the API reference (*https://oreil.ly/k3E7H*) to see that there are in fact quite a few more methods available. At some point you should invest in understanding the arguments of `init`, but all other methods likely won't be of interest to you, if you're not an administrator of your Ray Cluster.

Table 2-1. The six major API methods of Ray Core

API call	Description
ray.init()	Initializes your Ray Cluster. Pass in an address to connect to an existing cluster.
@ray.remote	Turns functions into tasks and classes into actors.
ray.put()	Puts values into Ray's object store.
ray.get()	Gets values from the object store. Returns the values you've put there or that were computed by a task or actor.
.remote()	Runs actor methods or tasks on your Ray Cluster and is used to instantiate actors.
ray.wait()	Returns two lists of object references, one with finished tasks we're waiting for and one with unfinished tasks.

Now that you've seen the Ray API in action, let's spend some time on its system architecture.

Understanding Ray System Components

You've seen how the Ray API can be used and understand the design philosophy behind Ray. Now it's time to get a better understanding of the underlying system components. In other words, how does Ray work and how does it achieve what it does?

Scheduling and Executing Work on a Node

You know that Ray Clusters consist of nodes. We'll first look at what happens on individual nodes, before we zoom out and discuss how the whole cluster interoperates.

As we've already discussed, a worker node consists of several worker processes or simply workers. Each worker has a unique ID, an IP address, and a port by which they can be referenced. Workers are called "workers" for a reason; they're components that blindly execute the work you give them. But who tells them what to do and when? A worker might be busy already, it may not have the proper resources to run a task (e.g., access to a GPU), and it might not even have the values it needs to run a given task. On top of that, workers have no knowledge of what happens before or after they've executed their workload; there's no coordination.

To address these issues, each worker node has a component called *Raylet*. Think of Raylets as the smart components of a node that manage the worker processes. Raylets are shared between jobs and consist of two components, a *task scheduler* and an *object store*.

Let's talk about object stores first. In the running example in this chapter, we've already used the concept of an object store loosely, without explicitly specifying it. Each node of a Ray Cluster is equipped with an object store, within that node's Raylet, and all objects stored collectively form the distributed object store of a cluster. The object store manages a *shared pool of memory* across workers on the same node and ensures that workers can access objects that were created on a different node. The object store is implemented in Plasma (*https://oreil.ly/RdrJZ*), which now belongs to the Apache Arrow project. Functionally, the object store takes care of memory management and ultimately makes sure workers have access to the objects they need.

The second component of a Raylet is its scheduler. The scheduler takes care of *resource management*, among other things. For instance, if a task requires access to four CPUs, the scheduler needs to make sure it can find a free worker process that can grant access to said resources. By default, the scheduler knows about and acquires information about the number of CPUs and GPUs, as well as the amount of memory available on its node. If a scheduler can't provide the required resources, it simply can't schedule execution of a task right away and needs to queue it. The scheduler limits which tasks are running concurrently to make sure that you don't run out of physical resources.

Apart from resources, the other requirement the scheduler takes care of is *dependency resolution*. That means it needs to ensure that each worker has all the objects it needs to execute a task in the local object store. For that to work, the scheduler will first resolve local dependencies by looking up values in its object store. If the required value is not available on this node's object store, the scheduler will communicate with other nodes (we'll tell you how in a bit) and pull in remote dependencies. Once the scheduler has ensured enough resources for a task, resolved all needed dependencies, and found a worker for a task, it can schedule the task for execution.

Task scheduling is a very difficult topic, even if we're talking only about single nodes. You can easily imagine scenarios in which an incorrectly or naively planned task execution can "block" downstream tasks because not enough resources remain. Especially in a distributed context, assigning work like this can be become tricky very quickly.

Now that you know about Raylets, let's briefly come back to worker processes and wrap up the discussion by explaining how Ray can recover from failures and the concepts needed to do so.

In short, workers store metadata for all the tasks they invoke and the object references returned by those tasks. This concept, called *ownership*, means the process that generates an object reference is also responsible for its resolution. In other words, each worker process "owns" the tasks it submits, which includes proper execution and ensuring availability of results. Worker processes need to track what they own, for instance in case of failures, which is why they have a so-called *ownership table*. This way, if a task fails and needs to be recomputed, the worker already owns all the information it needs to do so.[13] To give you a concrete example of an ownership relationship, as opposed to the concept of dependency discussed earlier, let's say we have a program that starts a simple task and internally calls another task:

```
@ray.remote
def task_owned():
    return


@ray.remote
def task(dependency):
    res_owned = task_owned.remote()
    return


val = ray.put("value")
res = task.remote(dependency=val)
```

Let's quickly analyze ownership and dependency for this example. We defined two tasks in task and task_owned, and we have three variables in total: val, res, and res_owned. Our main program defines both val (which puts "value" into the object store) and res, and it also calls task. In other words, the driver *owns* task, val, and res according to Ray's ownership definition. In contrast, res depends on task, but there's no ownership relationship between the two. When task gets called, it takes val as a dependency. It then calls task_owned and assigns res_owned and hence owns them both. Lastly, task_owned itself does not own anything, but certainly res_owned depends on it. Figure 2-2 sums up this discussion about worker nodes, showing all involved components.

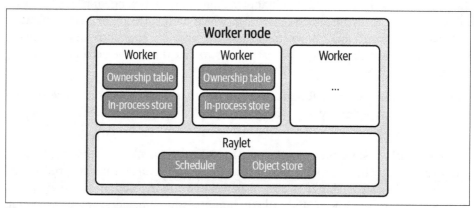

Figure 2-2. The system components comprising a Ray worker node

---

13 This is an extremely limited description of how Ray handles failures in general. After all, just having all the information to recover does not tell you how to do so. We refer you to the architecture whitepaper (*https://oreil.ly/_1SyA*) for an in-depth discussion on this topic.

The Head Node

We've already indicated in Chapter 1 that each Ray Cluster has one special node called a *head node*. So far you know that this node has a driver process.[14] Drivers can submit tasks themselves but can't execute them. You also know that the head node can have some worker processes, which is important to be able to run local clusters consisting of a single node.

The head node is identical to other worker nodes, but it additionally runs processes responsible for cluster management such as the autoscaler (that we cover in Chapter 9) and a component called *Global Control Service* (GCS). This is an important component that carries global information about the cluster. The GCS is a key-value store that stores information such as system-level metadata. For instance, it has a table with heartbeat signals for each Raylet to ensure they are still reachable. Raylets, in turn, send heartbeat signals to the GCS to indicate that they are alive. The GCS also stores the locations of Ray actors. The ownership model just discussed tells us that all object information is stored at their owner worker process, which avoids making the GCS a bottleneck.

Distributed Scheduling and Execution

Let's briefly talk about cluster orchestration and how nodes manage, plan, and execute tasks. When talking about worker nodes, we've indicated that there are several components to distributing workloads with Ray. Here's an overview of the steps and intricacies involved in this process:

Distributed memory
> The object stores of individual Raylets manage memory on a node. But sometimes objects need to be transferred between nodes, which is called *distributed object transfer*. This is needed for remote dependency resolution so that workers have the objects they need to run tasks.

Communication
> Most of the communication in a Ray Cluster, such as object transfer, takes place via *gRPC* (*https://grpc.io*).

Resource management and fulfillment
> On a node, Raylets are responsible for granting resources and *leasing* worker processes to task owners. All schedulers across nodes form the distributed scheduler, which effectively means that nodes can schedule tasks on other nodes.

---

14 In fact, it could have multiple drivers, but this is not essential for our discussion. Starting a single driver on the head node is the most common, but driver processes also can be started on any node in the cluster, and multiple drivers can be on a single cluster.

Through communication with the GCS, local schedulers know about other nodes' resources.

Task execution

Once a task has been submitted for execution, all its dependencies (local and remote data) need to be resolved, e.g., by retrieving large data from the object store, before execution can begin.

If the past few sections seem a bit involved technically, that's because they are. It's important to understand the basic patterns and ideas of the software you're using, but we'll admit that the details of Ray's architecture can be a bit tough to wrap your head around in the beginning. In fact, it's one of Ray's design principles to trade usability for architectural complexity. If you want to delve deeper into Ray's architecture, a good place to start is their architecture whitepaper (*https://oreil.ly/tadqC*).

Figure 2-3 summarizes what we know about Ray's architecture.

Now that you've learned the basics of the Ray Core API and know the fundamentals of Ray's Cluster architecture, let's compute one more complex example.

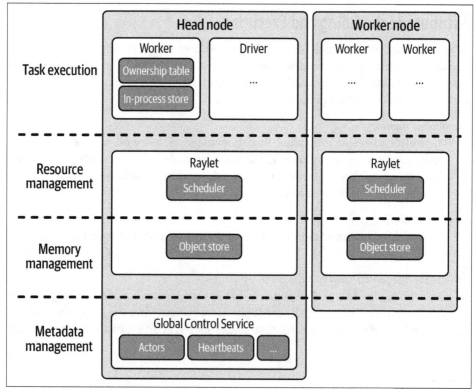

Figure 2-3. An overview of Ray's architectural components

Systems Related to Ray

With the architecture and functionality of it in mind, how does Ray relate to other systems? Here are the basics:

- Ray can be used as a parallelization framework for Python and shares properties with tools like `celery` or `multiprocessing`. In fact, there's a drop-in replacement (*https://oreil.ly/4Lrgf*) for the latter implemented in Ray.
- Ray is also related to data processing frameworks such as Spark, Dask, Flink, and MARS. We'll explore these relationships in Chapter 11, when talking about Ray's ecosystem.
- As a distributed computing tool, Ray also deals with the problems of cluster management and orchestration, and we'll see how Ray does that in relation to tools like Kubernetes in Chapter 9.
- Since Ray is implementing the actor model of concurrency, it's also interesting to explore its relationship with frameworks like Akka.
- Lastly, since Ray banks on a performant, low-level API for communication, there's a certain relationship with high-performance computing (HPC) frameworks and communication protocols like the message passing interface (MPI).

A Simple MapReduce Example with Ray

We can't let you go without discussing an example of one of the most important milestones in distributed computing in recent decades, namely, *MapReduce*. Many successful big data technologies like Hadoop are based on this programming model, and it's worth revisiting in the context of Ray. To keep things simple, we'll restrict our MapReduce implementation to a single use case, the task of counting word occurrences across several documents. This is an almost trivial task in single processing, but it becomes an interesting challenge once a massive corpus of documents is involved and you need multiple compute nodes to crunch the numbers.

Implementing a MapReduce word-count example might be the most well-known example we have in distributed computing,[15] so it's worth knowing. If you don't know about this classic paradigm, it's based on three straightforward steps:

1. Take a set of documents and transform or "map" its elements (for instance the words contained in them) according to a function you provide. This *map phase* produces key-value pairs by design, in which a *key* represents a document element and a *value* is simply a metric you want to compute for that element.

---

15 It's a *drosophila melanogaster* of sorts, not unlike computing a classifier on the ubiquitous MNIST dataset.

Since we're interested in counting words, whenever we encounter a word in a document, our *map function* will simply emit the pair (word, 1) to indicate that we found one occurrence of it.

2. Collect and group all the outputs of the map phase according to their key. Since we work in a distributed setup and the same key might be present on several compute nodes, this might require shuffling of data between nodes. For that reason this step is often referred to as the *shuffle phase*.[16] To give you an idea of what grouping might mean in our concrete use case, let's say we have a total of four (word, 1) occurrences produced in the map phase. The shuffle would then co-locate all occurrences of the same word on the same node.

3. Aggregate or "reduce" the elements from the shuffle step, which is why we refer to it as the *reduce phase*. Continuing with the example we laid out, we simply sum up all word occurrences on each node to get the final count. For instance, four occurrences of (word, 1) would be reduced to word: 4.

Evidently, MapReduce gets its name from the first and last of these three phases, but the second one is arguably just as important. While schematically these phases may look simple, their power lies in the fact that they can be massively parallelized across hundreds of machines.

In Figure 2-4 we illustrate an example of applying the three MapReduce phases to a corpus of documents that has been distributed across three partitions. To run MapReduce on a distributed corpus of documents, we first map each document to a set of key-value pairs, then shuffle the results to ensure that all key-value pairs with the same key are on the same node, and finally reduce the key-value pairs to compute the final word counts.

Let's implement the MapReduce algorithm for our word-count use case in Python and parallelize the computation using Ray. First, load example data so that you get a better idea of what we're operating on:

```python
import subprocess
zen_of_python = subprocess.check_output(["python", "-c", "import this"])
corpus = zen_of_python.split()  ❶

num_partitions = 3
chunk = len(corpus) // num_partitions
partitions = [  ❷
    corpus[i * chunk: (i + 1) * chunk] for i in range(num_partitions)
]
```

---

16 In general, a shuffle is any operation that requires redistributing data across its partitions. Shuffles can be quite costly. If your map phase operates on N partitions, it will produce $N \times N$ results that need to be shuffled.

---

❶ Our text corpus is the content of the Zen of Python.

❷ Split the corpus into three partitions.

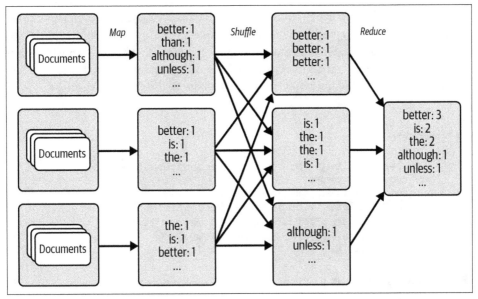

Figure 2-4. Running the MapReduce algorithm on a distributed corpus of documents

The data we're using is the so-called Zen of Python, a small set of guidelines by the Python community. The Zen is hidden in an "Easter egg" and gets printed when you type import this in a Python session. It's worth reading these guidelines as a Python programmer, but for this exercise we're only interested in counting the words they contain. Put simply, we load the Zen of Python, treat each line as a separate "document," and split it into three partitions.

To start our implementation of MapReduce, we'll first cover the map phase and discuss how Ray can help us take care of shuffling the results.

Mapping and Shuffling Document Data

To define the map phase, we need a map function that we apply to each document. In our case, we want to emit the pair (word, 1) for each word we find in a document. For simple text documents loaded as Python strings, it looks like this:[17]

---

17 Note the usage of yield in the map function. This is the quickest way of building a generator with the data we need in Python. You could also build and return a list of pairs, if that's clearer to you.

```
def map_function(document):
    for word in document.lower().split():
        yield word, 1
```

Next, we want to apply this map function to a whole corpus of documents. We do this by making the following apply_map function a Ray task via the @ray.remote decorator. When we call apply_map, we'll apply it to three partitions (num_partitions=3) of document data, just like we indicated in Figure 2-4. Note that apply_map will return three lists, one for each partition. As you will see in a moment, we do this so that Ray can automatically shuffle the results of the map phase to the right nodes for us:

```
import ray


@ray.remote
def apply_map(corpus, num_partitions=3):
    map_results = [list() for _ in range(num_partitions)]   ❶
    for document in corpus:
        for result in map_function(document):
            first_letter = result[0].decode("utf-8")[0]
            word_index = ord(first_letter) % num_partitions   ❷
            map_results[word_index].append(result)   ❸
    return map_results
```

❶ The Ray task apply_map returns one result for each data partition.

❷ Assign each (word, 1) pair to a partition by using the ord function to generate a word_index. This ensures that each occurrence of a word gets shuffled to the same partition.

❸ The pairs are then successively appended to the correct list.

For a text corpus that can be loaded on a single machine, this is overkill, and we could count the words instead. But in a distributed setting, in which we have to partition the data across several nodes, this map phase makes perfect sense.

To apply the map phase to our corpus of documents in parallel, we use a remote call on apply_map as we've done many times before in this chapter. The notable difference is that now we also instruct Ray to return three results (one for each partition) via the num_returns argument:

```
map_results = [
    apply_map.options(num_returns=num_partitions)   ❶
    .remote(data, num_partitions)   ❷
    for data in partitions   ❸
]

for i in range(num_partitions):
    mapper_results = ray.get(map_results[i])   ❹
```

```
    for j, result in enumerate(mapper_results):
        print(f"Mapper {i}, return value {j}: {result[:2]}")
```

❶ Use options to tell Ray to return num_partitions values.

❷ Execute apply_map remotely.

❸ Iterate over each of the partitions we defined.

❹ Inspect the results for illustration purposes only. Normally you would not call ray.get yet.

If you run this code, you will see that each map phase result consists of three lists, of which we print the first two elements of each:

```
Mapper 0, return value 0: [(b'of', 1), (b'is', 1)]
Mapper 0, return value 1: [(b'python,', 1), (b'peters', 1)]
Mapper 0, return value 2: [(b'the', 1), (b'zen', 1)]
Mapper 1, return value 0: [(b'unless', 1), (b'in', 1)]
Mapper 1, return value 1: [(b'although', 1), (b'practicality', 1)]
Mapper 1, return value 2: [(b'beats', 1), (b'errors', 1)]
Mapper 2, return value 0: [(b'is', 1), (b'is', 1)]
Mapper 2, return value 1: [(b'although', 1), (b'a', 1)]
Mapper 2, return value 2: [(b'better', 1), (b'than', 1)]
```

As you will see, we can make it so that all pairs from the j-th return value end up on the same node for the reduce phase.[18] Let's discuss this phase next.

Reducing Word Counts

In the reduce phase, we can now simply create a dictionary that sums up all word occurrences on each partition:

```
@ray.remote
def apply_reduce(*results):     ❶
    reduce_results = dict()
    for res in results:
        for key, value in res:
            if key not in reduce_results:
                reduce_results[key] = 0
            reduce_results[key] += value    ❷

    return reduce_results
```

---

18 By construction, all same-key pairs will end up on the same node this way. For instance, note how in the sample output we printed the word is that appears in the 0-th return value of two of the mappers. All occurrences of is will end up on the same partition for the reduce phase.

❶ Reduce the list of shuffled map results.

❷ Iterate over each `result` obtained from the map phase and increase word counts by one for each occurrence of a word.

We can now collect the j-th return value from each mapper and pass it to the j-th reducer as follows. Note that we use a toy dataset here, but this code would scale to datasets that don't fit on a single machine. That's because we're passing Ray object references to the reducers, not the actual data. The map and reduce phases are Ray tasks that can be executed on any Ray Cluster, and the shuffling of the data is handled by Ray as well:

```
outputs = []
for i in range(num_partitions):
    outputs.append(  ❶
        apply_reduce.remote(*[partition[i] for partition in map_results])
    )

counts = {k: v for output in ray.get(outputs) for k, v in output.items()}  ❷

sorted_counts = sorted(counts.items(), key=lambda item: item[1], reverse=True)  ❸
for count in sorted_counts:
    print(f"{count[0].decode('utf-8')}: {count[1]}")
```

❶ Gather one output from each map task and supply it to `apply_reduce`.

❷ Collect all reduce-phase results in a single Python `count` dictionary.

❸ Print the sorted word count over the full corpus.

Running this example will yield the following output:

```
is: 10
than: 8
better: 8
the: 6
to: 5
although: 3
...
```

If you want a deep dive into making MapReduce tasks scale to multiple nodes with Ray, including detailed memory considerations, we recommend studying the excellent blog post (*https://oreil.ly/ROSPr*) on this topic.

The important part about this MapReduce example is how *flexible Ray's programming model really is*. Surely, a production-grade MapReduce implementation takes a bit more effort. But being able to reproduce common algorithms like this one quickly goes a long way. Keep in mind that in the earlier phases of MapReduce, say around

2010, this paradigm was often the only thing you had to express your workloads. With Ray, a whole range of interesting distributed computing patterns become accessible to any intermediate Python programmer.[19]

Summary

You've seen the basics of the Ray API in action in this chapter. You know how to put values into the object store and how to get them back. Also, you're familiar with declaring Python functions as Ray tasks with the @ray.remote decorator, and you know how to run them on a Ray Cluster with the .remote() call. In much the same way, you understand how to declare a Ray actor from a Python class and how to instantiate it and leverage it for stateful, distributed computations.

On top of that, you also know the basics of Ray Clusters. After starting them with ray.init(...), you know that you can submit jobs consisting of tasks to your cluster. The driver process, sitting on the head node, will then distribute the tasks to the worker nodes. Raylets on each node will schedule the tasks, and worker processes will execute them. You've also seen a quick implementation of the MapReduce paradigm with Ray as an example of a common pattern of building Ray applications.

This quick tour through Ray Core should get you started with writing your own distributed programs. In Chapter 3 we'll test your knowledge by implementing a basic machine learning application.

---

19 We encourage you to check out Ray's in-depth patterns and anti-patterns for both tasks (*https://oreil.ly/ dWaSg*) and actors (*https://oreil.ly/s6eLw*).

## CHAPTER 3

Building Your First Distributed Application

Now that you've seen the basics of the Ray API in action, let's build something more realistic with it. By the end of this chapter, you will have built a reinforcement learning (RL) problem from scratch, implemented your first algorithm to tackle it, and used Ray tasks and actors to parallelize this solution to a local cluster—all in less than 250 lines of code.

This chapter is designed to work for readers who don't have any experience with RL. We'll work on a straightforward problem and develop the necessary skills to tackle it hands-on. Since Chapter 4 is devoted entirely to this topic, we'll skip all advanced RL topics and language and just focus on the problem at hand. But even if you're a quite advanced RL user, you'll likely benefit from implementing a classic algorithm in a distributed setting.

This is the last chapter working *only* with Ray Core. We hope you learn to appreciate how powerful and flexible it is and how quickly you can implement distributed experiments that would otherwise take considerable efforts to scale.

Before we jump into any implementation, let's quickly talk about the paradigm of RL in a bit more detail. Feel free to skip this section if you've worked with RL before.

Introducing Reinforcement Learning

One of my (Max's) favorite mobile apps can automatically classify or "label" individual plants in our garden. The app works by simply showing it a picture of the plant in question. That's immensely helpful; I'm terrible at distinguishing them. (I'm not bragging about the size of my garden; I'm just bad at it.) In the last couple of years we've seen a surge of impressive applications similar to this one.

Ultimately, the promise of AI is to build intelligent agents that go far beyond classifying objects. Imagine an AI application that not only knows your plants but can take care of them too. Such an application would have to do the following:

- Operate in dynamic environments (like the change of seasons)
- React to changes in the environment (like a heavy storm or pests)
- Take sequences of actions (like watering and fertilizing plants)
- Accomplish long-term goals (like prioritizing plant health)

By observing its environment, such an AI would also learn to explore the possible actions it could take and come up with better solutions over time. If you feel like this example is artificial or too far out, it's not difficult to come up with examples on your own that share all these requirements. Think of managing and optimizing a supply chain, strategically restocking a warehouse considering fluctuating demands, or orchestrating the processing steps in an assembly line. Another famous example of what you could expect from AI is Stephen Wozniak's famous "Coffee Test": if you're invited to a friend's house, you can navigate to the kitchen, spot the coffee machine and all necessary ingredients, figure out how to brew a cup of coffee, and sit down to enjoy it. A machine should be able to do the same, except the last part might be a bit of a stretch. What other examples can you think of?

You can frame all the requirements naturally in RL, a subfield of machine learning.[1] For now, it's enough to understand that RL is about agents interacting with their environment by observing it and emitting actions. In RL, agents evaluate their environments by attributing a reward (e.g., how healthy is my plant on a linear scale). The term "reinforcement" comes from the fact that agents will ideally learn to seek behavior that leads to good outcomes (high reward) and shy away from punishing situations (low or negative reward).

The interaction of agents with their environment is usually modeled by creating a computer simulation of it (although sometimes that's not feasible). So, let's build an example of such a simulation with agents acting in their environments to give you an idea of what this looks like in practice.

Setting Up a Simple Maze Problem

As with the previous chapters, we encourage you to code this chapter and build this application as we go. If you don't want to do that, you can simply follow the notebook for this chapter (*https://oreil.ly/ceW4X*).

---

1 We don't yet have gardening robots, and we don't know which AI paradigm will get us there. RL isn't necessarily the answer; it is just a paradigm that naturally fits into this specific discussion of AI goals.

To give you an idea, the app we're building is structured as follows:

- Implement a simple 2D-maze game in which a single player can move around in the four major directions.

- Initialize the maze as a 5 × 5 grid to which the player is confined. One of the 25 grid cells is the "goal" that a player called the *seeker* must reach.

- Employ an RL algorithm instead of hard-coding a solution so that the seeker learns to find the goal.

- Run simulations of the maze repeatedly, rewarding the seeker for finding the goal and smartly keeping track of which of the seeker's decisions worked and which didn't. Because running simulations can be parallelized and our RL algorithm can also be trained in parallel, we use the Ray API to parallelize the whole process.

We're not quite ready to deploy this application on an actual Ray Cluster composed of multiple nodes just yet, so for now we'll continue to work with local clusters. If you're interested in infrastructure topics and want to learn how to set up Ray Clusters, jump ahead to Chapter 9. In any case, make sure you have Ray installed with `pip install ray`.

Let's start by implementing the 2D maze we just sketched. The idea is to implement a simple grid in Python that spans a 5 × 5 grid starting at (0, 0) and ending at (4, 4) and properly define how a player can move around the grid. To do this, we first need an abstraction for moving in the four cardinal directions. These four actions, namely, moving up, down, left, and right, can be encoded in Python as a class we call `Discrete`. The abstraction of moving in several discrete actions is so useful that we'll generalize it to *n* directions, instead of just four. In case you're worried, this is not premature—we'll actually need a general `Discrete` class in a moment:

```
import random


class Discrete:
    def __init__(self, num_actions: int):
        """ Discrete action space for num_actions.
        Discrete(4) can be used as encoding moving in
        one of the cardinal directions.
        """
        self.n = num_actions

    def sample(self):
        return random.randint(0, self.n - 1)  ❶


space = Discrete(4)
print(space.sample())  ❷
```

❶ A discrete action can be uniformly sampled between 0 and $n - 1$.

❷ For instance, a Discrete(4) sample will give you 0, 1, 2, or 3.

Sampling from a Discrete(4) like in this example will randomly return 0, 1, 2, or 3. How we interpret these numbers is up to us, so let's say we go for "down," "left," "up," and "right" in that order.

Now that we know how to encode moving around the maze, let's code the maze itself, including the goal cell and the position of the seeker player that tries to find the goal. To this end we're going to implement a Python class called Environment. It's called that because the maze is the environment in which the player "lives." To make matters easy, we'll always put the seeker at (0, 0) and the goal at (4, 4). To make the seeker move and find the goal, we initialize the Environment with an action_space of Discrete(4).

We need to set up one last bit of information for our maze environment: an encoding of the seeker position. The reason is that we're going to implement an algorithm later that keeps track of which actions led to good results for which seeker positions. By encoding the seeker position as a Discrete(5*5), it becomes a single number that's much easier to work with. In RL lingo it is common to call the information of the game that is accessible to the player an *observation*. So, in an analogy to the actions we can carry out for our seeker, we can also define an observation_space for it. Here's the implementation of what we've just discussed:

```
import os


class Environment:
    def __init__(self,  *args, **kwargs):
        self.seeker, self.goal = (0, 0), (4, 4)   ❶
        self.info = {'seeker': self.seeker, 'goal': self.goal}

        self.action_space = Discrete(4)   ❷
        self.observation_space = Discrete(5*5)   ❸
```

❶ The seeker gets initialized in the top left, the goal in the bottom right of the maze.

❷ Our seeker can move down, left, up, and right.

❸ It can be in a total of 25 states, one for each position on the grid.

Note that we defined an `info` variable as well, which can be used to print information about the current state of the maze, for instance for debugging purposes. To play an actual game of find-the-goal from the perspective of the seeker, we have to define a few helper methods. Clearly, the game should be considered "done" when the seeker finds the goal. Also, we should reward the seeker for finding the goal. And when the game is over, we should be able to reset it to its initial state, to play again. To round things off, we also define a `get_observation` method that returns the encoded `seeker` position. Continuing our implementation of the `Environment` class, this translates into the following four methods:

```python
def reset(self):  ❶
    """Reset seeker position and return observations."""
    self.seeker = (0, 0)

    return self.get_observation()

def get_observation(self):
    """Encode the seeker position as integer"""
    return 5 * self.seeker[0] + self.seeker[1]  ❷

def get_reward(self):
    """Reward finding the goal"""
    return 1 if self.seeker == self.goal else 0  ❸

def is_done(self):
    """We're done if we found the goal"""
    return self.seeker == self.goal  ❹
```

❶ To play a new game, `reset` the grid to its original state.

❷ Convert the seeker tuple to a value from the environment's `observation_space`.

❸ The seeker is rewarded only upon reaching the goal.

❹ If the seeker is at the goal, the game is over.

The last essential method to implement is the `step` method. Imagine you're playing our maze game and decide to go right as your next move. The `step` method will take this action (namely, 3, the encoding of "right") and apply it to the internal state of the game. To reflect what changed, the `step` method will then return the seeker's observations, its reward, whether the game is over, and the `info` value of the game. Here's how the `step` method works:

```python
def step(self, action):
    """Take a step in a direction and return all available information."""
    if action == 0:  # move down
        self.seeker = (min(self.seeker[0] + 1, 4), self.seeker[1])
```

```
    elif action == 1:  # move left
        self.seeker = (self.seeker[0], max(self.seeker[1] - 1, 0))
    elif action == 2:  # move up
        self.seeker = (max(self.seeker[0] - 1, 0), self.seeker[1])
    elif action == 3:  # move right
        self.seeker = (self.seeker[0], min(self.seeker[1] + 1, 4))
    else:
        raise ValueError("Invalid action")

    obs = self.get_observation()
    rew = self.get_reward()
    done = self.is_done()
    return obs, rew, done, self.info   ❶
```

❶ Returns the observation, reward, whether we're done, and any additional information we might find useful after taking a step in the specified direction.

We said the step method was the last essential method, but we actually want to define one more helper method that's extremely useful for visualizing the game and helping us understand it. This render method will print the current state of the game to the command line:

```
def render(self, *args, **kwargs):
    """Render the environment, e.g., by printing its representation."""
    os.system('cls' if os.name == 'nt' else 'clear')   ❶

    grid = [['| ' for _ in range(5)] + ["|\n"] for _ in range(5)]
    grid[self.goal[0]][self.goal[1]] = '|G'
    grid[self.seeker[0]][self.seeker[1]] = '|S'   ❷
    print(''.join([''.join(grid_row) for grid_row in grid]))   ❸
```

❶ Clear the screen.

❷ Draw the grid and mark the goal as G and the seeker as S on it.

❸ The grid then gets rendered by printing it to your screen.

Great, now we have completed the implementation of our Environment class that's defining our 2D-maze game. We can step through this game, know when it's done, and reset it again. The player of the game, the seeker, can also observe its environment and get rewarded for finding the goal.

Let's use this implementation to play a game of find-the-goal for a seeker that simply takes random actions. This can be done by creating a new Environment, sampling and applying actions to it, and rendering the environment until the game is over:

```
import time

environment = Environment()
```

```
while not environment.is_done():
    random_action = environment.action_space.sample()   ❶
    environment.step(random_action)
    time.sleep(0.1)
    environment.render()   ❷
```

❶ We can test our environment by applying sampled actions until we're finished.

❷ To visualize the environment, render it after waiting for a tenth of a second
   (otherwise the code runs too fast to follow).

If you run this on your computer, eventually you'll see that the game is over and the
seeker has found the goal. It might take a while if you're unlucky.

In case you're objecting that this is an extremely simple problem, and to solve it,
all you have to do is take a total of eight steps, namely, going right and down four
times each in arbitrary order, we're not arguing with you. The point is that we want
to tackle this problem using machine learning, so that we can take on much harder
problems later. Specifically, we want to implement an algorithm that figures out on its
own how to play the game, merely by playing the game repeatedly: observing what's
happening, deciding what to do next, and getting rewarded for its actions.

If you want, now is a good time to make the game more complex. As long as you do
not change the interface we defined for the Environment class, you could modify this
game in many ways. Here are a few suggestions:

- Make it a 10 × 10 grid or randomize the initial position of the seeker.
- Make the outer walls of the grid dangerous. Whenever you touch them, you'll
  incur a reward of –100, i.e., a steep penalty.
- Introduce obstacles in the grid that the seeker cannot pass through.

If you're feeling really adventurous, you could also randomize the goal position. This
requires extra care, as currently the seeker has no information about the goal position
in terms of the get_observation method. Maybe come back to tackling this last
exercise after you've finished reading this chapter.

Building a Simulation

With the Environment class implemented, what does it take to tackle the problem of
"teaching" the seeker to play the game well? How can it find the goal consistently
in the minimum number of eight steps necessary? We've equipped the maze environment with reward information so that the seeker can use this signal to learn to play
the game. In RL, you play games repeatedly and learn from the experience you gain in
the process. The player of the game is often referred to as an *agent* that takes *actions*

in the environment, observes its *state*, and receives a *reward*.[2] The better an agent learns, the better it becomes at interpreting the current game state (observations) and finding actions that lead to more rewarding outcomes.

Regardless of the RL algorithm you want to use, you need to have a way of simulating the game repeatedly to collect experience data. For this reason, we're going to implement a simple Simulation class.

The other useful abstraction we need to proceed is that of a Policy, a way of specifying actions. Right now the only thing we can do to play the game is sample random actions for our seeker. What a Policy allows us to do is to get better actions for the current state of the game. In fact, we define a Policy to be a class with a get_action method that takes a game state and returns an action.

Remember that in our game the seeker has a total of 25 possible states on the grid and can carry out four actions. A simple idea would be to look at pairs of states and actions and assign a high value to a pair if carrying out this action in this state will lead to a high reward, and a low value otherwise. For instance, from your intuition of the game it should be clear that going down or right is always a good idea, whereas going left or up is not. Then, create a 25 × 4 lookup table of all possible state-action pairs and store it in our Policy. Then we could simply ask our policy to return the highest value of any action, given a state. Of course, implementing an algorithm that finds good values for these state-action pairs is the challenging part. Let's implement this idea of a Policy first and worry about a suitable algorithm later:

```python
import numpy as np

class Policy:

    def __init__(self, env):
        """A Policy suggests actions based on the current state.
        We do this by tracking the value of each state-action pair.
        """
        self.state_action_table = [
            [0 for _ in range(env.action_space.n)]
            for _ in range(env.observation_space.n)  ❶
        ]
        self.action_space = env.action_space

    def get_action(self, state, explore=True, epsilon=0.1):  ❷
        """Explore randomly or exploit the best value currently available."""
        if explore and random.uniform(0, 1) < epsilon:  ❸
            return self.action_space.sample()
        return np.argmax(self.state_action_table[state])  ❹
```

---

2 As we'll see in Chapter 4, you can run RL on multiplayer games too. Making the maze environment a so-called multi-agent environment, in which multiple seekers compete for the goal, is an interesting exercise.

❶ Define a nested list of values for each state-action pair, initialized to zero.

❷ `explore` random actions on demand so that we don't get stuck in suboptimal behavior.

❸ Introduce an `explore` parameter to the `get_action` method because we might want to explore actions randomly in the game. By default, this happens 10% of the time.

❹ Return the action with the highest value in the lookup table, given the current state.

We've snuck a little implementation detail into the `Policy` definition that might be a bit confusing. The `get_action` method has an `explore` parameter. Without it, if you learn an extremely poor policy (e.g., one that always wants you to move left), you have no chance of ever finding better solutions. In other words, sometimes you need to explore new ways and not "exploit" your current understanding of the game. As indicated before, we haven't discussed how to learn to improve the values in the `state_action_table` of our policy. For now, just keep in mind that the policy gives us the actions we want to follow when simulating the maze game.

Moving on to the `Simulation` class we spoke about earlier, a simulation should take an `Environment` and compute actions of a given `Policy` until the goal is reached and the game ends. The data we observe when "rolling out" a full game like this is what we call the *experience* we gained. Accordingly, our `Simulation` class has a `rollout` method that computes `experiences` for a full game and returns them. Here's what the implementation of the `Simulation` class looks like:

```
class Simulation(object):
    def __init__(self, env):
        """Simulates rollouts of an environment, given a policy to follow."""
        self.env = env

    def rollout(self, policy, render=False, explore=True, epsilon=0.1):  ❶
        """Returns experiences for a policy rollout."""
        experiences = []
        state = self.env.reset()  ❷
        done = False
        while not done:
            action = policy.get_action(state, explore, epsilon)  ❸
            next_state, reward, done, info = self.env.step(action)  ❹
            experiences.append([state, action, reward, next_state])  ❺
            state = next_state
            if render:  ❻
                time.sleep(0.05)
                self.env.render()
```

```
return experiences
```

❶ Compute a game "rollout" by following the actions of a policy, and optionally render the simulation.

❷ To be sure, reset the environment before each rollout.

❸ The passed-in policy drives the actions we take. The explore and epsilon parameters are passed through.

❹ Step through the environment by applying the policy's action.

❺ Define an experience as a (state, action, reward, next_state) quadruple.

❻ Optionally render the environment at each step.

Note that each entry of the experiences we collect in a rollout consists of four values: the current state, the action taken, the reward received, and the next state. The algorithm we're going to implement in a moment will use these experiences to learn from them. Other algorithms might use other experience values, but those are the ones we need to proceed.

We now have a policy that hasn't learned anything just yet, but we can already test its interface to see if it works. Let's try it out by initializing a Simulation object, calling its rollout method on a not-so-smart Policy, and then printing the state_action_table of it:

```
untrained_policy = Policy(environment)
sim = Simulation(environment)

exp = sim.rollout(untrained_policy, render=True, epsilon=1.0)  ❶
for row in untrained_policy.state_action_table:
    print(row)  ❷
```

❶ Roll out one full game with an "untrained" policy that we render.

❷ The state-action values are currently all zero.

If you feel like we haven't made much progress since the previous section, rest assured that things will come together in the next one. The prep work of setting up a Simulation and a Policy were necessary to frame the problem correctly. Now the only thing that's left is to devise a smart way to update the internal state of the Policy based on the experiences we've collected so that it actually learns to play the maze game.

Training a Reinforcement Learning Model

Imagine we have a set of experiences that we've collected from a couple of games. What would be a smart way to update the values in the `state_action_table` of our `Policy`? Here's one idea. Let's say you're sitting at position (3,5), and you've decided to go right, which puts you at (4,5), just one step away from the goal. Clearly you could then just go right and collect a reward of 1. That must mean the current state you're in, combined with an action of going "right," should have a high value. In other words, the value of this particular state-action pair should be high. In contrast, moving left in the same situation does not lead to anything, and the corresponding state-action pair should have a low value.

More generally, let's say you were in a given `state`, you decided to take an `action`, leading to a reward, and you're then in `next_state`. Remember that this is how we defined an experience. With our `policy.state_action_table` we can peek a little ahead and see if we can expect to gain anything from actions taken from `next_state`. That is, we can compute:

```
next_max = np.max(policy.state_action_table[next_state])
```

How should we compare the knowledge of this value to the current state-action value, which is `value = policy.state_action_table[state][action]`? There are many ways to go about this, but we clearly can't completely discard the current `value` and put too much trust in `next_max`. After all, this is just a single piece of experience we're using here. So as a first approximation, why don't we simply compute a weighted sum of the old and the expected value and go with `new_value = 0.9 * value + 0.1 * next_max`? Here, the values 0.9 and 0.1 have been chosen somewhat arbitrarily; the only important pieces are that the first value is high enough to reflect our preference to keep the old value and that both weights sum to 1. That formula is a good starting point, but the problem is that we're not at all factoring in the crucial information that we're getting from the `reward`. In fact, we should put more trust in the current `reward` value than in the projected `next_max` value, so it's a good idea to discount the latter a little, let's say by 10%. Updating the state-action value would then look like this:

```
new_value = 0.9 * value + 0.1 * (reward + 0.9 * next_max)
```

Depending on your level of experience with this kind of reasoning, the last few paragraphs might be a lot to digest. If you've understood the explanations up to this point, the remainder of this chapter will likely come easily to you. Mathematically, this was the last (and only) hard part of this example. If you've worked with RL before, you will have noticed that this is an implementation of the so-called Q-Learning algorithm. It's called that because the state-action table can be described as a function `Q(state, action)` that returns values for these pairs.

We're almost there, so let's formalize the procedure with an `update_policy` function for a policy and collected experiences:

```
def update_policy(policy, experiences, weight=0.1, discount_factor=0.9):
    """Updates a given policy with a list of (state, action, reward, state)
    experiences."""
    for state, action, reward, next_state in experiences:   ❶
        next_max = np.max(policy.state_action_table[next_state])   ❷
        value = policy.state_action_table[state][action]   ❸
        new_value = (1 - weight) * value + weight * \
                    (reward + discount_factor * next_max)   ❹
        policy.state_action_table[state][action] = new_value   ❺
```

❶ Loop through all experiences in order.

❷ Choose the maximum value among all possible actions in the next state.

❸ Extract the current state-action value.

❹ The new value is the weighted sum of the old value and the expected value, which is the sum of the current reward and the discounted `next_max`.

❺ After updating, set the new `state_action_table` value.

Having this function in place now makes it simple to train a policy to make better decisions. We can use the following procedure:

1. Initialize a policy and a simulation.

2. Run the simulation many times, let's say for a total of 10,000 runs.

3. For each game, first collect the experiences by running a `rollout`.

4. Then update the policy by calling `update_policy` on the collected experiences.

That's it! The following `train_policy` function implements this procedure:

```
def train_policy(env, num_episodes=10000, weight=0.1, discount_factor=0.9):
    """Training a policy by updating it with rollout experiences."""
    policy = Policy(env)
    sim = Simulation(env)
    for _ in range(num_episodes):
        experiences = sim.rollout(policy)   ❶
        update_policy(policy, experiences, weight, discount_factor)   ❷

    return policy


trained_policy = train_policy(environment)   ❸
```

❶ Collect experiences for each game.

❷ Update our policy with those experiences.

❸ Finally, train and return a policy for our `enviroment` from before.

Note that in the RL literature, the high-brow way of referring to a full play-through of the maze game is an *episode*. That's why we call the argument `num_episodes` in the `train_policy` function, rather than `num_games`.

Q-Learning

The Q-Learning algorithm we just implemented is often the first algorithm taught in RL classes, mostly because it is relatively easy to reason with. You collect and tabulate experience data that shows you how well state-action pairs work, and then you update the table according to the Q-Learning update rule.

For RL problems that have a huge number of either states or actions, the Q-table can become excessively large. The algorithm then becomes inefficient, because it would take too much time to collect enough experience data for all (relevant) state-action pairs.

One way to address this issue is to use a neural network to approximate the Q-table. By this we mean that you can employ a deep neural network to learn a function that maps states to actions. This approach is called Deep Q-Learning, and the networks used for learning are called Deep Q-Networks (DQN). From Chapter 4 on, we will exclusively use deep learning to tackle RL problems in this book.

Now that we have a trained policy, let's see how well it performs. We've run random policies twice before in this chapter, just to get an idea of how well they work for the maze problem. But let's now properly evaluate our trained policy on several games and see how it does on average. Specifically, we'll run our simulation for a couple of episodes and count how many steps it took per episode to reach the goal. So, let's implement an `evaluate_policy` function that does precisely that:

```
def evaluate_policy(env, policy, num_episodes=10):
    """Evaluate a trained policy through rollouts."""
    simulation = Simulation(env)
    steps = 0

    for _ in range(num_episodes):
        experiences = simulation.rollout(policy, render=True, explore=False)  ❶
        steps += len(experiences)  ❷

    print(f"{steps / num_episodes} steps on average "
          f"for a total of {num_episodes} episodes.")
```

```
    return steps / num_episodes
```

```
evaluate_policy(environment, trained_policy)
```

❶ This time, set `explore` to `False` to fully exploit the trained policy's learnings.

❷ The length of the `experiences` is the number of steps we took to finish the game.

Apart from seeing the trained policy crush the maze problem 10 times in a row, as we hoped it would, you should also see the following prompt:

```
8.0 steps on average for a total of 10 episodes.
```

In other words, the trained policy is able to find optimal solutions for the maze game. That means you've successfully implemented your first RL algorithm from scratch!

With the understanding you've built, do you think placing the `seeker` into randomized starting positions and then running this evaluation function would still work? Why don't you go ahead and make the changes necessary for that?

Another interesting question to ask yourself is what assumptions went into the algorithm we used. For instance, it's clearly a prerequisite for the algorithm that all state-action pairs can be tabulated. Do you think this would still work well if we had millions of states and thousands of actions?

Building a Distributed Ray App

We hope you have enjoyed the example so far, but you might be wondering how what we've done until now relates to Ray (which is a great question). As you'll see shortly, all we need to make the RL experiment a distributed Ray app is writing three short code snippets. This is what we're going to do:

1. Make the `Simulation` a Ray actor using just a few lines of code.

2. Define a parallel version of `train_policy` that's structurally similar to its original. For simplicity, we will parallelize only the rollouts, not the policy updates.

3. Train and evaluate the policy as before but using `train_policy_parallel`.

Let's tackle the first step of this plan by implementing a Ray actor called `Simulation Actor`:

```
import ray

ray.init()

@ray.remote
```

```
class SimulationActor(Simulation):   ❶
    """Ray actor for a Simulation."""
    def __init__(self):
        env = Environment()
        super().__init__(env)
```

❶ This Ray actor wraps our Simulation class in a straightforward way.

With the foundations on Ray Core you've developed in Chapter 2, you should have no problems reading this code. It might take some practice to be able to write it yourself, but conceptually you should be on top of this example.

Moving on, let's define a train_policy_parallel function that distributes this RL workload on your local Ray Cluster. To do so, we create a policy on the driver and a total of four SimulationActor instances that we can use for distributed rollouts. We then put the policy into the object store with ray.put and pass it to the remote rollout calls as an argument to collect experiences for a given number of training episodes. We then use ray.wait to get the finished rollouts (and account for the fact that some rollouts might finish earlier than others) and update our policy with the collected experiences. Finally, we return the trained policy:

```
def train_policy_parallel(env, num_episodes=1000, num_simulations=4):
    """Parallel policy training function."""
    policy = Policy(env)   ❶
    simulations = [SimulationActor.remote() for _ in range(num_simulations)]   ❷

    policy_ref = ray.put(policy)   ❸
    for _ in range(num_episodes):
        experiences = [sim.rollout.remote(policy_ref) for sim in simulations]   ❹

        while len(experiences) > 0:
            finished, experiences = ray.wait(experiences)   ❺
            for xp in ray.get(finished):
                update_policy(policy, xp)

    return policy
```

❶ Initialize a policy for the given environment.

❷ Instead of one simulation, create four simulation actors.

❸ Put the policy into the object store.

❹ For each of the 1,000 episodes, collect experience data in parallel using our simulation actors.

❺ Finished rollouts can be retrieved from the object store and used to update the policy.

This allows us to take the last step and run the training procedure in parallel and then evaluate the result as before:

```
parallel_policy = train_policy_parallel(environment)
evaluate_policy(environment, parallel_policy)
```

The result of those two lines is the same as before, when we ran the serial version of the RL training for the maze. We hope you appreciate how `train_policy_parallel` has the same high-level structure as `train_policy`. It's a good exercise to compare the two line-by-line.

Essentially, all it took to parallelize the training process was to use the `ray.remote` decorator on a class in a suitable way and then use the right `remote` calls. Of course, you need some experience to get this right. But notice how little time we spent on thinking about distributed computing and how much time we could spend on the actual application code. We didn't need to adopt an entirely new programming paradigm and could simply approach the problem in the most natural way. Ultimately, that's what you want—and Ray is great at giving you this kind of flexibility.

To wrap things up, let's have a quick look at the execution graph of the Ray application that we've just built. Figure 3-1 summarizes this task graph in a compact way.

 The running example in this chapter is an implementation of the pseudocode example used to illustrate the flexibility of Ray in the initial paper (*https://oreil.ly/ZKZFY*) by its creators. That paper has a figure similar to Figure 3-1 and is worth reading for context.

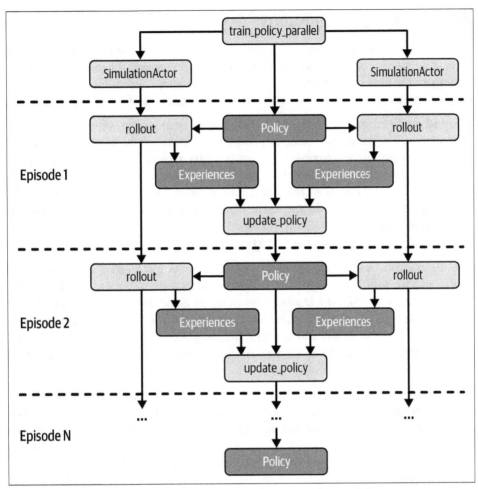

Figure 3-1. Parallel training of a reinforcement learning policy with Ray

Recapping RL Terminology

Before we wrap up this chapter, let's discuss the concepts we've encountered in the maze example in a broader context. Doing so will prepare you for more complex RL settings in the next chapter and show you where we simplified things a little for this chapter's running example. If you know RL well enough, you can skip this section.

Every RL problem starts with the formulation of an *environment*, which describes the dynamics of the "game" you want to play. The environment hosts a player or *agent* that interacts with its environment through a simple interface. The agent can request information from the environment, namely, its current *state* within the environment, the *reward* it has received in this state, and whether the game is *done* or not. In observing states and rewards, the agent can learn to make decisions based on the information it receives. Specifically, the agent will emit an *action* that can be executed by the environment by taking the next `step`.

The mechanism used by an agent to produce actions for a given state is called a *policy*, and we sometimes say that the agent follows a given policy. Given a policy, we can simulate or *roll out* a few steps or an entire game using that policy. During a rollout we can collect *experiences*, which collect information about the current state and reward, the next action, and the resulting state. An entire sequence of steps from start to finish is referred to as an *episode*, and the environment can be `reset` to its initial state to start a new episode.

The policy we used in this chapter was based on the simple idea of tabulating *state-action values* (also called *Q-values*), and the algorithm used to update the policy from the experiences collected during rollouts is called *Q-Learning*. More generally, you can consider the state-action table we implemented as the *model* used by the policy. In the next chapter you will see examples of more complex models, such as a neural network to learn state-action values. The policy can decide to *exploit* what it has learned about the environment by choosing the best available value of its model or *explore* the environment by choosing a random action.

Many of the basic concepts introduced here hold for any RL problem, but we've made a few simplifying assumptions. For instance, there could be *multiple agents* acting in the environment (imagine having multiple seekers competing for reaching the goal first), and we'll look into so-called multi-agent environments and multi-agent RL and in the next chapter. Also, we assumed that the *action space* of an agent was *discrete*, meaning that the agent could take only a fixed set of actions. You can, of course, also have *continuous* action spaces, and the cart–pole example from Chapter 1 is one example of this. Especially when you have multiple agents, action spaces can be more complicated, and you might need tuples of actions or even to nest them accordingly. The *observation space* we've considered for the maze game was also quite simple and was modeled as a discrete set of states. You can easily imagine that complex agents like robots interacting with their environments might work with image or video data as observations, which would require a more complex observation space too.

Another crucial assumption we made is that the environment is *deterministic*, meaning that when our agent chose to take an action, the resulting state would always reflect that choice. In general environments this is not the case, and there can be elements of randomness at play in the environment. For instance, we could have implemented a coin flip in the maze game, and whenever tails came up, the agent would get pushed in a random direction. In that scenario, we couldn't have planned ahead like we did in this chapter because actions would not deterministically lead to the same next state every time. To reflect this probabilistic behavior, in general we have to account for *state transition probabilities* in our RL experiments.

The last simplifying assumption I'd like to talk about here is that we've been treating the environment and its dynamics as a game that can be perfectly simulated. But the fact is that some physical systems can't be faithfully simulated. In that case you might still interact with this physical environment through an interface like the one we defined in our Environment class, but there would be some communication overhead involved. In practice, *reasoning* about RL problems as if they were games takes very little away from the experience.

Summary

To recap, we've implemented a simple maze problem in plain Python and then solved the task of finding the goal in that maze using a straightforward reinforcement learning algorithm. We then took this solution and ported it to a distributed Ray application in roughly 25 lines of code. We did so without having to plan up front how to work with Ray—we simply used the Ray API to parallelize our Python code. This example shows how Ray gets out of your way and lets you focus on your application code. It also demonstrates how custom workloads that use advanced techniques like RL can be efficiently implemented and distributed with Ray.

In Chapter 4, you'll build on what you've learned here and see how easy it is to solve our maze problem directly with the higher-level Ray RLlib library.

## CHAPTER 4

Reinforcement Learning with Ray RLlib

In Chapter 3 you built an RL environment, a simulation to play out some games, an RL algorithm, and the code to parallelize the training of the algorithm—all completely from scratch. It's good to know how to do all that, but in practice the only thing you really want to do when training RL algorithms is the first part, namely, specifying your custom environment, the "game" you want to play.[1] Most of your efforts will go into selecting the right algorithm, setting it up, finding the best parameters for the problem, and generally focusing on training a well-performing policy.

Ray RLlib is an industry-grade library for building RL algorithms at scale. You've already seen a first example of RLlib in Chapter 1, but in this chapter we'll go into much more depth. The great thing about RLlib is that it's a mature library for developers that comes with good abstractions to work with. As you will see, many of these abstractions you already know from the previous chapter.

We start out by giving you an overview of RLlib's capabilities. Then we quickly revisit the maze game from Chapter 3 and show you how to tackle it both with the RLlib CLI and the RLlib Python API in a few lines of code. You'll see how easy RLlib is to get started before learning about its key concepts, such as RLlib environments and algorithms.

We'll also take a closer look at some advanced RL topics that are extremely useful in practice but are not often properly supported in other RL libraries. For instance, you will learn how to create a curriculum for your RL agents so that they can learn simple scenarios before moving on to more complex ones. You will also see how RLlib deals

---

[1] We're using a simple game to illustrate the process of RL. There is a multitude of interesting industry applications of RL that are not games.

with having multiple agents in a single environment and how to leverage experience data that you've collected outside your current application to improve your agent's performance.

An Overview of RLlib

Before we dive into any examples, let's quickly discuss what RLlib is and what it can do. As part of the Ray ecosystem, RLlib inherits all the performance and scalability benefits of Ray. In particular, RLlib is distributed by default, so you can scale your RL training to as many nodes as you want.

Another benefit of being built on top of Ray is that RLlib integrates tightly with other Ray libraries. For instance, the hyperparameters of any RLlib algorithm can be tuned with Ray Tune, as we will see in Chapter 5. You can also seamlessly deploy your RLlib models with Ray Serve.[2]

What's extremely useful is that RLlib works with both of the predominant deep learning frameworks at the time of this writing: PyTorch and TensorFlow. You can use either one of them as your backend and can easily switch between them, often by changing just one line of code. That's a huge benefit, as companies are often locked into their underlying deep learning framework and can't afford to switch to another system and rewrite their code.

RLlib also has a track record of solving real-world problems and is a mature library used by many companies to bring their RL workloads to production. The RLlib API appeals to many engineers, as it offers the right level of abstraction for many applications while still being flexible enough to be extended.

Apart from these more general benefits, RLlib has a lot of RL-specific features that we will cover in this chapter. In fact, RLlib is so feature rich that it would deserve a book on its own, which means we can touch on just some aspects of it here. For instance, RLlib has a rich library of advanced RL algorithms to choose from. In this chapter we will focus on a few select ones, but you can track the growing list of options on the RLlib algorithms page (*https://oreil.ly/14JhM*). RLlib also has many options for specifying RL environments and is very flexible in handling them during training; for an overview of RLlib environments see the documentation (*https://oreil.ly/Vp6xY*).

---

2 We don't cover this integration in this book, but you can learn more about deploying RLlib models in the "Serving RLlib Models" tutorial (*https://oreil.ly/vsz0A*) in the Ray documentation.

Getting Started with RLlib

To use RLlib, make sure you have installed it on your computer:

```
pip install "ray[rllib]"==2.2.0"
```

 Check out the accompanying notebook for this chapter (*https://oreil.ly/KEhGx*) if you don't feel like typing the code yourself.

Every RL problem starts with having an interesting environment to investigate. In Chapter 1 we looked at the classical cart–pole balancing problem. Recall that we didn't implement this cart–pole environment; it came out of the box with RLlib.

In contrast, in Chapter 3 we implemented a simple maze game on our own. The problem with this implementation is that we can't directly use it with RLlib or any other RL library for that matter. The reason is that in RL you have ubiquitous standards, and our environments need to implement certain interfaces. The best known and most widely used library for RL environments is gym, an open source Python project (*https://gym.openai.com*) from OpenAI.

Let's have a look at what Gym is and how to convert our maze `Environment` from the previous chapter to a Gym environment compatible with RLlib.

Building a Gym Environment

If you look at the well-documented and easy-to-read `gym.Env` environment interface on GitHub (*https://oreil.ly/R3Ob1*), you'll notice that an implementation of this interface has two mandatory class variables and three methods that subclasses need to implement. You don't have to check the source code, but we do encourage you to have a look. You might just be surprised by how much you already know about these environments.

In short, the interface of a Gym environment looks like the following pseudocode:

```
import gym


class Env:

    action_space: gym.spaces.Space
    observation_space: gym.spaces.Space    ❶

    def step(self, action):    ❷
        ...
```

```
    def reset(self):  ❸
        ...

    def render(self, mode="human"):  ❹
        ...
```

❶ The gym.Env interface has an action and an observation space.

❷ The Env can run a step and returns a tuple of observations, reward, done condition, and further info.

❸ An Env can reset itself, which will return the initial observations of a new episode.

❹ We can render an Env for different purposes, such as for human display or as a string representation.

You'll recall from Chapter 3 that this is very similar to the interface of the maze Environment we built there. In fact, Gym has a so-called Discrete space implemented in gym.spaces, which means we can make our maze Environment a gym.Env as follows. We assume that you store this code in a file called *maze_gym_env.py* and that the code for the Environment from Chapter 3 is located at the top of that file (or is imported there):

```
# maze_gym_env.py  | Original definition of Environment goes at the top.

import gym
from gym.spaces import Discrete  ❶


class GymEnvironment(Environment, gym.Env):  ❷
    def __init__(self, *args, **kwargs):
        """Make our original Environment a gym `Env`."""
        super().__init__(*args, **kwargs)


gym_env = GymEnvironment()
```

❶ Replace our own Discrete implementation with that of Gym.

❷ Make the GymEnvironment implement a gym.Env. The interface is essentially the same as before.

Of course, we could have made our original Environment implement gym.Env by simply inheriting from it in the first place. But the point is that the gym.Env interface comes up so naturally in the context of RL that it is a good exercise to implement it without having to resort to external libraries.[3]

The gym.Env interface also comes with helpful utility functionality and many interesting example implementations. For instance, the CartPole-v1 environment we used in Chapter 1 is an example from Gym,[4] and there are many other environments (*https://oreil.ly/Mj6_t*) available to test your RL algorithms.

Running the RLlib CLI

Now that we have our GymEnvironment implemented as a gym.Env, here's how you can use it with RLlib. You've seen the RLlib CLI in action in Chapter 1, but this time the situation is a bit different. In the first chapter we simply ran a tuned example using the rllib example command.

This time around we want to bring our own gym environment class, namely, the class GymEnvironment that we defined in *maze_gym_env.py*. To specify this class in Ray RLlib, you use the full qualifying name of the class from where you're referencing it, so in our case that's maze_gym_env.GymEnvironment. If you had a more complicated Python project and your environment was stored in another module, you'd simply add the module name accordingly.

The following Python file specifies the minimal configuration needed to train an RLlib algorithm on the GymEnvironment class. To align as closely as possible with our experiment from Chapter 3, in which we used Q-Learning, we use a DQNConfig to define a DQN algorithm and store it in a file called *maze.py*:

```
from ray.rllib.algorithms.dqn import DQNConfig

config = DQNConfig().environment("maze_gym_env.GymEnvironment")\
    .rollouts(num_rollout_workers=2)
```

This gives a quick preview of RLlib's Python API, which we cover in the next section. To run this with RLlib, we're using the rllib train command. We do this by specifying the file we want to run: *maze.py*. To make sure we can control the time of training, we tell our algorithm to stop after running for a total of 10,000 time steps (timesteps_total):

```
rllib train file maze.py --stop '{"timesteps_total": 10000}'
```

---

3 From Ray 2.3.0 onward, RLlib will be using the Gymnasium library as drop-in replacement for Gym. This will likely introduce some breaking changes, so it's best to stick with Ray 2.2.0 to follow this chapter.

4 Gym comes with a variety of interesting environments that are worth exploring. For instance, you can find many of the Atari environments that were used in the famous "Playing Atari with Deep Reinforcement Learning" paper (*https://arxiv.org/abs/1312.5602*) from DeepMind, or advanced physics simulations using the MuJoCo engine.

This single line takes care of everything we did in Chapter 3, but in a better way:

- It runs a more sophisticated version of Q-Learning for us (DQN).[5]
- It takes care of scaling out to multiple workers under the hood (in this case two).
- It even creates checkpoints of the algorithm automatically for us.

From the output of that training script you should see that Ray will write training results to a directory located at ~/ray_results/maze_env. And if the training run finishes successfully,[6] you'll get a checkpoint and a copiable rllib evaluate command in the output, just as in the example from Chapter 1. Using this reported <checkpoint>, you can now evaluate the trained policy on our custom environment by running the following command:

```
rllib evaluate ~/ray_results/maze_env/<checkpoint>\
    --algo DQN\
    --env maze_gym_env.Environment\
    --steps 100
```

The algorithm used in --algo and the environment specified with --env have to match the ones used in the training run, and we evaluate the trained algorithm for a total of 100 steps. This should lead to output of the following form:

```
Episode #1: reward: 1.0
Episode #2: reward: 1.0
Episode #3: reward: 1.0
...
Episode #13: reward: 1.0
```

It should not come as a big surprise that the DQN algorithm from RLlib gets the maximum reward of 1 for the simple maze environment we tasked it with every single time.

Before moving on to the Python API, we should mention that the RLlib CLI uses Ray Tune under the hood, for instance, to create the checkpoints of your algorithms. You will learn more about this integration in Chapter 5.

---

5 To be precise, RLlib uses a double and dueling DQN.

6 In the GitHub repo for this book we've also included an equivalent *maze.yml* file that you could use via rllib train file maze.yml (no --type needed).

Using the RLlib Python API

In the end, the RLlib CLI is merely a wrapper around its underlying Python library. As you will likely spend most of your time coding your RL experiments in Python, we'll focus the rest of this chapter on aspects of this API.

To run RL workloads with RLlib from Python, the `Algorithm` class is your main entry point. Always start with a corresponding `AlgorithmConfig` class to define an algorithm. For instance, in the previous section we used a `DQNConfig` as a starting point, and the `rllib train` command took care of instantiating the DQN algorithm for us. All other RLlib algorithms follow the same pattern.

Training RLlib algorithms

Every RLlib `Algorithm` comes with reasonable default parameters, meaning that you *can* initialize them without having to tweak any configuration parameters for these algorithms.[7]

That said, it's worth noting that RLlib algorithms are highly configurable, as you will see in the following example. We start by creating a `DQNConfig` object. Then we specify its `environment` and set the number of rollout workers to two by using the `rollouts` method. This means that the DQN algorithm will spawn two Ray actors, each using a CPU by default, to run the algorithm in parallel. Also, for later evaluation purposes, we set `create_env_on_local_worker` to `True`:

```
from ray.tune.logger import pretty_print
from maze_gym_env import GymEnvironment
from ray.rllib.algorithms.dqn import DQNConfig

config = (DQNConfig().environment(GymEnvironment)    ❶
          .rollouts(num_rollout_workers=2, create_env_on_local_worker=True))

pretty_print(config.to_dict())

algo = config.build()    ❷

for i in range(10):
    result = algo.train()    ❸

print(pretty_print(result))    ❹
```

---

7 Of course, configuring your models is a crucial part of RL experiments. We will discuss configuration of RLlib algorithms in more detail in the next section.

❶ Set the environment to our custom `GymEnvironment` class and configure the number of rollout workers and ensure that an environment instance is created on the local worker.

❷ Use the `DQNConfig` from RLlib to `build` a DQN algorithm for training. This time we use two rollout workers.

❸ Call the `train` method to train the algorithm for 10 iterations.

❹ With the `pretty_print` utility, we can generate human-readable output of the training results.

Note that the number of training iterations has no special meaning, but it should be enough for the algorithm to learn to solve the maze problem adequately. The example just goes to show that you have full control over the training process.

From printing the `config` dictionary, you can verify that the `num_rollout_workers` parameter is set to 2.[8] The `result` contains detailed information about the state of the DQN algorithm and the training results, which are too verbose to show here. The part that's most relevant for us right now is information about the reward of the algorithm, which ideally indicates that the algorithm learned to solve the maze problem. You should see output of the following form (we're showing only the most relevant information for clarity):

```
...
episode_reward_max: 1.0
episode_reward_mean: 1.0
episode_reward_min: 1.0
episodes_this_iter: 15
episodes_total: 19
...
training_iteration: 10
...
```

In particular, this output shows that the minimum reward attained on average per episode is 1.0, which in turn means that the agent always reached the goal and collected the maximum reward (1.0).

---

8 If you set `num_rollout_workers` to 0, only the local worker on the head node will be created, and all sampling from the env is done there. This is particularly useful for debugging, as no additional Ray actor processes are spawned.

Saving, loading, and evaluating RLlib models

Reaching the goal for this simple example isn't too difficult, but let's see if evaluating the trained algorithm confirms that the agent can also do so in an optimal way, namely, by taking only the minimum number of eight steps to reach the goal.

To do so, we utilize another mechanism that you've already seen from the RLlib CLI: *checkpointing*. Creating algorithm checkpoints is useful to ensure you can recover your work in case of a crash or simply to track training progress persistently. You can create a checkpoint of an RLlib algorithm at any point in the training process by calling `algo.save()`. Once you have a checkpoint, you can easily restore your `Algorithm` with it. Evaluating a model is as simple as calling `algo.evaluate(checkpoint)` with the checkpoint you created. Here's how that looks if you put it all together:

```
from ray.rllib.algorithms.algorithm import Algorithm


checkpoint = algo.save()       ❶
print(checkpoint)

evaluation = algo.evaluate()   ❷
print(pretty_print(evaluation))

algo.stop()                    ❸
restored_algo = Algorithm.from_checkpoint(checkpoint)   ❹
```

❶ Save algorithms to create checkpoints.

❷ Evaluate RLlib algorithms at any point in time by calling `evaluate`.

❸ Stop an `algo` to free all claimed resources.

❹ Restore any `Algorithm` from a given checkpoint with `from_checkpoint`.

Looking at the output of this example, we can now confirm that the trained RLlib algorithm did indeed converge to a good solution for the maze problem, as indicated by episodes of length 8 in evaluation:

```
~/ray_results/DQN_GymEnvironment_2022-02-09_10-19-301o3m9r6d/checkpoint_000010/
checkpoint-10 evaluation:
  ...
  episodes_this_iter: 5
  hist_stats:
    episode_lengths:
    - 8
    - 8
    ...
```

Computing actions

RLlib algorithms have much more functionality than just the `train`, `evaluate`, `save`, and `from_checkpoint` methods we've seen so far. For example, you can directly compute actions given the current state of an environment. In Chapter 3 we implemented episode rollouts by stepping through an environment and collecting rewards. We can easily do the same with RLlib for our `GymEnvironment`:

```
env = GymEnvironment()
done = False
total_reward = 0
observations = env.reset()

while not done:
    action = algo.compute_single_action(observations)    ❶
    observations, reward, done, info = env.step(action)
    total_reward += reward
```

❶ To compute actions for given `observations`, use `compute_single_action`.

In case you should need to compute many actions at once, not just a single one, you can use the `compute_actions` method instead, which takes dictionaries of observations as input and produces dictionaries of actions with the same dictionary keys as output:

```
action = algo.compute_actions(    ❶
    {"obs_1": observations, "obs_2": observations}
)
print(action)
# {'obs_1': 0, 'obs_2': 1}
```

❶ For multiple actions, use `compute_actions`.

Accessing policy and model states

Remember that each reinforcement learning algorithm is based on a *policy* that chooses next actions given the agent's current observations of the environment. Each policy is in turn based on an underlying *model*.

In the case of vanilla Q-Learning that we discussed in Chapter 3, the model was a simple lookup table of state-action values, also called Q-values. And that policy used this model for predicting next actions in case it decided to *exploit* what the model had learned so far or to *explore* the environment with random actions otherwise.

When using Deep Q-Learning, the underlying model of the policy is a neural network that, loosely speaking, maps observations to actions. Note that for choosing next actions in an environment, we're ultimately not interested in the concrete values of the approximated Q-values, but rather in the *probabilities* of taking each action. The probability distribution over all possible actions is called an *action distribution*.

In the maze we're using as a running example, we can move up, right, down, or left. So, in our case an action distribution is a vector of four probabilities, one for each action. In the case of Q-Learning, the algorithm will always *greedily* choose the action with the highest probability of this distribution, while other algorithms will sample from it.

To make things concrete, let's look at how you access policies and models in RLlib:[9]

```
policy = algo.get_policy()
print(policy.get_weights())

model = policy.model
```

Both `policy` and `model` have many useful methods to explore. In this example we use `get_weights` to inspect the parameters of the model underlying the policy (which are called *weights* by standard convention).

To convince you that not just one model is at play here but in fact a collection of models,[10] we can access all the workers we used in training and then ask each worker's policy for their weights using `foreach_worker`:

```
workers = algo.workers
workers.foreach_worker(
    lambda remote_trainer: remote_trainer.get_policy().get_weights()
)
```

In this way, you can access every method available on an `Algorithm` instance on each of your workers. In principle, you can use this to *set* model parameters as well, or otherwise configure your workers. RLlib workers are ultimately Ray actors, so you can alter and manipulate them in almost any way you like.

We haven't talked about the specific implementation of Deep Q-Learning used in DQN, but the model used is a bit more complex than what we've described so far. Every RLlib model obtained from a policy has a `base_model` that has a neat `summary` method to describe itself:[11]

```
model.base_model.summary()
```

---

9 The `Policy` class in RLlib today will be replaced in a future release. The new `Policy` class will likely be a drop-in replacement for the most part and exhibit some minor differences. The idea of the class remains the same, though: a *policy* is a class that encapsulates the logic of choosing actions given observations, and it gives you access to the underlying models used.

10 Technically speaking, only the *local* model is used for actual training. The two worker models are used for action computation and data collection (rollouts). After each training step, the local model sends its current weights to the workers for synchronization. Fully distributed training, as opposed to distributed sampling, will be available across all RLlib algorithms in future Ray versions.

11 This is true by default, since we're using TensorFlow and Keras under the hood. Should you opt to change the `framework` specification of your algorithm to work with PyTorch directly, do `print(model)`, in which case `model` is-a `torch.nn.Module`. Access to the underlying model will be unified across all frameworks the future.

As you can see from the following output, this model takes in our observations. The shape of these observations is a bit strangely annotated as [(None, 25)], but essentially this means we have the expected 5 × 5 maze grid values correctly encoded. The model follows with two so-called Dense layers and predicts a single value at the end:[12]

```
Model: "model"

_____
Layer (type)                Output Shape       Param #     Connected to
========================================================================
observations (InputLayer)   [(None, 25)]       0
_____
fc_1 (Dense)                (None, 256)        6656        observations[0][0]
_____
fc_out (Dense)              (None, 256)        65792       fc_1[0][0]
_____
value_out (Dense)           (None, 1)          257         fc_1[0][0]
========================================================================
Total params: 72,705
Trainable params: 72,705
Non-trainable params: 0
_____
```

Note that it's perfectly possible to customize this model for your RLlib experiments. If your environment is complex and has a big observation space, for instance, you might need a bigger model to capture that complexity. However, doing so requires in-depth knowledge of the underlying neural network framework (in this case Tensor-Flow), which we don't assume you have.[13]

State-Action Values and State-Value Functions

So far we've been mostly concerned with the concept of state-action values, since this concept takes center stage in the formulation of Q-Learning that we used extensively so far. The model we just had a look at has a dedicated output (in deep learning terms called a *head*) for predicting Q-values. You can access and summarize this part of the model through model.q_value_head.summary().

In contrast it's also possible to ask how valuable a particular *state* is, without specifying an action that pairs with it. This leads to the concept of *state-value functions*, or simply *value functions*, that are very important in the RL literature. We can't go into more detail in this RLlib introduction, but note that you have access to a *value function head* as well through model.state_value_head.summary().

---

12 The "value" output of this network represents the Q-value of state-action pairs.

13 To learn more about customizing your RLlib models, check out the guide to custom models in the Ray documentation (*https://oreil.ly/cpRdf*).

Next, let's see if we can take some observations from our environment and pass them to the model we just extracted from our `policy`. This part is a bit technically involved because models are a bit more difficult to access directly in RLlib. Normally you would only interface with a model through your `policy`, which takes care of preprocessing the observations, among other things. Luckily, we can access the preprocessor used by the policy, `transform` the observations from our environment, and then pass them to the model:

```
from ray.rllib.models.preprocessors import get_preprocessor


env = GymEnvironment()
obs_space = env.observation_space
preprocessor = get_preprocessor(obs_space)(obs_space)   ❶

observations = env.reset()
transformed = preprocessor.transform(observations).reshape(1, -1)   ❷

model_output, _ = model({"obs": transformed})   ❸
```

❶ Use `get_preprocessor` to access the preprocessor used by the policy.

❷ You can use `transform` on any `observations` obtained from your `env` to the format expected by the model. Note that we need to reshape the observations too.

❸ Get the model output by calling the model on a preprocessed observation dictionary.

Having computed our `model_output`, we can now access the Q-values and the action distribution of the model for this output:

```
q_values = model.get_q_value_distributions(model_output)   ❶
print(q_values)

action_distribution = policy.dist_class(model_output, model)   ❷
sample = action_distribution.sample()   ❸
print(sample)
```

❶ The `get_q_value_distributions` method is specific to DQN models only.

❷ By accessing `dist_class` we get the policy's action distribution class.

❸ Action distributions can be sampled from.

Configuring RLlib Experiments

Now that you've seen the basic Python training API of RLlib in an example, let's take a step back and discuss in more depth how to configure and run RLlib experiments. By now you know that to define an `Algorithm`, you start with the respective `AlgorithmConfig` and then build your algorithm from it. So far we've used only the `rollout` method of an `AlgorithmConfig` to set the number of rollout workers to two, and set our `environment` accordingly.

If you want to alter the behavior of your RLlib training run, chain more utility methods onto the `AlgorithmConfig` instance and then call `build` on it at the end. As RLlib algorithms are fairly complex, they come with many configuration options. To make things easier, the common properties of algorithms are naturally grouped into useful categories.[14] Each such category comes with its own respective `AlgorithmConfig` method:

`training()`
> Takes care of all training-related configuration options of your algorithm. The `training` method is the one place that RLlib algorithms differ in their configuration. All the following methods are algorithm-agnostic.

`environment()`
> Configures all aspects of your environment.

`rollouts()`
> Modifies the setup and behavior of your rollout workers.

`exploration()`
> Alters the behavior of your exploration strategy.

`resources()`
> Configures the compute resources used by your algorithm.

`offline_data()`
> Defines options for training with so-called offline data, a topic we cover in "Working with Offline Data" on page 97.

`multi_agent()`
> Specifies options for training algorithms using *multiple agents*. We discuss an explicit example of this in the next section.

---

[14] We list only the methods we introduce in this chapter. Apart from those we mention, you also find options for evaluation of your algorithms, reporting, debugging, checkpointing, adding callbacks, altering your deep learning framework, requesting resources, and accessing experimental features.

The algorithm-specific configuration in `training()` becomes even more relevant once you've settled on an algorithm and want to squeeze it for performance. In practice, RLlib provides you with good defaults to get started.

For more details on configuring RLlib experiments, look up configuration arguments in the API reference for RLlib algorithms (*https://oreil.ly/4q1eo*). But before we move on to examples, you should learn about the most common configuration options in practice.

Resource Configuration

Whether you use Ray RLlib locally or on a cluster, you can specify the resources used for the training process. Here are the most important options to consider. We continue using the DQN algorithm as an example, but this would apply to any other RLlib algorithm as well:

```
from ray.rllib.algorithms.dqn import DQNConfig

config = DQNConfig().resources(
    num_gpus=1,  ❶
    num_cpus_per_worker=2,  ❷
    num_gpus_per_worker=0,  ❸
)
```

❶ Specify the number of GPUs to use for training. It's important to check whether your algorithm of choice supports GPUs first. This value can also be fractional. For example, if using four rollout workers in DQN (`num_rollout_workers=4`), you can set `num_gpus=0.25` to pack all four workers on the same GPU so that all rollout workers benefit from the potential speedup. This affects only the local learner process, not the rollout workers.

❷ Set the number of CPUs to use for each rollout worker.

❸ Set the number of GPUs used per worker.

Rollout Worker Configuration

RLlib lets you configure how your rollouts are computed and how to distribute them:

```
from ray.rllib.algorithms.dqn import DQNConfig

config = DQNConfig().rollouts(
    num_rollout_workers=4,  ❶
    num_envs_per_worker=1,  ❷
    create_env_on_local_worker=True,  ❸
)
```

❶ You've seen this already. It specifies the number of Ray workers to use.

❷ Specify the number of environments to evaluate per worker. This setting allows you to "batch" evaluation of environments. In particular, if your models take a long time to evaluate, grouping environments like this can speed up training.

❸ When `num_rollout_workers` > 0, the driver ("local worker") does not need an environment. That's because sampling and evaluation is done by the rollout workers. If you still want an environment on the driver, you can set this option to `True`.

Environment Configuration

```python
from ray.rllib.algorithms.dqn import DQNConfig

config = DQNConfig().environment(
    env="CartPole-v1",  ❶
    env_config={"my_config": "value"},  ❷
    observation_space=None,
    action_space=None,  ❸
    render_env=True,  ❹
)
```

❶ Specify the environment you want to use for training. This can be either a string of an environment known to Ray RLlib, such as any Gym environment, or the class name of a custom environment you've implemented.[15]

❷ Optionally specify a dictionary of configuration options for your environment that will be passed to the environment constructor.

❸ You can specify the observation and action spaces of your environment too. If you don't specify them, they will be inferred from the environment.

❹ `False` by default, this property allows you to turn on rendering of the environment, which requires you to implement the `render` method of your environment.

Note that we left out many available configuration options for each of the types we listed. On top of that, we can't touch on aspects here that alter the behavior of the RL training procedure in this introduction (like modifying the underlying model to use). But the good news is that you'll find all the information you need in the RLlib Training API documentation (*https://oreil.ly/mljW7*).

---

15 There's also a way to *register* your environments so that you can refer to them by name, but this requires using Ray Tune. You will learn about this feature in Chapter 5.

Working with RLlib Environments

So far we've introduced you to just Gym environments, but RLlib supports a wide variety of environments. After giving you a quick overview of all available options (see Figure 4-1), we'll show you two concrete examples of advanced RLlib environments in action.

An Overview of RLlib Environments

All available RLlib environments extend a common `BaseEnv` class. If you want to work with several copies of the same `gym.Env` environment, you can use RLlib's `VectorEnv` wrapper. Vectorized environments are useful, but they are straightforward generalizations of what you've seen already. The two other types of environments available in RLlib are more interesting and deserve more attention.

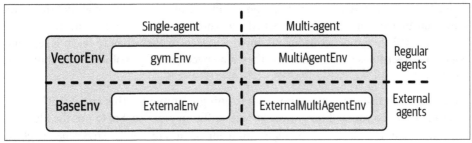

Figure 4-1. An overview of all available RLlib environments

The first is called `MultiAgentEnv`, which allows you to train a model with *multiple agents*. Working with multiple agents can be tricky. That's because you have to take care to define your agents within your environment with a suitable interface and account for the fact that each agent might have a completely different way of interacting with its environment.

What's more is that agents might interact with each other, and they have to respect each other's actions. In more advanced settings, there might even be a *hierarchy* of agents that explicitly depend on each other. In short, running multi-agent RL experiments is difficult, and we'll see how RLlib handles this in the next example.

The other type of environment we will look at is called `ExternalEnv`, which can be used to connect external simulators to RLlib. For instance, imagine our simple maze problem from earlier was a simulation of an actual robot navigating a maze. It might not be suitable in such scenarios to co-locate the robot (or its simulation, implemented in a different software stack) with RLlib's learning agents. To account for that, RLlib provides you with a simple client-server architecture for communicating with external simulators, which allows communication over a REST API. In case you want to work both in a multi-agent and external environment setting, RLlib offers a `MultiAgentExternalEnv` environment that combines both.

Working with Multiple Agents

The basic idea of defining multi-agent environments in RLlib is simple. You first assign each agent an agent ID. Then, whatever you previously defined as a single value in a Gym environment (observations, rewards, etc.), you now define as a dictionary with agent IDs as keys and values per agent. Of course, the details are a little more complicated than that in practice. But once you have defined an environment hosting several agents, you have to define how these agents should learn.

In a single-agent environment there's one agent and one policy to learn. In a multi-agent environment there are multiple agents that might map to one or several policies. For instance, if you have a group of homogenous agents in your environment, then you could define a single policy for all of them. If they all *act* the same way, then their behavior can be learned the same way. In contrast, you might have situations with heterogeneous agents in which each of them has to learn a separate policy. Between these two extremes, there's a spectrum of possibilities, as shown in Figure 4-2.

We continue to use our maze game as a running example for this chapter. This way you can check for yourself how the interfaces differ in practice. So, to put the ideas we just outlined into code, let's define a multi-agent version of the `GymEnvironment` class. Our `MultiAgentEnv` class will have precisely two agents, which we encode in a Python dictionary called `agents`, but in principle this works with any number of agents.

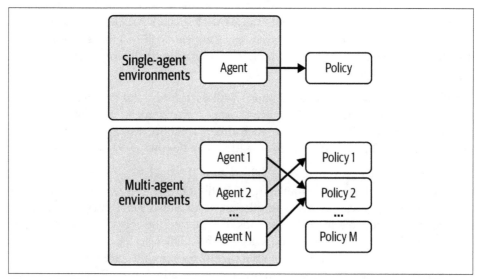

Figure 4-2. Mapping agents to policies in multi-agent reinforcement learning problems

We start by initializing and resetting our new environment:

```python
from ray.rllib.env.multi_agent_env import MultiAgentEnv
from gym.spaces import Discrete
import os


class MultiAgentMaze(MultiAgentEnv):

    def __init__(self, *args, **kwargs):        ❶
        self.action_space = Discrete(4)
        self.observation_space = Discrete(5*5)
        self.agents = {1: (4, 0), 2: (0, 4)}     ❷
        self.goal = (4, 4)
        self.info = {1: {'obs': self.agents[1]}, 2: {'obs': self.agents[2]}}    ❸

    def reset(self):
        self.agents = {1: (4, 0), 2: (0, 4)}

        return {1: self.get_observation(1), 2: self.get_observation(2)}    ❹
```

❶ Action and observation spaces stay exactly the same as before.

❷ We now have two seekers with (0, 4) and (4, 0) starting positions in an `agents` dictionary.

❸ For the `info` object, we're using agent IDs as keys.

❹ Observations are now per-agent dictionaries.

Notice that we didn't touch the action and observation spaces at all. That's because we're using two essentially identical agents here that can reuse the same spaces. In more complex situations you'd have to account for the fact that the actions and observations might look different for some agents.[16]

To continue, let's generalize our helper methods `get_observation`, `get_reward`, and `is_done` to work with multiple agents. We do this by passing in an `action_id` to their signatures and handling each agent the same way as before:

```python
    def get_observation(self, agent_id):
        seeker = self.agents[agent_id]
        return 5 * seeker[0] + seeker[1]

    def get_reward(self, agent_id):
        return 1 if self.agents[agent_id] == self.goal else 0
```

---

16 You can find a good example that defines different observation and action spaces for multiple agents in the RLlib documentation (*https://oreil.ly/4yyE-*).

```
def is_done(self, agent_id):
    return self.agents[agent_id] == self.goal
```

Next, to port the `step` method to our multi-agent setup, you have to know that `MultiAgentEnv` now expects the `action` passed to a `step` to be a dictionary with keys corresponding to the agent IDs, too. We define a step by looping through all available agents and acting on their behalf:[17]

```
def step(self, action):    ❶
    agent_ids = action.keys()

    for agent_id in agent_ids:
        seeker = self.agents[agent_id]
        if action[agent_id] == 0:  # move down
            seeker = (min(seeker[0] + 1, 4), seeker[1])
        elif action[agent_id] == 1:  # move left
            seeker = (seeker[0], max(seeker[1] - 1, 0))
        elif action[agent_id] == 2:  # move up
            seeker = (max(seeker[0] - 1, 0), seeker[1])
        elif action[agent_id] == 3:  # move right
            seeker = (seeker[0], min(seeker[1] + 1, 4))
        else:
            raise ValueError("Invalid action")
        self.agents[agent_id] = seeker    ❷

    observations = {i: self.get_observation(i) for i in agent_ids}    ❸
    rewards = {i: self.get_reward(i) for i in agent_ids}
    done = {i: self.is_done(i) for i in agent_ids}

    done["__all__"] = all(done.values())    ❹

    return observations, rewards, done, self.info
```

❶ Actions in a `step` are now per-agent dictionaries.

❷ After applying the correct action for each seeker, set the correct states of all agents.

❸ `observations`, `rewards`, and `dones` are also dictionaries with agent IDs as keys.

❹ Additionally, RLlib needs to know when all agents are done.

---

17 Note how this can lead to issues like deciding which agent gets to act first. In our simple maze problem the order of actions is irrelevant, but in more complex scenarios this becomes a crucial part of modeling the RL problem correctly.

The last step is to modify rendering the environment, which we do by denoting each agent by its ID when printing the maze to the screen:

```python
def render(self, *args, **kwargs):
    os.system('cls' if os.name == 'nt' else 'clear')
    grid = [['| ' for _ in range(5)] + ["|\n"] for _ in range(5)]
    grid[self.goal[0]][self.goal[1]] = '|G'
    grid[self.agents[1][0]][self.agents[1][1]] = '|1'
    grid[self.agents[2][0]][self.agents[2][1]] = '|2'
    grid[self.agents[2][0]][self.agents[2][1]] = '|2'
    print(''.join([''.join(grid_row) for grid_row in grid]))
```

Randomly rolling out an episode until *one* of the agents reaches the goal can, for instance, be done by the following code:[18]

```python
import time

env = MultiAgentMaze()

while True:
    obs, rew, done, info = env.step(
        {1: env.action_space.sample(), 2: env.action_space.sample()}
    )
    time.sleep(0.1)
    env.render()
    if any(done.values()):
        break
```

Note how we have to make sure to pass two random samples by means of a Python dictionary into the step method, and how we check if any of the agents are done yet. We use this break condition for simplicity because it's highly unlikely that both seekers find their way to the goal at the same time by chance. But of course we'd like both agents to complete the maze eventually.

In any case, equipped with our MultiAgentMaze, training an RLlib Algorithm works *exactly* the same way as before:

```python
from ray.rllib.algorithms.dqn import DQNConfig

simple_trainer = DQNConfig().environment(env=MultiAgentMaze).build()
simple_trainer.train()
```

This covers the simplest case of training a multi-agent reinforcement learning (MARL) problem. But if you remember what we said earlier, when using multiple agents, there's always a mapping between agents and policies. By not specifying such a mapping, both of our seekers were implicitly assigned to the same policy. This can

---

18 Deciding when an episode is done is a crucial part of multi-agent RL, and it depends entirely on the problem at hand and what you want to achieve.

be changed by calling the `.multi_agent` method on our `DQNConfig` and setting the `policies` and `policy_mapping_fn` arguments accordingly:

```
algo = DQNConfig()\
    .environment(env=MultiAgentMaze)\
    .multi_agent(
        policies={ ❶
            "policy_1": (
                None, env.observation_space, env.action_space, {"gamma": 0.80}
            ),
            "policy_2": (
                None, env.observation_space, env.action_space, {"gamma": 0.95}
            ),
        },
        policy_mapping_fn = lambda agent_id: f"policy_{agent_id}", ❷
    ).build()

print(algo.train())
```

❶ Define multiple `policies` for our agents, each with a different `"gamma"` value.

❷ Each agent can then be mapped to a policy with a custom `policy_mapping_fn`.

As you can see, running multi-agent RL experiments is a first-class citizen of RLlib, and there's a lot more that could be said about it. The support of MARL problems is probably one of RLlib's strongest features.

Working with Policy Servers and Clients

For the last example in this section, let's assume our original `GymEnvironment` can be simulated only on a machine that can't run RLlib, for instance because it doesn't have enough resources available. We can run the environment on a `PolicyClient` that can ask a respective *server* for suitable next actions to apply to the environment. The server, in turn, does not know about the environment. It only knows how to ingest input data from a `PolicyClient`, and it is responsible for running all RL-related code; in particular, it defines an RLlib `AlgorithmConfig` object and trains an `Algorithm`.

Typically, you want to run the server that trains your algorithm on a powerful Ray Cluster, and then the respective client runs outside that cluster. Figure 4-3 schematically illustrates this setup.

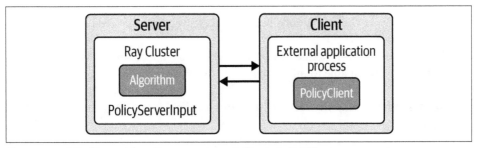

Figure 4-3. Working with policy servers and clients in RLlib

Defining a server

Let's start by defining the server side of such an application first. We define a so-called `PolicyServerInput` that runs on localhost on port 9900. This policy input is what the client will provide later. With this `policy_input` defined as `input` to our algorithm configuration, we can define yet another DQN to run on the server:

```
# policy_server.py
import ray
from ray.rllib.agents.dqn import DQNConfig
from ray.rllib.env.policy_server_input import PolicyServerInput
import gym


ray.init()


def policy_input(context):
    return PolicyServerInput(context, "localhost", 9900)  ❶


config = DQNConfig()\
    .environment(
        env=None,  ❷
        action_space=gym.spaces.Discrete(4),  ❸
        observation_space=gym.spaces.Discrete(5*5))\
    .debugging(log_level="INFO")\
    .rollouts(num_rollout_workers=0)\
    .offline_data(  ❹
        input=policy_input,
        input_evaluation=[])


algo = config.build()
```

❶ The `policy_input` function returns a `PolicyServerInput` object running on localhost on port 9900.

❷ We explicitly set the env to None because this server does not need one.

❸ We therefore need to define both an observation_space and an action_space, as the server is not able to infer them from the environment.

❹ To make this work, we need to feed our policy_input into the experiment's input.

With this algo defined,[19] we can now start a training session on the server like so:

```
# policy_server.py
if __name__ == "__main__":

    time_steps = 0
    for _ in range(100):
        results = algo.train()
        checkpoint = algo.save()  ❶
        if time_steps >= 1000:  ❷
            break
        time_steps += results["timesteps_total"]
```

❶ Train for a maximum of 100 iterations and store checkpoints after each iteration.

❷ If training surpasses 1,000 time steps, we stop the training.

In what follows we assume that you store the last two code snippets in a file called *policy_server.py*. If you want to, you can now start this policy server on your local machine by running python policy_server.py in a terminal.

Defining a client

Next, to define the corresponding client side of the application, we define a Policy Client that connects to the server we just started. Since we can't assume that you have several computers at home (or available in the cloud), contrary to what we said prior, we will start this client on the same machine. In other words, the client will connect to http://localhost:9900, but if you can run the server on a different machine, you could replace localhost with the IP address of that machine, provided it's available in the network.

Policy clients have a fairly lean interface. They can trigger the server to start or end an episode, get next actions from it, and log reward information to it (that it would otherwise not have). With that said, here's how you define such a client:

---

19 For technical reasons, we have to specify observation and action spaces here, which might not be necessary in future releases of RLlib, as it leaks environment information. Also note that we need to set input_evaluation to an empty list to make this server work.

```
# policy_client.py
import gym
from ray.rllib.env.policy_client import PolicyClient
from maze_gym_env import GymEnvironment

if __name__ == "__main__":
    env = GymEnvironment()
    client = PolicyClient("http://localhost:9900", inference_mode="remote")  ❶

    obs = env.reset()
    episode_id = client.start_episode(training_enabled=True)  ❷

    while True:
        action = client.get_action(episode_id, obs)  ❸

        obs, reward, done, info = env.step(action)

        client.log_returns(episode_id, reward, info=info)  ❹

        if done:
            client.end_episode(episode_id, obs)  ❺
            exit(0)  ❻
```

❶ Start a policy client on the server address with remote inference mode.

❷ Tell the server to start an episode.

❸ For given environment observations, we can get the next action from the server.

❹ It's mandatory for the client to log reward information to the server.

❺ If a certain condition is reached, we can stop the client process.

❻ If the environment is done, we have to inform the server about episode completion.

Assuming you store this code under *policy_client.py* and start it by running python policy_client.py, then the server that we started earlier will start learning with environment information solely obtained from the client.

Advanced Concepts

So far we've been working with simple environments that were easy enough to tackle with the most basic RL algorithm settings in RLlib. Of course, in practice you're not always that lucky and might have to come up with other ideas to tackle more difficult environments. In this section we're going to introduce a slightly harder version of the maze environment and discuss some advanced concepts to help you solve it.

Building an Advanced Environment

Let's make our maze `GymEnvironment` a bit more challenging. First, we increase its size from a 5 × 5 to an 11 × 11 grid. Then we introduce obstacles in the maze that the agent can pass through but only by incurring a penalty, a negative reward of –1. This way our seeker agent will have to learn to avoid obstacles while still finding the goal. Also, we randomize the agent's starting position. All of this makes the RL problem harder to solve. Let's look at the initialization of this new `AdvancedEnv` first:

```python
from gym.spaces import Discrete
import random
import os


class AdvancedEnv(GymEnvironment):

    def __init__(self, seeker=None, *args, **kwargs):
        super().__init__(*args, **kwargs)
        self.maze_len = 11
        self.action_space = Discrete(4)
        self.observation_space = Discrete(self.maze_len * self.maze_len)

        if seeker:  ❶
            assert 0 <= seeker[0] < self.maze_len and \
                   0 <= seeker[1] < self.maze_len
            self.seeker = seeker
        else:
            self.reset()

        self.goal = (self.maze_len-1, self.maze_len-1)
        self.info = {'seeker': self.seeker, 'goal': self.goal}

        self.punish_states = [  ❷
            (i, j) for i in range(self.maze_len) for j in range(self.maze_len)
            if i % 2 == 1 and j % 2 == 0
        ]
```

❶ Set the `seeker` position upon initialization.

❷ Introduce `punish_states` as obstacles for the agent.

Next, when resetting the environment, we want to make sure to reset the agent's position to a random state.[20] We also increase the positive reward for reaching the goal to 5 to offset the negative reward for passing through an obstacle (which will

---

20 In the definition of `reset`, we allow the seeker to reset on top of the goal to keep the definition simpler. Allowing this trivial edge case does not affect learning.

happen a lot before the RL algorithm picks up on the obstacle locations). Balancing rewards like this is a crucial task in calibrating your RL experiments:

```python
def reset(self):
    """Reset seeker position randomly, return observations."""
    self.seeker = (
        random.randint(0, self.maze_len - 1),
        random.randint(0, self.maze_len - 1)
    )
    return self.get_observation()

def get_observation(self):
    """Encode the seeker position as integer"""
    return self.maze_len * self.seeker[0] + self.seeker[1]

def get_reward(self):
    """Reward finding the goal and punish forbidden states"""
    reward = -1 if self.seeker in self.punish_states else 0
    reward += 5 if self.seeker == self.goal else 0
    return reward

def render(self, *args, **kwargs):
    """Render the environment, e.g. by printing its representation."""
    os.system('cls' if os.name == 'nt' else 'clear')
    grid = [['| ' for _ in range(self.maze_len)] +
            ["|\n"] for _ in range(self.maze_len)]
    for punish in self.punish_states:
        grid[punish[0]][punish[1]] = '|X'
    grid[self.goal[0]][self.goal[1]] = '|G'
    grid[self.seeker[0]][self.seeker[1]] = '|S'
    print(''.join([''.join(grid_row) for grid_row in grid]))
```

There are many other ways you could make this environment more difficult, like making it much bigger, introducing a negative reward for every step the agent takes in a certain direction, or punishing the agent for trying to walk off the grid. By now you should understand the problem setting well enough to customize the maze further.

While you might have success training this environment, this is a good opportunity to introduce some advanced concepts that you can apply to other RL problems.

Applying Curriculum Learning

One of the most interesting features of RLlib is providing an Algorithm with a *curriculum* to learn from. Instead of letting the algorithm learn from arbitrary environment setups, we cherry-pick states that are much easier to learn from and then slowly but surely introduce more difficult states. Building a learning curriculum is a great way to make your experiments converge to solutions quicker. To apply curriculum learning, the only thing you need is a view on which starting states are easier than others. This can be a challenge for many environments, but it's easy to come up with a simple curriculum for our advanced maze. Namely, the distance of the seeker from the goal can be used as a measure of difficulty. The distance measure we'll use for simplicity is the sum of the absolute distance of both seeker coordinates from the goal to define a difficulty.

To run curriculum learning with RLlib, we define a CurriculumEnv that extends both our AdvancedEnv and a so-called TaskSettableEnv from RLLib. The interface of TaskSettableEnv is very simple in that you have to define only how to get the current difficulty (get_task) and how to set a required difficulty (set_task). Here's the full definition of this CurriculumEnv:

```python
from ray.rllib.env.apis.task_settable_env import TaskSettableEnv


class CurriculumEnv(AdvancedEnv, TaskSettableEnv):

    def __init__(self, *args, **kwargs):
        AdvancedEnv.__init__(self)

    def difficulty(self):  ❶
        return abs(self.seeker[0] - self.goal[0]) + \
               abs(self.seeker[1] - self.goal[1])

    def get_task(self):  ❷
        return self.difficulty()

    def set_task(self, task_difficulty):  ❸
        while not self.difficulty() <= task_difficulty:
            self.reset()
```

❶ Define the difficulty of the current state as the sum of the absolute distance of both seeker coordinates from the goal.

❷ To define get_task we can then simply return the current difficulty.

❸ To set a task difficulty, we reset the environment until its difficulty is *at most* the specified task_difficulty.

To use this environment for curriculum learning, we need to define a curriculum function that tells the algorithm when and how to set the task difficulty. We have many options here, but we use a schedule that simply increases the difficulty by one every 1,000 time steps trained:

```python
def curriculum_fn(train_results, task_settable_env, env_ctx):
    time_steps = train_results.get("timesteps_total")
    difficulty = time_steps // 1000
    print(f"Current difficulty: {difficulty}")
    return difficulty
```

To test this curriculum function, we need to add it to our RLlib algorithm `config` by setting the `env_task_fn` property to our `curriculum_fn`. Note that before training a DQN for 15 iterations, we also set an *output* folder in our config. This will store experience data of our training run to the specified *temp* folder:[21]

```python
from ray.rllib.algorithms.dqn import DQNConfig
import tempfile


temp = tempfile.mkdtemp()  ❶

trainer = (
    DQNConfig()
    .environment(env=CurriculumEnv, env_task_fn=curriculum_fn)  ❷
    .offline_data(output=temp)  ❸
    .build()
)

for i in range(15):
    trainer.train()
```

❶ Create a *temp* file to store our training data for later use.

❷ Set the `CurriculumEnv` as our environment in the `environment` part of our config and assign our `curriculum_fn` to the `env_task_fn` property.

❸ Use the `offline_data` method to store output in our *temp* folder.

Running this algorithm, you should see how the task difficulty increases over time, thereby giving the algorithm easy examples to start with so that it can learn from them and progress to more difficult tasks.

Curriculum learning is a great technique to be aware of and RLlib allows you to easily incorporate it into your experiments through the curriculum API we just discussed.

Working with Offline Data

In our previous curriculum learning example we stored training data to a temporary folder. What's interesting is that you already know from Chapter 3 that in Q-Learning you can collect experience data first and decide when to use it in a training step later. This separation of data collection and training opens up many possibilities. For instance, maybe you have a good heuristic that can solve your problem in an

---

21 Note that if you run the notebook for this chapter (*https://oreil.ly/KEhGx*) on the cloud, the training process could take a while to finish.

imperfect yet reasonable manner. Or you have records of human interaction with your environment, demonstrating how to solve the problem by example.

The topic of collecting experience data for later training is often discussed as working with *offline data*. It's called "offline" because it's not directly generated by a policy interacting online with the environment. Algorithms that don't rely on training on their own policy output are called *off-policy algorithms*, and Q-Learning, particularly DQN, is just one such example. Algorithms that don't share this property are called on-policy algorithms. In other words, off-policy algorithms can be used to train on offline data.[22]

To use the data we stored in the *temp* folder, we can create a new DQNConfig that takes this folder as input. We will also set explore to False, since we simply want to exploit the data previously collected for training—the algorithm will not explore according to its own policy.

Using the resulting RLlib algorithm works exactly as before, which we demonstrate by training it for 10 iterations and then evaluating it:

```
imitation_algo = (
    DQNConfig()
    .environment(env=AdvancedEnv)
    .evaluation(off_policy_estimation_methods={})
    .offline_data(input_=temp)
    .exploration(explore=False)
    .build())

for i in range(10):
    imitation_algo.train()

imitation_algo.evaluate()
```

Note that we called the algorithm imitation_algo. That's because this training procedure intends to *imitate* the behavior reflected in the data we collected before. This type of learning by demonstration in RL is therefore often called *imitation learning* or *behavior cloning*.

Other Advanced Topics

Before concluding this chapter, let's have a look at a few other advanced topics that RLlib has to offer. You've already seen how flexible RLlib is: working with a range of different environments, configuring your experiments, training on a curriculum, or running imitation learning. This section gives you a taste of what else is possible.

---

22 Note that RLlib has a wide range of on-policy algorithms like PPO as well.

With RLlib, you can completely customize the models and policies used under the hood. If you've worked with deep learning before, you know how important it can be to have a good model architecture in place. In RL this is often not as crucial as in supervised learning, but it is still a vital part of successfully running advanced experiments.

You can also change the way your observations are preprocessed by providing custom preprocessors. For our simple maze examples, there was nothing to preprocess, but when working with image or video data, preprocessing is often a crucial step.

In our AdvancedEnv we introduced states to avoid. Our agents had to learn to do this, but RLlib has a feature to automatically avoid them through so-called *parametric action spaces*. Loosely speaking, what you can do is "mask out" all undesired actions from the action space for each point in time. In some cases it can also be necessary to have variable observation spaces, which is also fully supported by RLlib.

We briefly touched on the topic of offline data. RLlib has a full-fledged Python API for reading and writing experience data that can be used in various situations.

We have worked solely with DQN here for simplicity, but RLlib has an impressive range of training algorithms. To name just one, the MARWIL algorithm is a complex hybrid algorithm with which you can run imitation learning from offline data, while also mixing in regular training on data generated "online."

Summary

You've seen a selection of interesting RLlib features in this chapter. We covered training multi-agent environments, working with offline data generated by another agent, setting up a client-server architecture to split simulations from RL training, and using curriculum learning to specify increasingly difficult tasks.

We've also given you a quick overview of the main concepts underlying RLlib and how to use its CLI and Python API. In particular, we've shown how to configure your RLlib algorithms and environments to your needs. As we've covered only a small part of RLlib's possibilities, we encourage you to read its documentation and explore its API (*https://oreil.ly/OmQYE*).

In the next chapter you'll learn how to tune the hyperparameters of your RLlib models and policies with Ray Tune.

## CHAPTER 5

Hyperparameter Optimization with Ray Tune

In Chapter 4 you learned how to build and run various reinforcement learning experiments. Running such experiments can be expensive, in terms of both compute resources and the time it takes to run them. This expense only gets amplified as you move on to more challenging tasks, since it is unlikely that you can just pick an algorithm out of the box and run it to get a good result. In other words, at some point you'll need to tune the hyperparameters of your algorithms to get the best results. As we'll see in this chapter, tuning machine learning models is hard, but Ray Tune is an excellent choice to help you tackle this task.

Ray Tune is a powerful tool for hyperparameter optimization (HPO). Not only does it work in a distributed manner by default (and works in any other Ray library discussed in this book), but it's also one of the most feature-rich HPO libraries available. To top this off, Tune integrates with some of the most prominent HPO libraries out there, such as Hyperopt, Optuna, and many more. This makes Tune an ideal candidate for distributed HPO experiments, whether you're coming from other libraries or starting from scratch.

In this chapter we'll first revisit in a bit more depth why HPO is hard to do and how you could naively implement it yourself with Ray. We then teach you the core concepts of Ray Tune and how you can use it to tune the RLlib models built in the previous chapter. To wrap things up, we'll also have a look at how to use Tune for supervised learning tasks, using frameworks like Keras. Along the way, we demonstrate how Tune integrates with other HPO libraries and introduce you to some of its more advanced features.

Tuning Hyperparameters

Let's briefly recap the basics of hyperparameter optimization. If you're familiar with HPO, you can skip this section, but since we're also discussing aspects of distributed HPO, you might still benefit from following along. As always, you can find a notebook for this chapter in the book's GitHub repository (*https://oreil.ly/-afF8*).

In our first RL experiment introduced in Chapter 3, we defined a very basic Q-Learning algorithm whose internal *state-action values* were updated according to an explicit update rule. After initialization, we never touched these *model parameters* directly; they were learned by the algorithm. By contrast, in setting up the algorithm, we explicitly chose a `weight` and a `discount_factor` parameter prior to training. We didn't tell you how we chose to set these parameters back then; we simply accepted that they were good enough to crack the problem at hand.

In the same way, in Chapter 4 we initialized an RLlib algorithm with a `config` that used two rollout workers for our DQN algorithm by setting `num_rollout_workers=2`. Parameters like these are called *hyperparameters*, and finding good choices for them can be crucial for successful experiments. The field of hyperparameter optimization is devoted to efficiently finding such good choices.

Building a Random Search Example with Ray

Hyperparameters like the `weight` or the `discount_factor` of our Q-Learning algorithm are *continuous* parameters, so we can't possibly test all combinations of them. What's more, these parameter choices may not be independent of each other. If we want them to be selected for us, we also need to specify a *value range* for each of them (both hyperparameters need to be between 0 and 1 in this case). So, how do we determine good or even optimal hyperparameters?

Let's look at an example that implements a naive yet effective approach to tuning hyperparameters. This example will also allow us to introduce some terminology that we'll use later. The core idea is that we can attempt to *randomly sample* hyperparameters, run the algorithm for each sample, and then select the best run based on the results. But to do the theme of this book justice, we don't just want to run this in a sequential loop; we want to compute our runs in parallel using Ray.

To keep things simple we'll revisit our simple Q-Learning algorithm from Chapter 3. We defined the signature of the main training function as `train_policy(env, num_episodes=10000, weight=0.1, discount_factor=0.9)`. That means we can tune the `weight` and `discount_factor` parameters of our algorithm by passing in different values to the `train_policy` function and see how the algorithm performs. To do that, let's define a so-called *search space* for our hyperparameters. For both parameters in question we uniformly sample values between 0 and 1, for a total of 10 choices.

Here's what that looks like:

```
import random
search_space = []
for i in range(10):
    random_choice = {
        'weight': random.uniform(0, 1),
        'discount_factor': random.uniform(0, 1)
    }
    search_space.append(random_choice)
```

Next, we define an *objective function*, or simply *objective*. The role of an objective function is to evaluate the performance of a given set of hyperparameters for a desired task. In our case, we want to train our RL algorithm and evaluate the trained policy. Recall that in Chapter 3 we also defined an `evaluate_policy` function for precisely this purpose. The `evaluate_policy` function was defined to return the average number of steps it took for an agent to reach the goal in the underlying maze environment. In other words, we want to find a set of hyperparameters that minimizes the result of our objective function. To parallelize the objective function, we'll use the `ray.remote` decorator to make our `objective` a Ray task:

```
import ray


@ray.remote
def objective(config):    ❶
    environment = Environment()
    policy = train_policy(    ❷
        environment,
        weight=config["weight"],
        discount_factor=config["discount_factor"]
    )
    score = evaluate_policy(environment, policy)    ❸
    return [score, config]    ❹
```

❶ Pass in a dictionary with a hyperparameter sample into our objective.

❷ Train our RL policy using the chosen hyperparameters.

❸ Afterward we can evaluate the policy to retrieve the score we want to minimize.

❹ Return both score and hyperparameter choice for later analysis.

Finally, we can run the objective function in parallel using Ray by iterating over the search space and collecting the results:

```
result_objects = [objective.remote(choice) for choice in search_space]
results = ray.get(result_objects)

results.sort(key=lambda x: x[0])
print(results[-1])
```

The actual results of this hyperparameter run are not very interesting because the problem is easy to solve (most runs will return the optimum of eight steps, regardless of the hyperparameters chosen). What's more interesting here is how easy it is to parallelize the objective function with Ray. In fact, we'd like to encourage you to rewrite the preceding example to simply loop through the search space and call the objective function for each sample, just to confirm how painfully slow such a serial loop can be.

Conceptually, the three steps we took to run that example are representative of how hyperparameter tuning works in general. First, you define a search space, then you define an objective function, and finally you run an analysis to find the best hyperparameters. In HPO it is common to speak of one evaluation of the objective function per hyperparameter sample as a *trial*, and all trials form the basis for your analysis. How parameters are sampled from the search space (in our case, randomly) is up to a *search algorithm* to decide. In practice, finding good hyperparameters is easier said than done, so let's have a closer look at why this problem is so hard.

Why Is HPO Hard?

If you zoom out from the previous example, you can see several intricacies involved in making the process of hyperparameter tuning work well. Here's a quick overview of the most important ones:

- Your search space can be composed of a large number of hyperparameters. These parameters might have different data types and ranges. Some parameters might be correlated or even depend on others. Sampling good candidates from complex, high-dimensional spaces is a difficult task.

- Picking parameters at random can work surprisingly well, but it's not always the best option. In general, you need to test more complex search algorithms to find the best parameters.

- In particular, even if you parallelize your hyperparameter search like we just did, a single run of your objective function can take a long time to complete. That means you can't afford to run too many searches overall. For instance, training neural networks can take hours to complete, so your hyperparameter search needs to be efficient.

- When distributing search, you need to have enough compute resources available to run searches over the objective function effectively. For instance, you might need a GPU to compute your objective function fast enough, so all your search runs need to have access to a GPU. Allocating the necessary resources for each trial is critical for speeding up your search.

- You need convenient tooling for your HPO experiments, like stopping bad runs early, saving intermediate results, restarting from previous trials, or pausing and resuming runs.

As a mature, distributed HPO framework, Ray Tune addresses all these topics and provides a simple interface for running hyperparameter tuning experiments. Before we look into how Tune works, let's rewrite our previous example to use Tune.

An Introduction to Tune

To get your first taste of Tune, porting over our naive Ray Core implementation of random search to Tune is straightforward and follows the same three steps as before. First, we define a search space, but this time using `tune.uniform`, instead of the random library:

```
from ray import tune


search_space = {
    "weight": tune.uniform(0, 1),
    "discount_factor": tune.uniform(0, 1),
}
```

Next, we can define an objective function that looks almost the same as before. We designed it like that. The only differences are that this time we return the score as a dictionary, and we don't need a `ray.remote` decorator because Tune will take care of distributing this objective function for us internally:

```
def tune_objective(config):
    environment = Environment()
    policy = train_policy(
        environment,
        weight=config["weight"],
        discount_factor=config["discount_factor"]
    )
    score = evaluate_policy(environment, policy)

    return {"score": score}
```

With this `tune_objective` function defined, we can pass it to a `tune.run` call, together with the search space we defined. By default, Tune will run a random search for you, but you can also specify other search algorithms, as you will see soon.[1] Calling tune.run generates random search trials for your objective and returns an analysis object that contains information about the hyperparameter search. We can get the best hyperparameters found by calling get_best_config and specifying the metric and mode arguments (we want to minimize our score):

```
analysis = tune.run(tune_objective, config=search_space)
print(analysis.get_best_config(metric="score", mode="min"))
```

This quick example covers the basics of Tune, but there's a lot more to unpack. The tune.run function is quite powerful and takes a lot of arguments for you to configure your runs. To understand these different configuration options, we first need to introduce you to the key concepts of Tune.

How Does Tune Work?

To effectively work with Tune, you must understand six key concepts, four of which you used in the previous example. Here's an overview of Ray Tune's components and how you should think about them:

Search spaces

These spaces determine which parameters to select. Search spaces define the range of values for each parameter and how they should be sampled. They are defined as dictionaries and use Tune's sampling functions to specify valid hyperparameter values. You have already seen tune.uniform, but there are many more options to choose from (*https://oreil.ly/6beij*).

Trainables

A Trainable is Tune's formal representation of an objective you want to "tune." Tune has a class-based API as well, but we will use only the function-based API in this book. For us, a Trainable is a function with a single argument: a search space, which reports scores to Tune. The easiest way to report a score is by returning a dictionary with the value you're interested in.

Trials

By triggering tune.run(...), Tune will set up trials and schedule them for execution on your cluster. A trial contains all the necessary information about a single run of your objective, given a set of hyperparameters.

---

1 Tune uses the same resource model as Ray Core. Each tune_objective run will be executed on a different CPU core by default. If you want, you can also specify a (fractional) GPU to be used for each trial.

Analyses

Completing a `tune.run` call returns an `ExperimentAnalysis` object, with the results of all trials. You can use this object to drill down into the results of your trials.

Search algorithms

Tune supports a large variety of search algorithms, which are at the core of how to tune your hyperparameters. So far you've implicitly encountered Tune's default search algorithm, which randomly selects hyperparameters from the search space.

Schedulers

The last, crucial component of a Tune experiment is that of a *scheduler*. Schedulers plan and execute what the search algorithm selects. By default, Tune schedules trials selected by your search algorithm on a first-in-first-out (FIFO) basis. In practice, you can think of schedulers as a way to speed up your experiments, for instance by stopping unsuccessful trials early.

Figure 5-1 sums up these major Tune components and their relationships.

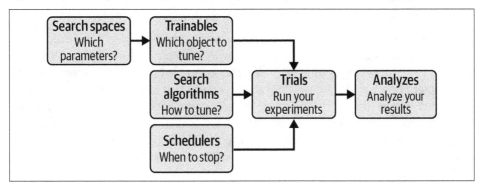

Figure 5-1. The core components of Ray Tune

In this chapter we exclusively use `tune.run` to illustrate Tune's functionality. Tune also had an API called `Tuner` added in Ray 2.0 as part of Ray AIR, which you will learn more about in Chapter 7 and use within Ray AIR in Chapter 10.

At the time of this writing, `tune.run` is still the more mature API. For instance, experiments using `tune.run(...)` return an `ExperimentAnalysis` object, a powerful tool for analyzing your results. Analogous calls using the `Tuner` API return a so-called `ResultGrid` instead. In the long run `ResultGrid` will succeed `ExperimentAnalysis`, but it is not yet at feature parity.

To learn more, see the Tune API documentation on this topic (*https://oreil.ly/pITtJ*).

Note that internally Tune runs are started on the driver process of your Ray Cluster, which spawns several worker processes (using Ray actors) that execute individual trials of your HPO experiment. Your trainables, defined on the driver, have to be sent to the workers, and trial results need to be communicated to the driver running `tune.run(...)`.

Search spaces, trainables, trials, and analyses don't need much additional explanation, and we'll see more examples of each of those components in the rest of this chapter. But search algorithms, *searchers* for short, and schedulers need a bit more elaboration.

Search algorithms

All advanced search algorithms provided by Tune, and the many third-party HPO libraries it integrates with, fall under the umbrella of *Bayesian optimization*. Unfortunately, going into the details of specific Bayesian search algorithms is far beyond the scope of this book. The basic idea is that you update your beliefs about which hyperparameter ranges are worth exploring based on the results of your previous trials. Techniques using this principle make more informed decisions and, hence, tend to be more efficient than independently sampling parameters (e.g., at random).

Apart from the basic random search we've seen already, and *grid search*, which picks hyperparameters from a predefined "grid" of choices, Tune integrates with a wide range of Bayesian optimization searchers. For instance, Tune integrates with the popular Hyperopt and Optuna libraries,[2] and you can use the popular TPE (Tree-structured Parzen Estimator) searcher with Tune through both of these libraries. Not only that, Tune also integrates with tools such as Ax, BlendSearch, FLAML, Dragonfly, scikit-Optimize, Bayesian optimization, HpBandSter, Nevergrad, ZOOpt, SigOpt, and HEBO. If you need to run HPO experiments with any of these tools on a cluster or want to easily switch between them, Tune is the way to go.

To make things more concrete, let's rewrite our basic random search Tune example from earlier to use the Bayesian optimization library. To do so, make sure you install this library in your Python environment first, e.g., with `pip install bayesian-optimization`:

```
from ray.tune.suggest.bayesopt import BayesOptSearch


algo = BayesOptSearch(random_search_steps=4)
```

---

2 In open source software, it's important to determine who is responsible for maintaining an integration. We will discuss this more in Chapter 11, which covers Ray's ecosystem as a whole. In the case of Tune, among the integrations listed here, the Hyperopt and Optuna integrations are maintained by the Ray Tune team; the rest are community-sponsored.

```
tune.run(
    tune_objective,
    config=search_space,
    metric="score",
    mode="min",
    search_alg=algo,
    stop={"training_iteration": 10},
)
```

Note that we "warm start" our Bayesian optimization with four random steps at the beginning, and we explicitly stop the trial runs after 10 training iterations.

Because we're not just randomly selecting parameters with BayesOptSearch: the search_alg we use in our Tune run needs to know which metric to optimize for and whether to minimize or optimize this metric. As we've argued before, we want to achieve a "min" "score".

Schedulers

Next, let's discuss how to use *trial schedulers* in Tune to make your runs more efficient. We also use this section to introduce a slightly different way to report your metrics to Tune within an objective function.

So let's say that instead of computing a score straight-up, like we did in the previous examples, we compute an *intermediate score* in a loop. This is a situation that often occurs in supervised machine learning scenarios, when training a model for several iterations (we'll see concrete applications of this in "Machine Learning with Tune" on page 115). With good hyperparameter choices selected, this immediate score might stagnate way before the loop in which it is computed. In other words, if we're not seeing enough incremental changes, why not stop the trial early? This is exactly one of the cases Tune's schedulers are built for.

Here's a quick example of such an objective function. This is a toy example, but it will help us think about the optimal hyperparameters we want Tune to find more easily than if we started with a complex example:

```
def objective(config):
    for step in range(30):      ❶
        score = config["weight"] * (step ** 0.5) + config["bias"]
        tune.report(score=score)    ❷


search_space = {"weight": tune.uniform(0, 1), "bias": tune.uniform(0, 1)}
```

❶ Often you may want to compute intermediate scores, e.g., in a "training loop."

❷ You can use tune.report to let Tune know about these intermediate scores.

The score we want to minimize here is the square root of a positive number times a weight, plus adding a bias term. It's clear that both of these hyperparameters need to be as small as possible to minimize the score for any positive x. Given that the square root function "flattens out," we might not have to compute all 30 passes through the loop to find sufficiently good values for our two hyperparameters. If each score computation took an hour, stopping early could be a huge boost in making your experiments run quicker.

Let's illustrate this idea by using the popular Hyperband algorithm as our trial scheduler. This scheduler needs to be passed a metric and mode (again, we min-imize our score). We also make sure to run for 10 samples so as not to stop prematurely:

```
from ray.tune.schedulers import HyperBandScheduler


scheduler = HyperBandScheduler(metric="score", mode="min")


analysis = tune.run(
    objective,
    config=search_space,
    scheduler=scheduler,
    num_samples=10,
)

print(analysis.get_best_config(metric="score", mode="min"))
```

Note that in this case we did not specify a search algorithm, which means that Hyperband will run on parameters selected by random search. We also could have *combined* this scheduler with another search algorithm instead. This would have allowed us to pick better trial hyperparameters and stop bad trials early. However, note that not every scheduler can be combined with search algorithms. Check Tune's scheduler compatibility matrix (*https://oreil.ly/B—eH*) for more information.

To wrap up this discussion, apart from Hyperband, Tune includes distributed implementations of early stopping algorithms such as the Median Stopping Rule, ASHA, Population Based Training (PBT), and Population Based Bandits (PB2).

Configuring and Running Tune

Before looking into more concrete machine learning examples using Ray Tune, let's dive into some useful topics that help you get more out of your Tune experiments, such as properly utilizing resources, stopping and resuming trials, adding callbacks to your Tune runs, or defining custom and conditional search spaces.

Specifying resources

By default, each Tune trial will run on one CPU and leverage as many CPUs as available for concurrent trials. For instance, if you run Tune on a laptop with 8 CPUs, any of the experiments computed so far in this chapter will spawn eight concurrent trials and allocate one CPU for each trial. Changing this behavior can be controlled using the `resources_per_trial` argument of a Tune run.

You can also determine the number of GPUs used per trial. Plus, Tune allows you to use *fractional resources*; i.e., you can share resources between trials. So, let's say that you have a machine with 12 CPUs and 2 GPUs and you request the following resources for your `objective`:

```
from ray import tune

tune.run(
    objective,
    config=search_space,
    num_samples=10,
    resources_per_trial={"cpu": 2, "gpu": 0.5}
)
```

That means Tune can schedule and execute up to four concurrent trials on your machine, as this would max out GPU utilization on this machine (while you'd still have four idle CPUs for other tasks). If you want, you can also specify the amount of `"memory"` used by a trial by passing the number of bytes into `resources_per_trial`. Also note that should you need to explicitly *restrict* the number of concurrent trials, you can do so by passing in the `max_concurrent_trials` parameter to your `tune.run(...)`. In the preceding example, if you want to always keep one GPU available for other tasks, you can limit the number of concurrent trials to two by setting `max_concurrent_trials = 2`.

Note that everything we just exemplified for resources on a single machine naturally extends to any Ray Cluster and its available resources. In any case, Ray will always try to schedule the next trials, but it will wait and ensure enough resources are available before executing them.

Callbacks and metrics

If you've spent some time investigating the outputs of the Tune runs we've started in this chapter so far, you'll have noticed that each trial comes equipped with a lot of information by default, such as the trial ID, its execution date, and much more. What's interesting is that Tune not only allows you to customize the metrics you want to report, you can also hook into a `tune.run` by providing *callbacks*. Let's compute a quick, representative example that does both.

Slightly modifying a previous example, let's say we want to log a specific message whenever a trial returns a result. To do so, all you need to do is implement the on_trial_result method on a Callback object from the ray.tune package.[3] Here's how that would look for an objective function that reports a score:

```python
from ray import tune
from ray.tune import Callback
from ray.tune.logger import pretty_print


class PrintResultCallback(Callback):
    def on_trial_result(self, iteration, trials, trial, result, **info):
        print(f"Trial {trial} in iteration {iteration}, "
              f"got result: {result['score']}")


def objective(config):
    for step in range(30):
        score = config["weight"] * (step ** 0.5) + config["bias"]
        tune.report(score=score, step=step, more_metrics={})
```

Note that, apart from the score, we also report step and more_metrics to Tune. In fact, you could expose any other metric you'd like to track there, and Tune would add it to its trial metrics. Here's how you'd run a Tune experiment with our custom callback and print the custom metrics we just defined:

```python
search_space = {"weight": tune.uniform(0, 1), "bias": tune.uniform(0, 1)}

analysis = tune.run(
    objective,
    config=search_space,
    mode="min",
    metric="score",
    callbacks=[PrintResultCallback()])

best = analysis.best_trial
print(pretty_print(best.last_result))
```

Running this code will result in the following outputs (additional to what you'll see in any other Tune run). Note that we need to specify mode and metric explicitly here so that Tune knows what we mean by best_result. First, you should see the output of our callback, while the trials are running:

```
...
Trial objective_85955_00000 in iteration 57, got result: 1.5379782083952644
Trial objective_85955_00000 in iteration 58, got result: 1.5539087627537493
Trial objective_85955_00000 in iteration 59, got result: 1.569535794562848
```

---

3 If you want to learn more about how to use callbacks in Tune or create your own callbacks, check out the user guide on callbacks and metrics in Tune (*https://oreil.ly/1CDj2*).

```
Trial objective_85955_00000 in iteration 60, got result: 1.5848760187255326
Trial objective_85955_00000 in iteration 61, got result: 1.5999446700996236
...
```

Then, at the very end of the program, we print the metrics of the best available trial, which includes the three custom metrics we defined. The following output omits some default metrics to make it more readable. We recommend that you run an example like this on your own, in particular to get used to reading the outputs of Tune trials (which can be a bit overwhelming due to their concurrent nature):

```
Result logdir: /Users/maxpumperla/ray_results/objective_2022-05-23_15-52-01
...
done: true
experiment_id: ea5d89c2018f483183a005a1b5d47302
experiment_tag: 0_bias=0.73356,weight=0.16088
hostname: mac
iterations_since_restore: 30
more_metrics: {}
score: 1.5999446700996236
step: 29
trial_id: '85955_00000'
...
```

We used on_trial_result as an example of a method to implement a custom Tune Callback, but you have many other useful options that are relatively self-explanatory. It's not very helpful to list them all here, but some particularly useful callback methods are on_trial_start, on_trial_error, on_experiment_end, and on_checkpoint. The latter hints at an important aspect of Tune runs that we'll discuss next.

Checkpoints, stopping, and resuming

The more Tune trials you kick off and the longer they each run individually, especially in a distributed setting, the more you need a mechanism to protect you against failures, stop a run, or pick a run up again from previous results. Tune makes this possible by periodically creating *checkpoints* for you. The checkpoint cadence is dynamically adjusted by Tune to ensure at least 95% of the time is spent on running trials, and not too many resources are devoted to storing checkpoints.

In the example we just computed, the checkpoint directory, or *logdir*, used by default is of the form ~/ray_results/<your-objective>_<date>_<time>. If you know this checkpoint directory of your experiment, you can easily resume it like so:

```
analysis = tune.run(
    objective,
    name="<your-logdir>",
    resume=True,
    config=search_space)
```

Similarly, you can *stop* your trials by defining stopping conditions and explicitly passing them to your tune.run. The easiest option for doing that is by providing a dictionary with a stopping condition. Here's how you stop running our `objective` analysis after reaching a `training_iteration` count of 10, a built-in metric of all Tune runs:

```
tune.run(
    objective,
    config=search_space,
    stop={"training_iteration": 10})
```

One of the drawbacks of specifying a stopping condition this way is that it assumes the metric in question is *increasing*. For instance, the `score` we compute starts high and is something we want to minimize. To formulate a flexible stopping condition for our `score`, the best way is to provide a stopping function as follows:

```
def stopper(trial_id, result):
    return result["score"] < 2


tune.run(
    objective,
    config=search_space,
    stop=stopper)
```

In situations that require a stopping condition with more context or explicit state, you can also define a custom `Stopper` class (*https://oreil.ly/1GBqm*) to pass into the `stop` argument of your Tune run, but we won't cover this case here.

Custom and conditional search spaces

The last more advanced topic we'll cover here is that of complex search spaces. So far, we've looked only at hyperparameters that were independent of each other, but in practice, some often depend on others. Also, while Tune's built-in search spaces have quite a lot to offer, sometimes you want to sample parameters from a more exotic distribution or your own modules.

Here's how you can handle both situations in Tune. Continuing with our simple `objective` example, let's say that instead of Tune's `tune.uniform` you want to use the `random.uniform` sampler from the `numpy` package for your `weight` parameter. And then your `bias` parameter should be `weight` times a standard normal variable. Using `tune.sample_from` you can tackle this situation (or more complex and nested ones) like this:

```
from ray import tune
import numpy as np

search_space = {
    "weight": tune.sample_from(
        lambda context: np.random.uniform(low=0.0, high=1.0)
    ),
```

```
    "bias": tune.sample_from(
        lambda context: context.config.weight * np.random.normal()
    )}

tune.run(objective, config=search_space)
```

There are many more interesting features to explore in Ray Tune, but let's switch gears here and look into some machine learning applications using Tune.

Machine Learning with Tune

As we've seen, Tune is versatile and allows you to tune hyperparameters for any objective you give it. In particular, you can use it with any machine learning framework you're interested in. This section provides two examples. First, we're going to use Tune to optimize parameters of an RLlib experiment, and then we'll tune a Keras model using Optuna through Tune.

Using RLlib with Tune

RLlib and Tune have been designed to work together, so you can quite easily set up an HPO experiment for your existing RLlib code. In fact, RLlib trainers can be passed into the first argument of `tune.run`, as `Trainable`. You can choose between the actual trainer class, like `DQNTrainer`, or its string representation, like `"DQN"`. As Tune `metric` you can pass any metric tracked by your RLlib experiment, for instance `"episode_reward_mean"`. And the `config` argument to `tune.run` is just your RLlib trainer configuration, but you can use the full power of Tune's search space API to sample hyperparameters like the learning rate or training batch size.[4] Here's a full example of what we just described, running a tuned RLlib experiment on the CartPole-v0 Gym environment:

```
from ray import tune

analysis = tune.run(
    "DQN",
    metric="episode_reward_mean",
    mode="max",
    config={
        "env": "CartPole-v1",
        "lr": tune.uniform(1e-5, 1e-4),
        "train_batch_size": tune.choice([10000, 20000, 40000]),
    },
)
```

---

4 In case you were wondering why the "config" argument in `tune.run` was not called `search_space`, the historical reason lies in this interoperability with RLlib `config` objects.

Tuning Keras Models

To wrap up this chapter, let's look at a slightly more involved example. As we mentioned, this is not primarily a machine learning book but rather an introduction to Ray and its libraries. Thus we can neither introduce you to the basics of ML nor spend much time on introducing ML frameworks in detail. So, in this section we assume familiarity with Keras and its API and some basic knowledge about supervised learning. If you do not have these prerequisites, you should still be able to follow along and focus on the Ray Tune–specific parts. You can view the following example as a more realistic scenario of applying Tune to machine learning workloads.

From a bird's-eye view, we'll take the following steps:

1. Load a common dataset.

2. Prepare it for an ML task.

3. Define a Tune objective by creating a deep learning model with Keras that reports an accuracy metric to Tune.

4. Use Tune's Hyperopt integration to define a search algorithm that tunes a set of hyperparameters of our Keras model.

The Tune workflow remains the same: we define an objective and a search space and then use tune.run with the configuration we want. On a high level, the process of using Tune with any ML framework works as shown in Figure 5-2.

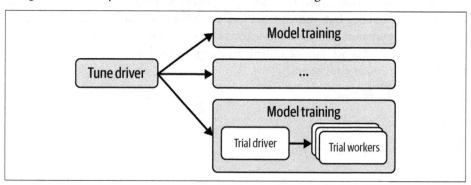

Figure 5-2. Tune sets up a distributed HPO for your ML models by executing trials on Ray workers in your cluster and reporting metrics back to the driver

To define a dataset to train on, let's write a simple load_data utility function that loads the famous MNIST data that ships with Keras. MNIST consists of 28 × 28 pixel images of handwritten digits. We normalize the pixel values to be between 0 and 1 and make the labels for those 10 digits *categorical variables*. Here's how you can do this purely with Keras's built-in functionality (make sure to use pip install tensorflow before running this):

```
from tensorflow.keras.datasets import mnist
from tensorflow.keras.utils import to_categorical


def load_data():
    (x_train, y_train), (x_test, y_test) = mnist.load_data()
    num_classes = 10
    x_train, x_test = x_train / 255.0, x_test / 255.0
    y_train = to_categorical(y_train, num_classes)
    y_test = to_categorical(y_test, num_classes)
    return (x_train, y_train), (x_test, y_test)


load_data()
```

Note that after defining load_data, we call it once so that the data gets downloaded locally. That's because when you call mnist.load_data(), it first looks for a locally cached copy. If we didn't load the data first, several Tune workers would try to download the data in parallel, which can lead to problems.[5]

Next, we define a Tune objective function, or trainable, by loading the data we just defined, setting up a sequential Keras model with hyperparameters selected from the config we pass into our objective, and then compile and fit the model. To define our deep learning model, we first flatten the MNIST input images to vectors and then add two fully connected layers (called Dense in Keras) and a Dropout layer in between.

The hyperparameters we want to tune are the activation function of the first Dense layer, the Dropout rate, and the number of "hidden" output units of the first layer. We could tune any other hyperparameter of this model the same way; this selection is just an example.

We could manually report a metric of interest in the same way we did in other examples in this chapter (e.g., by returning a dictionary in our objective or using tune.report(...)). But since Tune comes with a proper Keras integration, we can use the so-called TuneReportCallback as a custom Keras callback that we pass into our model's fit method. This is what our Keras objective function looks like:

```
from tensorflow.keras.models import Sequential
from tensorflow.keras.layers import Flatten, Dense, Dropout
from ray.tune.integration.keras import TuneReportCallback
```

---

5 This can even lead to a rare condition in which one worker starts downloading the data and another one checks for and sees a local copy. But since the download is not complete, the second worker will try to open a potentially corrupted file. This goes to show that, while Ray takes care of a lot of things in the background, you still need to be mindful about how you write your code.

```
def objective(config):
    (x_train, y_train), (x_test, y_test) = load_data()
    model = Sequential()
    model.add(Flatten(input_shape=(28, 28)))
    model.add(Dense(config["hidden"], activation=config["activation"]))
    model.add(Dropout(config["rate"]))
    model.add(Dense(10, activation="softmax"))

    model.compile(loss="categorical_crossentropy", metrics=["accuracy"])
    model.fit(x_train, y_train, batch_size=128, epochs=10,
              validation_data=(x_test, y_test),
              callbacks=[TuneReportCallback({"mean_accuracy": "accuracy"})])
```

Next, let's use a custom search algorithm to tune this objective. Specifically, we're using the HyperOptSearch algorithm, which gives us access to Hyperopt's TPE algorithm through Tune. To use this integration, make sure to install Hyperopt on your machine (for instance with pip install hyperopt==0.2.7). HyperOptSearch allows us to define a list of promising initial hyperparameter choices to investigate.

This is entirely optional, but sometimes you might have good guesses to start from. In our case, we go with a dropout "rate" of 0.2, 128 "hidden" units, and a rectified linear unit (ReLU) "activation" function initially. Other than that, we can define a search space with the tune utility just as we did before. Finally, we can get an analysis object to determine the best hyperparameters found by passing everything into a tune.run call:

```
from ray import tune
from ray.tune.suggest.hyperopt import HyperOptSearch

initial_params = [{"rate": 0.2, "hidden": 128, "activation": "relu"}]
algo = HyperOptSearch(points_to_evaluate=initial_params)

search_space = {
    "rate": tune.uniform(0.1, 0.5),
    "hidden": tune.randint(32, 512),
    "activation": tune.choice(["relu", "tanh"])
}


analysis = tune.run(
    objective,
    name="keras_hyperopt_exp",
    search_alg=algo,
    metric="mean_accuracy",
    mode="max",
    stop={"mean_accuracy": 0.99},
    num_samples=10,
    config=search_space,
)
print("Best hyperparameters found were: ", analysis.best_config)
```

Note that we're using the full power of Hyperopt here, without having to learn any of its specifics. Hyperopt itself is not distributed (by default). By using Hyperopt through the Tune API, we can leverage it for distributed HPO on a Ray Cluster.

We chose the combination of Keras and Hyperopt as example of using Tune with an advanced ML framework and a third-party HPO library. But we could have chosen any other machine learning library and practically any other HPO library supported by Tune. If you're interested in diving deeper into any of the many integrations Tune has to offer, check out the Ray Tune documentation examples (*https://oreil.ly/rKtZr*).

Summary

Tune is arguably one of the most versatile HPO tools you can choose today. It's feature-rich, offering many search algorithms, advanced schedulers, complex search spaces, custom stoppers, and many other features that we couldn't cover in this chapter. Also, it seamlessly integrates with most notable HPO tools, such as Optuna or Hyperopt, making it easy to migrate from these tools or simply leverage their features through Tune. You can view Ray Tune as a flexible, distributed HPO framework that *extends* others that might work only on single machines.

## CHAPTER 6

Data Processing with Ray

Edward Oakes

In Chapter 5 you learned how to tune hyperparameters for your machine learning experiments. Of course, the key component to applying machine learning in practice is data. In this chapter we'll explore the core set of data processing capabilities on Ray: Ray Data.

While not meant to replace more general data processing systems such as Apache Spark or Apache Hadoop, Ray Data offers basic data processing capabilities and a standard way to load, transform, and pass data to different parts of a Ray application. This enables an ecosystem of libraries on Ray to speak the same language so users can mix and match functionality in a framework-agnostic way to meet their needs.

The central component of the Ray Data ecosystem, Ray Datasets, offers the core abstractions for loading, transforming, and passing references to data in a Ray Cluster. Datasets are the "glue" that enables different libraries to interoperate on top of Ray. You'll see this in action in "External Library Integrations" on page 134, where we show how you can do dataframe processing using the full expressiveness of the Dask API using Dask on Ray and transform the result into a dataset. The main benefits of Ray Datasets are:

Flexibility
> It supports a wide range of data formats, work seamlessly with library integrations like Dask on Ray, and can be passed between Ray tasks and actors without copying data.

Performance for ML workloads
> It offers important features like accelerator support, pipelining, and global random shuffles that accelerate ML training and inference workloads.

This chapter will familiarize you with the core concepts for doing data processing on Ray and help you understand how to accomplish common patterns as well as why you would choose to use different pieces to accomplish a task. We assume a basic familiarity with data processing concepts such as map, filter, groupby, and partition, but it's not intended to be a tutorial on data science in general or a deep dive into the internals of how these operations are implemented. Readers with a limited data science background should not have a problem following along.

We'll start introducing the core building block: Ray Datasets. This will cover the architecture, basics of the API, and an example of how Ray Datasets can enable building complex data-intensive applications. Then, we'll briefly cover external library integrations on Ray, focusing on Dask on Ray. Finally, we'll bring it all together by building a scalable end-to-end machine learning pipeline in a single Python script.

 The notebook for this chapter is available on GitHub (*https://oreil.ly/CjHSJ*) along with the data used in the end-to-end example (*https://oreil.ly/5Ga8-*).

Ray Datasets

The main goal of Ray Datasets is to support a scalable, flexible abstraction for data processing on Ray. Datasets are intended to be the standard way to read, write, and transfer data across the full ecosystem of Ray libraries. One of the most powerful uses of Ray Datasets is acting as the data ingest and preprocessing layer for machine learning workloads, allowing you to efficiently scale up training using Ray Train and Ray Tune. We explore this in more detail in "Building an ML Pipeline" on page 136.

If you've worked with other distributed data processing APIs such as Apache Spark's Resilient Distributed Datasets in the past, the Ray Datasets API will be very familiar. The core of the API leans on functional programming and offers standard functionality such as reading and writing different data sources; performing basic transformations like map, filter, and sort; and performing some simple aggregations such as groupby.

Under the hood, Ray Datasets implements distributed Apache Arrow (*https://arrow.apache.org*). Apache Arrow is a unified columnar data format for data processing libraries and applications. Integrating with Apache Arrow means that Datasets get interoperability with many of the most popular processing libraries, such as NumPy and Pandas, out of the box.

A Ray Dataset consists of a list of Ray object references, each of which points at a "block" of data. These blocks are either Arrow tables or Python lists (for data that isn't supported by the Arrow format) in Ray's shared memory object store, and the compute over the data such as for map or filter operations happens in Ray tasks (and sometimes actors).

Because Ray Datasets relies on the core Ray primitives of tasks and objects in the shared memory object store, it inherits key benefits of Ray: scalability to hundreds of nodes, efficient memory usage due to sharing memory across processes on the same node, as well as object spilling and recovery to gracefully handle failures. Additionally, because Datasets are just lists of object references, they can also be passed between tasks and actors efficiently without needing to make a copy of the data, which is crucial for making data-intensive applications and libraries scalable.

Ray Datasets Basics

This section will give an overview of Ray Datasets, covering how to get started reading, writing, and transforming datasets. This is not a comprehensive reference but rather an introduction to the basic concepts so we can build up to some interesting examples later, showing what makes Ray Datasets powerful. For up-to-date information on what's supported and exact syntax, see the Ray Datasets documentation (*https://oreil.ly/aRTsX*).

To follow along with the examples in this section, make sure Ray Datasets is installed locally:

```
pip install "ray[data]==2.2.0"
```

Creating a Ray Dataset

First, let's create a simple Dataset and perform some basic operations on it:

```
import ray

# Create a dataset containing integers in the range [0, 10000).
ds = ray.data.range(10000)

# Basic operations: show the size of the dataset, get a few samples,
# print the schema.
print(ds.count())   # -> 10000
print(ds.take(5))   # -> [0, 1, 2, 3, 4]
print(ds.schema())  # -> <class 'int'>
```

Here we created a Dataset containing the numbers from 0 to 10,000 and then printed some basic information about it: the total number of records, a few samples, and the schema.

Reading from and writing to storage

Of course, for real workloads you'll often want to read from and write to persistent storage to load your data and write the results. Writing and reading Ray Datasets is simple; for example, to write a Dataset to a CSV file and then load it back into memory, we just need to use the built-in `write_csv` and `read_csv` utilities:

```
# Save the dataset to a local file and load it back.
ray.data.range(10000).write_csv("local_dir")
ds = ray.data.read_csv("local_dir")
print(ds.count())
```

Datasets supports a number of common serialization formats such as CSV, JSON, and Parquet and can read from or write to local disk as well as remote storage like HDFS or AWS S3.

In the preceding example, we provided just a local file path (`"local_dir"`) so the dataset was written to a directory on the local machine. If we wanted to write to and read from S3 instead, we would provide a path like `"s3://my_bucket/"` and Datasets would automatically handle efficiently reading and writing remote storage,[1] parallelizing the requests across many tasks to improve throughput.

Note that Ray Datasets also supports custom data sources that you can use to write to any external data storage system that isn't supported out of the box.

Built-in transformations

Now that we understand the basic APIs around how to create and inspect Datasets, let's take a look at some of the built-in operations we can do on them. The following code sample shows three basic operations that Ray Datasets supports:

```
ds1 = ray.data.range(10000)
ds2 = ray.data.range(10000)
ds3 = ds1.union(ds2)  ❶
print(ds3.count())  # -> 20000

# Filter the combined dataset to only the even elements.
ds3 = ds3.filter(lambda x: x % 2 == 0)  ❷
print(ds3.count())  # -> 10000
print(ds3.take(5))  # -> [0, 2, 4, 6, 8]

# Sort the filtered dataset.
ds3 = ds3.sort()  ❸
print(ds3.take(5))  # -> [0, 0, 2, 2, 4]
```

❶ union two Datasets together. The result is a new Dataset that contains all the records of both.

---

1 If you're interested in following an example that reads actual data from an S3 bucket, see the Batch Inference example in Ray's documentation (*https://oreil.ly/9C82a*).

❷ `filter` the elements of a Dataset to include only even integers by providing a custom filter function.

❸ `sort` the Dataset.

In addition to these operations, Datasets also support common aggregations you might expect such as `groupby`, `sum`, `min`, etc. You can also pass a user-defined function for custom aggregations.

Blocks and repartitioning

One important thing to keep in mind when using Ray Datasets is the concept of *blocks*. Blocks are the underlying chunks of data that make up a Dataset; operations are applied to the underlying data one block at a time. If the number of blocks in a Dataset is too high, each block will be small, and there will be a lot of overhead for each operation. If the number of blocks is too small, operations won't be able to be parallelized as efficiently.

If we take a peek under the hood of the previous example, we can see that the initial datasets we created each had 200 blocks by default. When we combined them, the resulting Dataset had 400 blocks. Given that the number of blocks is important for efficiency, we may want to reshuffle the data to match our original 200 blocks and retain the same parallelism. This process of changing the number of blocks is called *repartitioning*, and Ray Datasets offers a simple `.repartition(num_blocks)` API to achieve it. Let's use the API to repartition our resulting dataset back into 200 blocks:

```
ds1 = ray.data.range(10000)
print(ds1.num_blocks())  # -> 200
ds2 = ray.data.range(10000)
print(ds2.num_blocks())  # -> 200
ds3 = ds1.union(ds2)
print(ds3.num_blocks())  # -> 400

print(ds3.repartition(200).num_blocks())  # -> 200
```

Blocks also control the number of files that are created when we write a Dataset to storage (so if you want all of the data to be coalesced into a single output file, you should call `.repartition(1)` before writing it).

Schemas and data formats

To this point, we've been operating on simple Ray Datasets made up only of integers. However, for more complex data processing we often want to have a schema, allowing us to more easily comprehend the data and enforce types on each column.

Given that Datasets are meant to be the point of interoperation for applications and libraries on Ray, they are designed to be agnostic to a specific datatype and offer flexibility to read, write, and convert between many popular data formats. Datasets support Arrow's columnar format, which enables converting between different types of structured data such as Python dictionaries, DataFrames, and serialized Parquet files.

The simplest way to create a Dataset with a schema is to create it from a list of Python dictionaries:

```
ds = ray.data.from_items([{"id": "abc", "value": 1}, {"id": "def", "value": 2}])
print(ds.schema())  # -> id: string, value: int64
```

In this case, the schema was inferred from the keys in the dictionaries we passed in. We can also convert to/from data types from popular libraries such as Pandas:

```
pandas_df = ds.to_pandas()  # pandas_df will inherit the schema from our Dataset.
```

Here we went from a Dataset to a Pandas DataFrame, but this also works in reverse: if you create a Dataset from a DataFrame, it will automatically inherit the schema from the DataFrame.

Computing Over Ray Datasets

In the previous section, we introduced some of the functionality built in with Ray Datasets such as filtering, sorting, and creating unions. However, one of the most powerful parts of Ray Datasets is that it allows you to harness the flexible compute model of Ray and perform computations efficiently over large amounts of data.

The primary way to perform a custom transformation on a Dataset is using .map(). This allows you to pass a custom function that will be applied to the records of a Dataset. A basic example might be to square the records of a Dataset:

```
ds = ray.data.range(10000).map(lambda x: x ** 2)
ds.take(5)  # -> [0, 1, 4, 9, 16]
```

In this example, we passed a simple lambda function, and the data we operated on was integers, but we could pass any function here and operate on structured data that supports the Arrow format.

We can also choose to map batches of data instead of individual records using .map_batches(). Some types of computations are much more efficient when they're *vectorized*, meaning that they use an algorithm or implementation that is more efficient operating on a set of items instead of one at a time.

Revisiting our simple example of squaring the values in the Dataset, we can rewrite it to be performed in batches and use the numpy.square-optimized implementation instead of the naive Python implementation:

```
import numpy as np
```

```
ds = ray.data.range(10000).map_batches(lambda batch: np.square(batch).tolist())
ds.take(5)  # -> [0, 1, 4, 9, 16]
```

Vectorized computations are especially useful on GPUs when performing deep learning training or inference. However, generally performing computations on GPUs also has significant fixed cost due to needing to load model weights or other data into the GPU RAM. For this purpose, Ray Datasets supports mapping data using Ray actors. Ray actors are long-lived and can hold state, as opposed to stateless Ray tasks, so we can cache expensive operations costs by running them in the actor's constructor (such as loading a model onto a GPU).

For example, to perform batch inference using Datasets, we need to pass a class instead of a function, specify that this computation should run using actors, and use .map_batches() so we can perform vectorized inference. Datasets will automatically autoscale a group of actors to perform the map operation:

```
def load_model():
    # Returns a dummy model for this example.
    # In reality, this would likely load some model weights onto a GPU.
    class DummyModel:
        def __call__(self, batch):
            return batch

    return DummyModel()


class MLModel:
    def __init__(self):
        # load_model() will only run once per actor that's started.
        self._model = load_model()

    def __call__(self, batch):
        return self._model(batch)


ds.map_batches(MLModel, compute="actors")
```

To run the inference on a GPU, we would pass num_gpus=1 to the map_batches call to specify that the actors running the map function each require a GPU.

Dataset Pipelines

By default, Dataset operations are blocking, meaning they run synchronously from start to finish and there is only a single operation happening at a time. This pattern can be very inefficient for some workloads, however. For example, consider the following set of Dataset transformations on Parquet data that might be used to do batch inference for a machine learning model:[2]

```
ds = (ray.data.read_parquet("s3://my_bucket/input_data")  ❶
    .map(cpu_intensive_preprocessing)  ❷
    .map_batches(gpu_intensive_inference, compute="actors", num_gpus=1)  ❸
    .repartition(10))  ❹

ds.write_parquet("s3://my_bucket/output_predictions")  ❺
```

There are five stages to this process, and each stresses different parts of the system:

❶ Reading from remote storage requires ingress bandwidth to the cluster and may be limited by the throughput of the storage system. In this stage, a group of Ray tasks is spawned that will read from remote storage in parallel, and the resulting blocks of data are stored in the Ray object store.

❷ Preprocessing the inputs requires CPU resources. The objects from the first phase are passed into a group of tasks that will execute the `cpu_intensive_preprocessing` function on each block.

❸ Vectorized inference on the model requires GPU resources. The same process as in the second stage is repeated for `gpu_intensive_inference`, except this time the function is run on actors that are each allocated a GPU, and multiple blocks are passed into each function call (in batches). Actors are used for this step to avoid repeatedly reloading the model used for inference onto the GPU.

❹ Repartitioning requires network bandwidth within the cluster. After completing stage 3, more tasks are spawned to repartition the data into 10 blocks and write each of those 10 blocks to remote storage.

❺ Writing to remote storage requires egress bandwidth from the cluster and may be limited by the throughput of storage once again.

Figure 6-1 depicts a basic implementation where each stage runs in sequence. This naive implementation idles resources because each stage is blocking and run in sequence. For example, because GPU resources are used only in the final stage, they will be idle waiting for all of the data to be loaded and preprocessed.

---

2 Parquet is a structured, column-oriented format that enables efficient compression, data storage, and data retrieval. Many example and real-world datasets use Parquet, so it is used in the example provided. However, the code could easily be modified to use a different format by changing the read_parquet and write_parquet calls.

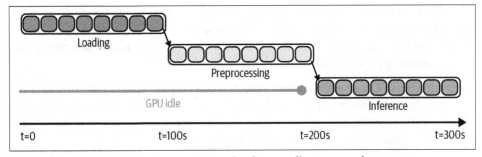

Figure 6-1. A naive Dataset computation, leading to idle resources between stages

In this scenario, it would be more efficient to *pipeline* the stages instead and allow them to overlap as shown in Figure 6-2. This means that as soon as some data has been read from storage, it is fed into the preprocessing stage, then to the inference stage, and so on.

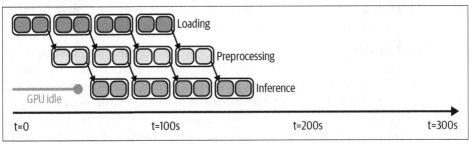

Figure 6-2. An optimized DatasetPipeline that enables overlapping compute between stages and reduces idle resources

This pipelining will improve the overall resource usage of the end-to-end workload, improving throughput and therefore decreasing the cost it takes to run the computation (fewer idle resources is better!).

Datasets can be converted to DatasetPipelines (*https://oreil.ly/Hr2d_*) using ds.win dow(), enabling the pipelining behavior that we want in this scenario. A window specifies the number of blocks that will be passed through a stage in the pipeline before being passed to the next stage. This behavior can be tuned using the blocks_per_window parameter, which defaults to 10.

Let's rewrite the inefficient pseudocode to use a DatasetPipeline instead:

```
ds = (ray.data.read_parquet("s3://my_bucket/input_data")
    .window(blocks_per_window=5)
    .map(cpu_intensive_preprocessing)
    .map_batches(gpu_intensive_inference, compute="actors", num_gpus=1)
    .repartition(10))
ds.write_parquet("s3://my_bucket/output_predictions")
```

The only modification made was the addition of a `.window()` call after `read_parquet` and before the preprocessing stage. Now the Dataset has been converted to a DatasetPipeline and its stages will proceed in parallel in five-block windows, decreasing idle resources and improving efficiency.

DatasetPipelines can also be created using `ds.repeat()` to repeat stages in a pipeline a finite or infinite number of times. This will be explored further in the next section, where we'll use it for a training workload. Of course, pipelining can be equally beneficial for training performance in addition to inference.

Example: Training Copies of a Classifier in Parallel

One of the key benefits of Datasets is that they can be passed between tasks and actors. In this section, we'll explore how this functionality can be used to write efficient implementations of complex distributed workloads such as distributed hyperparameter tuning and machine learning training. We'll implement an example of *distributed* training of ML models in this section, a topic that we'll cover in much more detail in Chapter 7 when we introduce you to Ray Train.

As discussed in Chapter 5, a common pattern in machine learning training is to explore a range of hyperparameters to find the ones that result in the best model. We may want to run across a wide range of hyperparameters, and doing this naively could be very expensive. Ray Data allows us to easily share the same in-memory data across a range of parallel training runs in a single Python script: we can load and preprocess the data once and then pass a reference to it to many downstream actors who can read the data from shared memory.

Additionally, sometimes when working with very large datasets, it is not feasible to load the full training data into memory in a single process or on a single machine. In this case, it's common to *shard* the data, which means to give each worker its own subset of the data that can fit into memory. This local subset of the data is called a *data shard*. After each worker trains on its shard of data in parallel, the results are combined either synchronously or asynchronously using a parameter server. Two important considerations can make this difficult to get right:

- Many distributed training algorithms take a *synchronous* approach, requiring the workers to synchronize their weights after each training epoch. This means there needs to be some coordination between the workers to maintain consistency between which batch of data they are operating on.

- It's important that each worker gets a random sample of the data during each epoch. A global random shuffle has been shown to perform better than local shuffle or no shuffle.

Figure 6-3 illustrates how the `ray.data` package is used to create shards of data forming a Ray Dataset from a given input dataset.

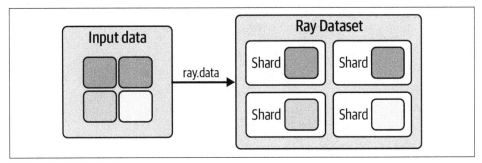

Figure 6-3. Creating a Ray Dataset from input data with the `ray.data` package

Let's walk through an example of how we can implement this type of pattern using Ray Datasets. In the example, we will train multiple copies of a machine learning model using different hyperparameters across different workers in parallel.

We'll be training a scikit-learn `SGDClassifier` algorithm on a generated binary classification dataset, and the hyperparameter we'll tune is the regularization term of this classifier.[3] The actual details of the ML task and model aren't too important to this example: you could replace the model and data with any number of examples. The main thing to focus on here is how we orchestrate the data loading and computation using Datasets.

To follow along with the examples in this section, make sure you have Ray Datasets and scikit-learn installed locally:[4]

```
pip install "ray[data]==2.2.0" "scikit-learn==1.0.2"
```

First, let's define our `TrainingWorker` that will train a copy of the classifier on the data:

```
from sklearn import datasets
from sklearn.linear_model import SGDClassifier
from sklearn.model_selection import train_test_split


@ray.remote
class TrainingWorker:
```

---

3 SGD stands for *stochastic gradient descent*, which is a common optimization algorithm used in machine learning, and specifically deep learning.

4 In this and the following two chapters, we're discussing more advanced ML examples that need additional dependencies. We pin the versions of these dependencies here and in the book's GitHub repo (*https://oreil.ly/learning_ray_repo*) to ensure the examples work as expected. Having said that, the examples very likely work with a relatively wide range of versions, as long as you make sure they're not too old.

```
def __init__(self, alpha: float):
    self._model = SGDClassifier(alpha=alpha)

def train(self, train_shard: ray.data.Dataset):
    for i, epoch in enumerate(train_shard.iter_epochs()):
        X, Y = zip(*list(epoch.iter_rows()))
        self._model.partial_fit(X, Y, classes=[0, 1])

    return self._model

def test(self, X_test: np.ndarray, Y_test: np.ndarray):
    return self._model.score(X_test, Y_test)
```

There are three important things to note about the `TrainingWorker`:

- It's a simple wrapper around the `SGDClassifier` and instantiates it with a given alpha value.

- The main training function happens in the `train` method. For each epoch, it trains the classifier on the data available.

- We also have a `test` method that can be used to run the trained model against a testing set.

Now, let's instantiate a number of `TrainingWorker` instances with different hyperparameters (`alpha` values):

```
ALPHA_VALS = [0.00008, 0.00009, 0.0001, 0.00011, 0.00012]

print(f"Starting {len(ALPHA_VALS)} training workers.")
workers = [TrainingWorker.remote(alpha) for alpha in ALPHA_VALS]
```

Next, we generate training and validation data and convert the training data to a Dataset. Here, we're using `.repeat()` to create a DatasetPipeline. This defines the number of epochs that our training will run for. In each epoch, the subsequent operations will be applied to the Dataset, and the workers will be able to iterate over the resulting data. We also shuffle the data randomly and shard it to be passed to the training workers, each getting an equal chunk:

```
X_train, X_test, Y_train, Y_test = train_test_split(   ❶
    *datasets.make_classification()
)

train_ds = ray.data.from_items(list(zip(X_train, Y_train)))   ❷
shards = (train_ds.repeat(10)   ❸
        .random_shuffle_each_window()   ❹
        .split(len(workers), locality_hints=workers))   ❺

ray.get([
    worker.train.remote(shard)
```

```
    for worker, shard in zip(workers, shards
)]) ❻
```

❶ Generate training and validation data for a classification problem.

❷ Convert the training data to a Dataset by using `from_items`.

❸ Define a DatasetPipeline using `.repeat`. This is similar to using `.window` as we showed earlier, but it allows us to iterate over the same dataset multiple times (in this case, 10).

❹ Shuffle the data randomly each time it is repeated.

❺ We want each worker to have its own local shard of the data, so we `split` the `DatasetPipeline` into multiple smaller ones that can be passed to each worker.

❻ Wait for training to complete on all the workers.

To run the training on the workers, we invoke their `train` method and pass in one shard of the `DatasetPipeline` to each. We then block, waiting for training to complete across all the workers. To summarize what happens during this phase:

1. Each epoch, each worker gets a random shard of the data.
2. The worker trains its local model on the shard of data assigned to it.
3. Once a worker has finished training on the current shard, it blocks until the other workers have finished.
4. The preceding three steps repeat for the remaining epochs (in this case, 10 total).

Finally, we can test the trained models from each worker on some test data to determine which alpha value produced the most accurate model:

```
# Get validation results from each worker.
print(ray.get([worker.test.remote(X_test, Y_test) for worker in workers]))
```

In reality, for this type of workload you should reach for Ray Tune or Ray Train, which we'll cover in the next chapter, but this example conveys the power of Ray Datasets for machine learning workloads. In just a few snippets of Python code, we implemented a complex distributed hyperparameter tuning and training workflow that could easily be scaled up to hundreds of machines and is agnostic to any framework or specific ML task.

External Library Integrations

While Ray Datasets supports a number of common data processing functionalities out of the box, as we've discussed, it's not a replacement for full data processing systems. Instead, as shown in Figure 6-4, it's more focused on performing "last mile" processing such as basic data loading, cleaning, and featurization before ML training or inference.

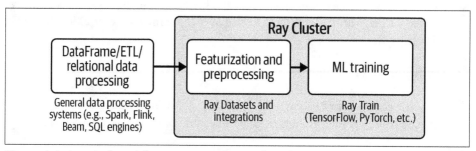

Figure 6-4. A typical workflow using Ray for machine learning: use external systems for primary data processing and ETL, use Ray Datasets for last-mile preprocessing

However, a number of other, more fully featured DataFrame and relational data processing systems integrate with Ray, such as:

- Dask on Ray
- RayDP (Spark on Ray)
- Modin (Pandas on Ray)
- MARS on Ray

These are standalone data processing libraries you may be familiar with outside the context of Ray. Each of these tools has an integration with the Ray Core that enables more expressive data processing than comes with the built-in Ray Datasets while still using Ray's deployment tooling, scalable scheduling, and shared memory object store for exchanging data. As shown in Figure 6-5, this complements Ray Datasets and enables end-to-end data processing on Ray.

Figure 6-5 shows the benefit of Ray Data ecosystem integrations, enabling more expressive data processing on Ray. These libraries integrate with Ray Datasets to feed into downstream libraries such as Ray Train.

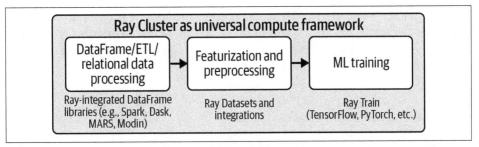

Figure 6-5. Ray Data ecosystem integrations enable more expressive data processing on Ray

For the purposes of this book, we'll explore Dask on Ray in slightly more depth to give you a feel for what these integrations look like. If you're interested in the details of a specific integration, see the latest Ray documentation (*https://oreil.ly/5MpG-*) for up-to-date information.

To follow along with the examples in this section, install Ray and Dask:

```
pip install "ray[data]==2.2.0" "dask==2022.2.0"
```

Dask (*https://dask.org*) is a Python library for parallel computing that is specifically targeted at scaling analytics and scientific computing workloads to a cluster. One of the most popular features of Dask is Dask DataFrames (*https://oreil.ly/k3yJb*), which offers a subset of the Pandas DataFrame API that can be scaled to a cluster of machines in cases where processing in memory on a single node is not feasible. DataFrames work by creating a *task graph* that is submitted to a scheduler for execution. The most typical way to execute Dask DataFrames operations is using the Dask distributed scheduler, but there is a pluggable API that allows other schedulers to execute these task graphs as well.

Ray comes packaged with a Dask scheduler backend, allowing Dask DataFrame task graphs to be executed as Ray tasks and therefore use the Ray scheduler and shared memory object store. This doesn't require modifying the core DataFrames code at all; instead, to run using Ray, all you need to do is first connect to a running Ray Cluster (or run Ray locally) and then enable the Ray scheduler backend:

```
import ray
from ray.util.dask import enable_dask_on_ray

ray.init()  # Start or connect to Ray.
enable_dask_on_ray()  # Enable the Ray scheduler backend for Dask.
```

Now we can run regular Dask DataFrames code and have it scaled across the Ray Cluster. For example, we might want to do some time-series analysis using standard DataFrame operations like `filter` and `groupby` and compute the standard deviation (example taken from Dask documentation):

```
import dask

df = dask.datasets.timeseries()
df = df[df.y > 0].groupby("name").x.std()
df.compute()  # Trigger the task graph to be evaluated.
```

If you're used to Pandas or other DataFrame libraries, you might wonder why we need to call `df.compute()`. This is because Dask is *lazy* by default and will compute results only on demand, allowing it to optimize the task graph that will be executed across the cluster.

One of the most powerful aspects of Dask on Ray is that it integrates very nicely with Ray Datasets. We can convert a Ray Dataset to a Dask DataFrame and vice versa using built-in utilities:

```
import ray
ds = ray.data.range(10000)

# Convert the Dataset to a Dask DataFrame.
df = ds.to_dask()
print(df.std().compute())  # -> 2886.89568

# Convert the Dask DataFrame back to a Dataset.
ds = ray.data.from_dask(df)
print(ds.std())  # -> 2886.89568
```

This simple example might not look impressive because we're able to compute the standard deviation using either Dask DataFrames or Ray Datasets. However, as you'll see in the next section when we build an end-to-end ML pipeline, this enables powerful workflows. For example, we can use the full expressiveness of DataFrames to do our featurization and preprocessing and then pass the data directly into downstream operations such as distributed training or inference while keeping everything in memory. This highlights how Ray Datasets enables a wide range of use cases on top of Ray and how integrations like Dask on Ray make the ecosystem even more powerful.

Building an ML Pipeline

Although we were able to build a simple distributed training application from scratch in the previous section, there were many edge cases, opportunities for performance optimization, and usability features that we would want to address to build a real-world application. As you've learned in Chapters 4 and 5, Ray has an ecosystem of libraries that enable us to build production-ready ML applications. In this section, we'll explore how to use Datasets as the "glue layer" to build an ML pipeline from end to end.

To successfully productionize a machine learning model, we need to collect and catalog data using standard ETL processes. However, that's not the end of the story: to train a model, we also often need to do featurization of the data before feeding into our training process, and how we feed the data into training can strongly impact cost and performance. After training a model, we'll also want to run inference across many different datasets—that's the whole point of training the model, after all!

Though this might seem like just a chain of steps, in practice the data processing workflow for ML is an iterative process of experimentation to define the right set of features and train a high-performing model on them. Efficiently loading, transforming, and feeding the data into training and inference is also crucial for performance, which translates directly to cost for compute-intensive models. Implementing such ML pipelines often means stitching together multiple systems and materializing intermediate results to remote storage between the stages. This has two major downsides:

- It requires orchestrating many different systems and programs for a single workflow. This can be a lot for any ML practitioner to handle, so many people use workflow orchestration systems like Apache Airflow (*https://airflow.apache.org*). While Airflow has its benefits, it's also a lot of complexity to introduce (especially in development).

- Running our ML workflow across multiple systems means we need to read from and write to storage between each stage.[5] This incurs significant overhead and cost due to data transfer and serialization.

In contrast, using Ray we are able to build a complete ML pipeline as a single application that can be run as a single Python script as depicted in Figure 6-6. The ecosystem of built-in and third-party libraries makes it possible to mix and match the right functionality for a given use case and build scalable, production-ready pipelines. Importantly, Ray Datasets acts as the glue layer that enables efficient data loading, preprocessing, and computing while avoiding expensive serialization costs and keeping intermediate data in shared memory.

Figure 6-6 shows a simplified version of the typical ML workflow and where Ray fits in that flow. ML's multiple steps often require iteration; without Ray this means stitching together many independent systems for one end-to-end process. Ray acts

---

5 Another challenge of relying on many tools is cultural. Knowledge transfer of best practices can be costly, especially in larger companies.

as a unified compute layer, enabling most of the workflow to be run as a single application.

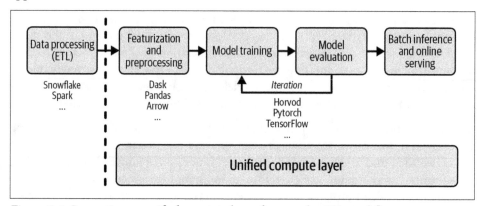

Figure 6-6. Ray acting as unified compute layer for complex ML workflows

In the next chapter we're going to show you a concrete example of building an end-to-end ML pipeline using Ray Datasets and other libraries in the Ray ecosystem in practice.

Summary

This chapter introduced Ray Datasets, a core building block in Ray. Ray Datasets offers built-in functionality for distributed data processing, but its true power lies in its integrations with both first- and third-party libraries. We've covered only a small portion of its functionality. For more details, API references, and examples, see the documentation (*https://oreil.ly/fmokZ*).

We've also shown you a simple example of distributed training of a scikit-learn classifier using Ray Datasets and discussed external library integrations such as Dask on Ray. Lastly, we've indicated the value of building end-to-end ML pipelines using the Ray ecosystem, which allows you to run your entire workflow in a single Python script. For data scientists and machine learning engineers, this means faster iteration time, better ML models, and ultimately more business value.

## CHAPTER 7

Distributed Training with Ray Train

Edward Oakes & Richard Liaw

In Chapter 6 we discussed how to train copies of a simple model on shards of data using Ray Datasets—but there's much more to distributed training than that. As we indicated in Chapter 1, Ray has a dedicated library for distributed training called Ray Train. It comes with an extensive suite of machine learning training integrations and allows you to scale your experiments seamlessly on Ray Clusters.

We will start this chapter by showing you why you might need to scale your ML training and then introduce you to the different ways of doing so. After that, we'll introduce Ray Train and walk through an extensive end-to-end example. We'll also cover some key concepts you need to know to use Ray Train, such as preprocessors, trainers, and checkpoints. Finally, we'll cover some of the more advanced functionality that Ray Train provides. As always, you can use the notebook for this chapter (*https://oreil.ly/vc5ej*) to follow along.

The Basics of Distributed Model Training

Machine learning often requires a lot of heavy computation. Depending on the type of model that you're training, whether it be a gradient boosted tree or a neural network, you may face some common problems with training ML models:

- The time it takes to finish training is too long.
- The data is too large to fit into one machine.
- The model itself is too large to fit into a single machine.

For the first case, training can be accelerated by processing data with increased throughput. Some ML algorithms, such as neural networks, can parallelize parts of the computation to speed up training.[1]

In the second case, your choice of algorithm may require you to fit all the available data from a dataset into memory, but the given single-node memory may not be sufficient. If that's the case, you would need to split the data across multiple nodes and train in a distributed manner. On the other hand, sometimes your algorithm may not require data to be distributed, but if you're using a distributed database system to begin with, you still want a training framework that can leverage your distributed data.

When your model doesn't fit into a single machine, you may need to split it up into multiple parts spread across multiple machines. The approach of splitting models across multiple machines is called *model parallelism*. To run into this issue, you first need a model that is large enough to not fit into a single machine. Usually, large companies like Google or Meta need model parallelism, and they also rely on in-house solutions to handle the distributed training.

The first two problems often arise much earlier in ML development than the third. The solutions we just sketched for these problems fall under the umbrella of data-parallel training. Instead of splitting up the model across multiple machines, you rely on distributed data to speed up training.

Specifically for the first problem, if you can speed up your training process, hopefully with minimal or no loss in accuracy, and you can do so cost-efficiently, why not go for it? And if you have distributed data, whether by necessity for your algorithm or the way you store your data, you need a training solution to deal with it. As you will see, Ray Train is built for efficient, data-parallel training. Figure 7-1 summarizes the two basic types of distributed training.

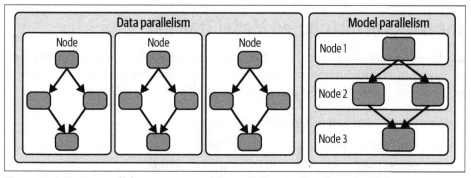

Figure 7-1. Data parallelism versus model parallelism in distributed training

---

1 This applies specifically to the gradient computation in neural networks.

Introduction to Ray Train by Example

Ray Train is a library for distributed data-parallel training on Ray. It offers key tools for different parts of the training workflow, from feature processing to scalable training to integrations with ML tracking tools, to export mechanisms for models.

In a basic ML training pipeline you will use the following key components of Ray Train:

Trainers
> Ray Train has several Trainer classes that make it possible to do distributed training. Trainers are wrapper classes around third-party training frameworks like XGBoost, Pytorch, and TensorFlow providing integration with core Ray actors (for distribution), Ray Tune, and Ray Datasets.

Predictors
> Once you have a trained model, you can use it to get predictions. For batches of input data you use so-called batch predictors, which are also used to evaluate the performance of a model on a validation set.

Additionally, Ray Train provides several common *Preprocessor* objects and utilities to process dataset objects into consumable features for Trainers. Finally, Ray Train provides a *Checkpoint* class that allows you to save and restore the state of a training run. In our first walk-through we will not use any preprocessors, but we will cover them in more detail later.

Ray Train is built with first-class support for training on large datasets. Along the same philosophy that you should not have to think about *how* to parallelize your code, you can simply "connect" your large dataset to Ray Train without thinking about how to ingest and feed your data into different parallel workers.

Let's put these components into practice by walking through our first Ray Train example. To load the training data, we're going to leverage our knowledge from Chapter 6 and make heavy use of Ray Datasets.

Predicting Big Tips in NYC Taxi Rides

This section walks through a practical, end-to-end example of building a deep learning pipeline using Ray. We will build a binary classification model to predict whether a taxi ride will result in a big tip (>20% of the fare) using the public New York City Taxi and Limousine Commission (TLC) Trip Record Data (*https://oreil.ly/nrJgK*). Our workflow will closely resemble that of a typical ML practitioner:

1. Load the data, do some basic preprocessing, and compute features we'll use in our model.

2. Define a neural network and train it using distributed data-parallel training.

3. Apply the trained neural network to a fresh batch of data.

The example will use Dask on Ray and train a PyTorch neural network, but note that nothing here is specific to either of those libraries: Ray Datasets and Ray Train can be used with a wide range of popular machine learning tools. To follow along with the example code in this section, install Ray, PyTorch, and Dask:

```
pip install "ray[data,train]==2.2.0" "dask==2022.2.0" "torch==1.12.1"
pip install "xgboost==1.6.2" "xgboost-ray>=0.1.10"
```

In the following examples, we'll be loading the data from local disk to make it easy to run the examples on your machine. The data is available in the book's GitHub repository (*https://oreil.ly/DhcUB*). The file paths in the next examples assume you've cloned the repository and are running from within its top-level directory.

Loading, Preprocessing, and Featurization

The first step in training our model is to load and preprocess it. To do this, we'll be using Dask on Ray, for which you've already seen a first example in Chapter 6. Dask on Ray gives us a convenient DataFrames API and the ability to scale up the preprocessing across a cluster and efficiently pass it into our training and inference operations. Here is our code for preprocessing data and building features for our model, defined in a single `load_dataset` function:

```
import ray
from ray.util.dask import enable_dask_on_ray

import dask.dataframe as dd

LABEL_COLUMN = "is_big_tip"
FEATURE_COLUMNS = ["passenger_count", "trip_distance", "fare_amount",
                   "trip_duration", "hour", "day_of_week"]

enable_dask_on_ray()


def load_dataset(path: str, *, include_label=True):
    columns = ["tpep_pickup_datetime", "tpep_dropoff_datetime", "tip_amount",
               "passenger_count", "trip_distance", "fare_amount"]
    df = dd.read_parquet(path, columns=columns)    ❶

    df = df.dropna()    ❷
    df = df[(df["passenger_count"] <= 4) &
            (df["trip_distance"] < 100) &
            (df["fare_amount"] < 1000)]

    df["tpep_pickup_datetime"] = dd.to_datetime(df["tpep_pickup_datetime"])
    df["tpep_dropoff_datetime"] = dd.to_datetime(df["tpep_dropoff_datetime"])

    df["trip_duration"] = (df["tpep_dropoff_datetime"] -
```

```
                        df["tpep_pickup_datetime"]).dt.seconds
df = df[df["trip_duration"] < 4 * 60 * 60] # 4 hours.
df["hour"] = df["tpep_pickup_datetime"].dt.hour
df["day_of_week"] = df["tpep_pickup_datetime"].dt.weekday  ❸

if include_label:
    df[LABEL_COLUMN] = df["tip_amount"] > 0.2 * df["fare_amount"]  ❹

df = df.drop(  ❺
    columns=["tpep_pickup_datetime", "tpep_dropoff_datetime", "tip_amount"]
)

return ray.data.from_dask(df).repartition(100)  ❻
```

❶ Drop unused columns of the initial Dask DataFrame loaded from Parquet files.

❷ Do basic cleaning, and drop null values and outliers.

❸ Add three new features: trip duration, hour the trip started, and day of the week.

❹ Calculate the label column: if the tip was more or less than 20% of the fare.

❺ Drop all unused columns.

❻ Return a repartitioned Ray Dataset created *from Dask*.

This involves basic data loading and cleaning as well as transforming some columns into a format that can be used as features in our ML model. For instance, we transform the pickup and drop-off date-times, which are provided as a string, into three numerical features: trip_duration, hour, and day_of_week. This is made easy by Dask's built-in support for Python datetime utilities (*https://oreil.ly/sZPhd*). If this data is going to be used for training, we also need to compute the label column.

Finally, once we've computed our preprocessed Dask DataFrame, we transform it into a Ray Dataset so we can pass it into our training and inference processes later.

Defining a Deep Learning Model

Now that we've cleaned and prepared the data, we need to define a model architecture that we'll use for the model. In practice, this would likely be an iterative process and involve researching the state of the art for similar problems. For the sake of our example, we'll keep things simple and use a basic PyTorch neural network that we call FarePredictor. The neural network has three linear transformations starting with the dimension of our feature vector, and then it outputs a value between 0 and 1 using a Sigmoid activation function. We also use *batch normalization* layers in the network to improve training. This output value will be rounded to produce the binary prediction of whether or not the ride will result in a big tip:

```python
import torch
import torch.nn as nn
import torch.nn.functional as F


class FarePredictor(nn.Module):
    def __init__(self):
        super().__init__()

        self.fc1 = nn.Linear(6, 256)
        self.fc2 = nn.Linear(256, 16)
        self.fc3 = nn.Linear(16, 1)

        self.bn1 = nn.BatchNorm1d(256)
        self.bn2 = nn.BatchNorm1d(16)

    def forward(self, x):
        x = F.relu(self.fc1(x))
        x = self.bn1(x)
        x = F.relu(self.fc2(x))
        x = self.bn2(x)
        x = torch.sigmoid(self.fc3(x))

        return x
```

Distributed Training with Ray Train

Now that we've defined the neural network architecture, we need a way to efficiently train it on our data. This dataset is very large, so our best bet is to perform *data-parallel training*.

This means we train the model on multiple machines in parallel, each of which has a copy of the model and a subset of the data. We will use Ray Train to define a scalable training process that will use PyTorch DataParallel (*https://oreil.ly/A_xcS*) under the hood. We won't go into conceptual details of the training process here, but we'll discuss them in the sections following this end-to-end example.

The upcoming example uses imports from the ray.air module. We mentioned Ray AIR in Chapter 1 and will introduce it formally in Chapter 10. For now, treat this module as a useful utility for defining and running your distributed training processes.

In particular, we're using a so-called AIR session that can be used to report metrics collected during the training process. This follows a usage pattern similar to the tune.report API that we discussed in Chapter 5.

The first thing we need to do is define the core logic needed to train on a batch of data on each worker in each epoch. This will take in a local shard of the full dataset, run it through the local copy of the model, and perform backpropagation to update the model weights. After each epoch, the worker will use Ray Train utilities to report the result and save the current model weights for use later:

```python
from ray.air import session
from ray.air.config import ScalingConfig
import ray.train as train
from ray.train.torch import TorchCheckpoint, TorchTrainer


def train_loop_per_worker(config: dict):    ❶
    batch_size = config.get("batch_size", 32)
    lr = config.get("lr", 1e-2)
    num_epochs = config.get("num_epochs", 3)

    dataset_shard = session.get_dataset_shard("train")    ❷

    model = FarePredictor()
    dist_model = train.torch.prepare_model(model)    ❸

    loss_function = nn.SmoothL1Loss()
    optimizer = torch.optim.Adam(dist_model.parameters(), lr=lr)

    for epoch in range(num_epochs):    ❹
        loss = 0
        num_batches = 0
        for batch in dataset_shard.iter_torch_batches(    ❺
                batch_size=batch_size, dtypes=torch.float
        ):
            labels = torch.unsqueeze(batch[LABEL_COLUMN], dim=1)
            inputs = torch.cat(
                [torch.unsqueeze(batch[f], dim=1) for f in FEATURE_COLUMNS],
                dim=1
            )
            output = dist_model(inputs)
            batch_loss = loss_function(output, labels)
            optimizer.zero_grad()
            batch_loss.backward()
            optimizer.step()

            num_batches += 1
            loss += batch_loss.item()

        session.report(    ❻
            {"epoch": epoch, "loss": loss},
            checkpoint=TorchCheckpoint.from_model(dist_model)
        )
```

❶ Pass a `config` dictionary into our training loop to specify some parameters at runtime.

❷ Retrieve the data shard for the current worker, using Ray Train's `get_data_shard` utility.

❸ Prepare the PyTorch model for distributed training by applying `prepare_model`.

❹ Define a standard PyTorch training loop, iterating over batches of data and performing backpropagation.

❺ The only nonstandard part is the use of `iter_torch_batches` to iterate over the data shard.

❻ After each epoch, `report` the `loss` computed and a *model checkpoint* using a Ray `session`.

In case you're not familiar with PyTorch, note that the code between the definition of the `loss_function` and aggregating the `batch_loss` to our `loss` is a standard training loop for a PyTorch model (except for iterating over batches of the dataset shard, which is specific to Ray).

Now that the training process has been defined, we need to load the training and validation data to feed into our training workers. Here, we call the `load_dataset` function defined earlier that will do preprocessing and featurization.[2]

This dataset is passed into a `TorchTrainer` along with some configuration parameters such as the batch size, number of epochs, and number of workers to use. Each worker will have access to a shard of the data locally and can iterate over it. After training has completed, we can fetch the final trained checkpoint from the returned result object:

```
trainer = TorchTrainer(
    train_loop_per_worker=train_loop_per_worker,  ❶
    train_loop_config={  ❷
        "lr": 1e-2, "num_epochs": 3, "batch_size": 64
    },
    scaling_config=ScalingConfig(num_workers=2),  ❸
    datasets={  ❹
        "train": load_dataset("nyc_tlc_data/yellow_tripdata_2020-01.parquet")
    },
)
```

---

2 The code loads only a subset of the data for testing; to run at scale we would use all partitions of the data when calling `load_dataset` and increase `num_workers` when training the model.

```
result = trainer.fit()  ❺
trained_model = result.checkpoint
```

❶ Each `TorchTrainer` requires you to specify a `train_loop_per_worker`.

❷ Optionally, if your train loop takes in a `config` dictionary, you can specify it as `train_loop_config`.

❸ Every Ray Train `Trainer` needs a so-called `ScalingConfig` to know how to scale training on your Ray Cluster.

❹ Another required argument of each `Trainer` is a `datasets` dictionary. We define a `"train"` Dataset here, and that is what we use in our training loop.

❺ You can simply `.fit()` a `TorchTrainer` to start training.

The last line exports our trained model as a checkpoint for later use in downstream applications like serving and inference. Ray Train generates these checkpoints to serialize intermediate state for training. Checkpoints can include both models and other training artifacts, such as preprocessors.

Distributed Batch Inference

Once we've trained a model and gotten the best accuracy, the next step is to actually apply it in practice. Sometimes this means powering a low-latency service, which we'll explore in Chapter 8, but often the task is to apply the model across batches of data as they come in.

Let's use the trained model weights from our `trained_model` and apply them across a new batch of data (in this case, it'll just be another chunk of the same public dataset). To do this, first we need to load, preprocess, and featurize the data in the same way we did for training. Then we will load our model and `map` it across the whole dataset. Ray Datasets allows us to do this efficiently with Ray actors, even using GPUs just by changing one parameter. We simply load the trained model checkpoint and call `.predict_pipelined()` on it. This will use Ray Datasets to perform distributed batch inference across the data:

```
from ray.train.torch import TorchPredictor
from ray.train.batch_predictor import BatchPredictor

batch_predictor = BatchPredictor(trained_model, TorchPredictor)
ds = load_dataset(
    "nyc_tlc_data/yellow_tripdata_2021-01.parquet", include_label=False)

batch_predictor.predict_pipelined(ds, blocks_per_window=10)
```

This example showed how Ray Train and Datasets can be used to implement an end-to-end machine learning workflow as a single application. We were able to featurize the dataset, train and validate an ML model, and then apply that model across a different dataset in a single Python script. Ray Datasets acted as the glue layer, connecting the different stages and avoiding expensive serialization costs between them. We also used checkpoints to store the model and ran a Ray Train batch prediction job to apply the model to a new dataset.

Now, that you've seen your first example of Ray Train, let's take a closer look at its primary abstraction, the `Trainer`.

More on Trainers in Ray Train

As you've seen in the example of using a `TorchTrainer`, Trainers are framework-specific classes that run model training in a distributed fashion. All Ray `Trainer` classes share a common interface. At this point, it's enough to know about two aspects of this interface, namely:

- The `.fit()` method, which fits a given `Trainer` with the given datasets, configuration, and desired scaling properties
- The `.checkpoint` property, which returns the Ray `Checkpoint` object for this Trainer

Ray Train's Trainers integrate with common machine learning frameworks such as PyTorch, Hugging Face, TensorFlow, Horovod, scikit-learn, and more. There's even a `Trainer` specifically for RLlib models, which we don't cover here. Let's discuss another PyTorch example to point out specific aspects of the `Trainer` API, with an emphasis on how to migrate an existing PyTorch model to Ray Train.

Gradient Boosting Frameworks

Ray Train also offers support for gradient boosted decision tree frameworks.

XGBoost is an optimized distributed gradient boosting library designed to be highly efficient, flexible, and portable. It implements ML algorithms under the gradient boosting framework. XGBoost provides a parallel tree boosting that solves many data science problems quickly and accurately.

LightGBM is a gradient boosting framework based on tree-based learning algorithms. Compared to XGBoost, it is a relatively new framework but one that is quickly becoming popular in both academic and production use cases.

To use these frameworks, you can use the `XGBoostTrainer` and `LightGBMTrainer` classes, respectively.

In this example we want to focus on the details of Ray Train itself, so we'll use a much simpler training dataset and a small neural network that takes random noise as input. We define a three-layer NeuralNetwork, an explicit training_loop, similar to the one we saw in the previous section, that you can use to train the model. For clarity, we extract the training code run for each epoch in a helper function called train_one_epoch:

```
import torch
import torch.nn as nn
import torch.nn.functional as F
from ray.data import from_torch

num_samples = 20
input_size = 10
layer_size = 15
output_size = 5
num_epochs = 3


class NeuralNetwork(nn.Module):
    def __init__(self):
        super().__init__()
        self.fc1 = nn.Linear(input_size, layer_size)
        self.relu = nn.ReLU()
        self.fc2 = nn.Linear(layer_size, output_size)

    def forward(self, x):
        x = F.relu(self.fc1(x))
        x = self.fc2(x)
        return x


def train_data():
    return torch.randn(num_samples, input_size)    ❶


input_data = train_data()
label_data = torch.randn(num_samples, output_size)
train_dataset = from_torch(input_data)    ❷


def train_one_epoch(model, loss_fn, optimizer):    ❸
    output = model(input_data)
    loss = loss_fn(output, label_data)
    optimizer.zero_grad()
    loss.backward()
    optimizer.step()


def training_loop():    ❹
    model = NeuralNetwork()
```

```
loss_fn = nn.MSELoss()
optimizer = torch.optim.SGD(model.parameters(), lr=0.1)
for epoch in range(num_epochs):
    train_one_epoch(model, loss_fn, optimizer)
```

❶ Use a randomly generated dataset.

❷ Create a Ray Dataset from this data with `from_torch`.

❸ Extract the PyTorch code to train one epoch into a helper function.

❹ This training loop can be run as is to train your PyTorch model on a single machine.

Typically, if you wanted to distribute your training without Ray Train, you would need to do these two things:

- Establish a backend that coordinates interprocess communication.
- Instantiate multiple parallel processes on each node that you want to distribute your training across.

In contrast, let's see how easy it is to use Ray Train to distribute your training process.

Migrating to Ray Train with Minimal Code Changes

With Ray Train, you can make a one-line change to your code to take care of both interprocess communication and process instantiation under the hood.

The code change is made by calling `prepare_model` on the PyTorch model that you plan to train. This change is literally the only difference between the `training_loop` defined before and the following `distributed_training_loop`:

```
from ray.train.torch import prepare_model


def distributed_training_loop():
    model = NeuralNetwork()
    model = prepare_model(model)   ❶
    loss_fn = nn.MSELoss()
    optimizer = torch.optim.SGD(model.parameters(), lr=0.1)
    for epoch in range(num_epochs):
        train_one_epoch(model, loss_fn, optimizer)
```

❶ Prepare the model for distributed training by calling `prepare_model`.

Then, we can instantiate a `TorchTrainer` model, which has three required arguments:

`train_loop_per_worker`
This function trains your model for each worker. It has access to the `datasets` provided and can be fed an optional `config` dictionary that can be passed to your trainer as `train_loop_config`. This function will typically report metrics, e.g., via a `session`.

`datasets`
This dictionary can contain several keys with Ray Datasets as values. It's kept flexible so that you can have training data, validation data, or any other type of data needed for your training loop.

`scaling_config`
This `ScalingConfig` object specifies how your training should scale. For instance, you can specify the number of training workers with `num_workers` and the use of GPUs with the `use_gpu` flag. We'll elaborate on this more in the next section.

Here's how you set up your Trainer in our example:

```
from ray.air.config import ScalingConfig
from ray.train.torch import TorchTrainer


trainer = TorchTrainer(
    train_loop_per_worker=distributed_training_loop,
    scaling_config=ScalingConfig(
        num_workers=2,
        use_gpu=False
    ),
    datasets={"train": train_dataset}
)

result = trainer.fit()
```

With an initialized Trainer, you can call `fit()`, which will execute the training across your Ray Cluster. Figure 7-2 summarizes working with a `TorchTrainer`.

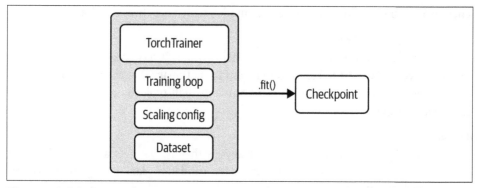

Figure 7-2. Working with a TorchTrainer requires you to specify a training loop, datasets, and a scaling configuration

Scaling Out Trainers

The Ray Train philosophy is that the user should not need to think about how to parallelize their code. Specifying a `scaling_config` allows you to scale your training without writing distributed logic and to declaratively specify the *compute resources* used by a Trainer. The nice thing about this specification is that you don't need to think about the underlying hardware. In particular, you can use hundreds of workers by specifying the parameters of your cluster nodes in your `ScalingConfig` accordingly:

```
import ray
from ray.air.config import ScalingConfig
from ray.train.xgboost import XGBoostTrainer

ray.init(address="auto")  ❶

scaling_config = ScalingConfig(num_workers=200, use_gpu=True)  ❷

trainer = XGBoostTrainer(  ❸
    scaling_config=scaling_config,
    # ...
)
```

❶ Connect to an existing, large Ray Cluster here.

❷ Define a `ScalingConfig` according to the cluster's available resources.

❸ We can then use Ray Train's XGBoost integration to train a model on this cluster.

Preprocessing with Ray Train

Data preprocessing is a common technique for transforming raw data into features for an ML model, and we've seen many examples in this and the previous chapter. So far we've "manually" preprocessed our data by writing custom functions to transform our data into the right format. But Ray Train has several built-in preprocessors for common use cases and also provides interfaces to define your own custom logic.

The `Preprocessor` is the core class offered by Ray Train for handling data preprocessing. Each preprocessor has the following APIs:

`.transform()`
> Used to process and apply a processing transformation to a dataset.

`.fit()`
> Used to calculate and store aggregate state about the dataset on a preprocessor. Returns `self` for chaining.

`.fit_transform()`
> Syntactic sugar for performing transformations that require aggregate state. May be optimized at the implementation level for specific preprocessors.

`.transform_batch()`
> Used to apply the same transformation on batches for prediction.

We often want to make sure we can use the same data preprocessing operations at training time and at serving time. Training-serving skew, a major problem in deploying ML, describes a situation where there is a difference between performance during training and performance during serving. This skew is often caused by a discrepancy between how you handle data in the training and serving pipelines. Thus, you want to make sure you have consistent data handling for training and serving.

You can use the preceding preprocessors by passing them to the constructor of a `trainer`. That means once you've created a `preprocessor`, you don't have to apply it to your Ray Datasets manually. Instead, you can pass it to your `trainer`, and Ray Train will take care of applying it in a distributed fashion. Here is how this works schematically:

```
from ray.data.preprocessors import StandardScaler
from ray.train.xgboost import XGBoostTrainer


trainer = XGBoostTrainer(
    preprocessor=StandardScaler(...),
    # ...
)
result = trainer.fit()
```

Some preprocessing operators such as one-hot encoders are easy to run in training and transfer to serving. However, other operators such as those that do standardization are a bit trickier, since you don't want to do large data crunching (to find the mean of a particular column) during serving time.

Fortunately, the Ray Train preprocessors are serializable so you can easily get consistency from training to serving just by serializing these operators. For instance, you can simply pickle a preprocessor like this:

```
import pickle
from ray.data.preprocessors import StandardScaler

preprocessor=StandardScaler(...)
pickle.dumps(preprocessor)
```

Next, let's discuss a concrete example of a training procedure using preprocessors, by also showing you how to tune your Trainer's hyperparameters.

Integrating Trainers with Ray Tune

Ray Train provides an integration with Ray Tune that allows you to perform HPO in just a few lines of code. Tune will create one trial per hyperparameter configuration. In each trial, a new Trainer will be initialized and run the training function with its generated configuration.

In the following code, we create an XGBoostTrainer and specify hyperparameter ranges for common hyperparameters. Specifically, we're going to choose between two different *preprocessors* in our training scenario. To be precise, we will use a StandardScaler, which translates and scales each specified column by its mean and standard deviation (the resulting columns will thus follow a standard normal distribution) and MinMaxScaler, which simply scales each column to the range [0, 1].

Here's the corresponding parameter space we will search over next:

```
import ray

from ray.air.config import ScalingConfig
from ray import tune
from ray.data.preprocessors import StandardScaler, MinMaxScaler


dataset = ray.data.from_items(
    [{"X": x, "Y": 1} for x in range(0, 100)] +
    [{"X": x, "Y": 0} for x in range(100, 200)]
)
prep_v1 = StandardScaler(columns=["X"])
prep_v2 = MinMaxScaler(columns=["X"])

param_space = {
    "scaling_config": ScalingConfig(
```

```
            num_workers=tune.grid_search([2, 4]),
            resources_per_worker={
                "CPU": 2,
                "GPU": 0,
            },
        ),
        "preprocessor": tune.grid_search([prep_v1, prep_v2]),
        "params": {
            "objective": "binary:logistic",
            "tree_method": "hist",
            "eval_metric": ["logloss", "error"],
            "eta": tune.loguniform(1e-4, 1e-1),
            "subsample": tune.uniform(0.5, 1.0),
            "max_depth": tune.randint(1, 9),
        },
    }
```

We can now create a `Trainer` as before, this time going with an `XGBoostTrainer` and then passing it to an instance of a `Tuner` from Ray Tune, which we can `.fit()` just like the `trainer` itself:

```
from ray.train.xgboost import XGBoostTrainer
from ray.air.config import RunConfig
from ray.tune import Tuner


trainer = XGBoostTrainer(
    params={},
    run_config=RunConfig(verbose=2),
    preprocessor=None,
    scaling_config=None,
    label_column="Y",
    datasets={"train": dataset}
)

tuner = Tuner(
    trainer,
    param_space=param_space,
)

results = tuner.fit()
```

Note that we're using another component of a Ray Trainer here that you haven't seen before, the `RunConfig`. This configuration is used for all runtime options of a Trainer, in our case the log verbosity of the experiment (0 would be silent; 1 gives only status updates; 2, the default, gives status updates and brief results; and 3 gives detailed results).

Compared to other distributed hyperparameter tuning solutions, Ray Tune and Ray Train have some unique features. Ray's solution is fault-tolerant, and it has the ability to specify the dataset and preprocessor as a parameter, as well as to adjust the number of workers during training time.

Using Callbacks to Monitor Training

To explore one more feature of Ray Train, you may want to plug in your training code with your favorite experiment management framework. Ray Train provides an interface to fetch intermediate results and callbacks to process or log them. It comes with built-in callbacks for popular tracking frameworks, but you can implement your own callback via Tune's `LoggerCallback` interface.

For instance, you can log results in JSON format using the `JsonLoggerCallback`, to TensorBoard using the `TBXLoggerCallback`, or to MLflow using the `MLFLowLogger Callback`.[3] The following example shows how you can use all three in one single training run by specifying a list of `callbacks`:

```
from ray.air.callbacks.mlflow import MLflowLoggerCallback
from ray.tune.logger import TBXLoggerCallback, JsonLoggerCallback

training_loop = ...
trainer = ...

trainer.fit(
    training_loop,
    callbacks=[
        MLflowLoggerCallback(),
        TBXLoggerCallback(),
        JsonLoggerCallback()
    ])
```

Summary

In this chapter, we've discussed the basics of distributed model training and showed you how to run data-parallel training with Ray Train. We walked you through an extensive example that used both Ray Data and Ray Train on an interesting dataset. Specifically, we demonstrated how to use Dask on Ray to load, preprocess, and featurize your datasets, and then use Ray Train to run a distributed PyTorch training loop. We then discussed Ray Trainers in more detail and showed how they integrate with Ray Tune via Tuners, how you can use them with preprocessors, and how you can use callbacks to monitor training.

---

3 MLflow and TensorBoard are open source projects for ML experiment tracking and visualization. They are very useful for monitoring the progress of your machine learning model.

## CHAPTER 8

Online Inference with Ray Serve

Edward Oakes

In Chapters 6 and 7 you learned how to use Ray to process data, train ML models, and apply them in a batch inference setting. However, many of the most exciting use cases for machine learning involve *online inference*.

Online inference is the process of using ML models to enhance API endpoints that users interact with directly or indirectly. This is important in situations where latency matters: you can't simply apply models to data behind the scenes and serve the results. There are many real-world examples of use cases where online inference can provide a lot of value, for example:

Recommendation systems
Providing recommendations for products (e.g., online shopping) or content (e.g., social media) is a bread-and-butter use case for machine learning. While it's possible to do this offline, recommendation systems often benefit from reacting to users' preferences in real time. This requires performing online inference using recent behavior as a key feature.

Chat bots
Online services often have real-time chat windows to provide support to customers from the comfort of their keyboard. Traditionally, these chat windows were staffed by customer support staff, but a recent trend to reduce labor costs and improve time-to-resolution is replacing them with ML-powered chat bots that can be online 24/7. These chat bots require a sophisticated mix of multiple machine learning techniques and must be able to respond to customer input in real time.

Estimating arrival times

Ride sharing, navigation, and food delivery services all rely on being able to provide an accurate estimate of arrival times (e.g., for your driver, yourself, or your dinner). Providing accurate estimates is very difficult because it requires accounting for real-world factors such as traffic patterns, weather, and accidents. Estimates are also refreshed many times over the course of one trip.

These are just a few examples of how applying machine learning in an online setting can provide a lot of value in application domains that are traditionally very difficult (imagine writing logic by hand to estimate arrival times!). The list of applications goes on: a number of nascent domains such as self-driving cars, robotics, and video-processing pipelines are also being redefined by machine learning.

All these applications share one crucial requirement: latency. In the case of online services, low latency is paramount for providing a good user experience. For applications that interact with the real world (such as robotics or self-driving cars), higher latency can have even stronger implications for safety or accuracy.

This chapter will provide a gentle introduction to Ray Serve, a Ray-native library that enables building online inference applications on top of Ray. First, we will discuss the challenges of online inference that Ray Serve addresses. Then, we'll cover the architecture of Ray Serve and introduce its core functionality. Finally, we will use Ray Serve to build an end-to-end online inference API consisting of multiple natural language processing models. You can follow along with the code in the notebook for this chapter (*https://oreil.ly/k9VlL*).

Key Characteristics of Online Inference

In the previous section we discussed that the main goal of online inference is to interact with ML models with low latency. However, this has long been a key requirement for API backends and web servers, so a natural question is: what's different about serving ML models?

ML Models Are Compute Intensive

Many of the challenges in online inference are a result of one key characteristic: ML models are very compute intensive. Compared to traditional web serving where requests are primarily handled by I/O-intensive database queries or other API calls, most ML models boil down to performing many linear algebra computations: provide a recommendation, estimate an arrival time, or detect an object in an image. This is especially true for the recent trend of "deep learning," which is an arm of ML characterized by neural networks that are growing larger over time. Often, deep learning models can also benefit significantly from using specialized hardware such as GPUs or TPUs, which have special-purpose instructions optimized for ML computations and enable vectorized computations across multiple inputs in parallel.

Many online inference applications must be run 24/7. When combined with the fact that ML models are compute intensive, operating online inference services can be very expensive, requiring allocation of many CPUs and GPUs at all times. The primary challenges of online inference boil down to serving models in a way that minimizes end-to-end latency while also reducing cost. Key properties that online inference systems provide to satisfy these requirements include:

- Support for specialized hardware such as GPUs and TPUs.
- The ability to scale the resources used for a model up and down in response to request load.
- Support for request batching to take advantage of vectorized computations.

ML Models Aren't Useful in Isolation

Often when ML is discussed in the academic or research setting, the focus is on an individual, isolated task such as object recognition or classification. However, real-world applications are not usually so clear cut and well defined. Instead, a combination of multiple ML models and business logic is required to solve a problem from end to end. For example, consider a product recommendation use case. While we could apply a multitude of known ML techniques to the core problem of making a recommendation, a lot of equally important challenges exist around the edges, many of which will be specific to each use case:

- Validating inputs and outputs to ensure the result returned to the user makes sense semantically. Often, we may have some manual rules such as avoiding returning the same recommendation to a user multiple times in succession.
- Fetching up-to-date information about the user and available products and converting it into features for the model (in some cases, this may be performed by an online feature store).
- Combining the results of multiple models using manual rules such as filtering the top results or selecting the model with highest confidence.

Implementing an online inference API requires the ability to integrate all of these pieces into one unified service. Therefore, it's important to have the flexibility to compose multiple models along with custom business logic. These pieces can't be viewed in isolation: the "glue" logic often needs to evolve alongside the models themselves.

An Introduction to Ray Serve

Ray Serve is a scalable compute layer for serving ML models on top of Ray. Serve is framework-agnostic, meaning that it isn't tied to a specific ML library; rather, it treats models as ordinary Python code. Additionally, it allows you to flexibly combine normal Python business logic alongside ML models. This makes it possible to build online inference services completely: a Serve application could validate user input, query a database, perform scalable inference across multiple ML models, and combine, filter, and validate the output—all in the process of handling a single inference request. Indeed, combining the results of multiple ML models is one of the key strengths of Ray Serve, as you'll see in "Multimodel Inference Graphs" on page 166.

While flexible, Ray Serve has purpose-built features for compute-heavy ML models, enabling dynamic scaling and resource allocation to ensure that request load can be handled efficiently across many CPUs and/or GPUs. Here, Serve inherits a lot of benefits from being built on top of Ray: it's scalable to hundreds of machines, offers flexible scheduling policies, and offers low-overhead communication across processes using Ray's core APIs.

This section incrementally introduces core functionality from Ray Serve with a focus on how it helps address the challenges of online inference previously outlined. To follow along with the code samples in this section, you'll need the following Python packages installed locally:

```
pip install "ray[serve]==2.2.0" "transformers==4.21.2" "requests==2.28.1"
```

Running the examples assumes that you have the code saved locally in a file named *app.py* in the current working directory.

Architectural Overview

Ray Serve is built on top of Ray, so it inherits a lot of benefits such as scalability, low-overhead communication, an API well suited to parallelism, and the ability to leverage shared memory via the object store. The core primitive in Ray Serve is a *deployment*, which you can think of as a managed group of Ray actors that can be addressed together and that will handle requests load-balanced across them. Each actor in a deployment is called a *replica* in Ray Serve. Often, a deployment will map one-to-one with an ML model, but deployments can contain arbitrary Python code, so they might also house business logic.

Ray Serve enables exposing deployments over HTTP and defining the input parsing and output logic. However, one of the most important features of Ray Serve is that deployments can also call into each other directly using a native Python API, which will translate to direct actor calls between the replicas. This enables flexible, high-performance composition of models and business logic; you'll see this in action later in the section.

Figure 8-1 provides a basic view of how a Ray Serve application runs on top of a Ray Cluster: multiple deployments are placed across a Ray Cluster. Each deployment is made up of one more "replicas," each of which is a Ray actor. Incoming traffic is routed through an HTTP proxy that will load-balance requests across the replicas.[1]

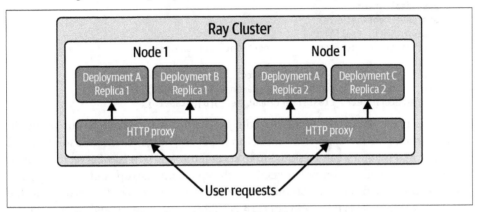

Figure 8-1. The architecture of a Ray Serve application

Under the hood, the deployments making up a Ray Serve application are managed by a centralized *controller* actor. This is a detached actor managed by Ray that will be restarted upon failure. The controller is in charge of creating and updating replica actors, broadcasting updates to other actors in the system, and performing health checking and failure recovery. If a replica or an entire Ray node crashes for any reason, the controller will detect the failures and ensure that the actors are recovered and can continue serving traffic.

Defining a Basic HTTP Endpoint

This section will introduce Ray Serve by defining a simple HTTP endpoint wrapping a single ML model. The model we'll deploy is a sentiment classifier: given a text input, it will predict if the output had a positive or negative sentiment. We'll be using a pretrained sentiment classifier from the Hugging Face Transformers library (*https://huggingface.co*), which provides a simple Python API for pretrained models that will abstract away the details of the model and allow us to focus on the serving logic.

To deploy this model using Ray Serve, we need to define a Python class and turn it into a Serve *deployment* using the @serve.deployment decorator. The decorator allows us to pass a number of useful options to configure the deployment; we will explore some of those options in "Scaling and Resource Allocation" on page 163:

---

1 Deployments can also send traffic to each other directly. This enables building more complex applications involving model composition or mixing ML models with business logic.

```
from ray import serve

from transformers import pipeline


@serve.deployment
class SentimentAnalysis:
    def __init__(self):
        self._classifier = pipeline("sentiment-analysis")

    def __call__(self, request) -> str:
        input_text = request.query_params["input_text"]
        return self._classifier(input_text)[0]["label"]
```

There are a few important points to note here. First, we instantiate our model in the constructor of the class. This model may be very large, so downloading it and loading it into memory can be slow (up to several minutes). In Ray Serve, the code in the constructor will be run only once in each replica on startup, and any properties can be cached for future use. Second, we define the logic to handle a request in the __call__ method. This takes a Starlette HTTP request as input and can return any JSON-serializable output. In this case, we'll return a single string from the output of our model: "POSITIVE" or "NEGATIVE".

Once a deployment is defined, we use the .bind() API to instantiate a copy of it. This is where we can pass optional arguments to the constructor to configure the deployment (such as a remote path to download model weights from). Note that this doesn't actually run the deployment but packages it with its arguments (this will be more important later when we combine multiple models):

```
basic_deployment = SentimentAnalysis.bind()
```

We can run the bound deployment using the serve.run Python API or corresponding serve run CLI command. Assuming you save the preceding code in a file called *app.py*, you can run it locally with the following command:

```
serve run app:basic_deployment
```

This will instantiate a single replica of our deployment and host it behind a local HTTP server. To test it, we can use the Python requests package:

```
import requests

print(requests.get(
    "http://localhost:8000/", params={"input_text": "Hello friend!"}
).json())
```

Testing the sentiment classifier on a sample input text of "Hello friend!", it correctly classifies the text as positive!

This example is effectively the "hello world" of Ray Serve: we deployed a single model behind a basic HTTP endpoint. Note, however, that we had to manually parse the input HTTP request and feed it into our model. For this basic example it was just a single line of code, but real-world applications often take a more complex schema as input, and hand-writing HTTP logic can be tedious and error-prone. To enable writing more expressive HTTP APIs, Serve integrates with the FastAPI Python framework (*https://oreil.ly/fLnjY*).[2]

A Serve deployment can wrap a `FastAPI` app, using its expressive APIs for parsing inputs and configuring HTTP behavior. In the following example, we rely on `FastAPI` to handle parsing the `input_text` query parameter, allowing removal of the boiler-plate parsing code:

```
from fastapi import FastAPI

app = FastAPI()


@serve.deployment
@serve.ingress(app)
class SentimentAnalysis:
    def __init__(self):
        self._classifier = pipeline("sentiment-analysis")

    @app.get("/")
    def classify(self, input_text: str) -> str:
        return self._classifier(input_text)[0]["label"]


fastapi_deployment = SentimentAnalysis.bind()
```

The modified deployment should have exactly the same behavior on this example (try it using `serve run`!), but it will gracefully handle invalid inputs. These may look like minor benefits for this simple example, but for more complex APIs this can make a world of difference. We won't delve deeper into the details of FastAPI here, but for more information on its features and syntax, check out their excellent documentation (*https://oreil.ly/vrxao*).

Scaling and Resource Allocation

As mentioned, machine learning models are often compute hungry. Therefore, it's important to be able to allocate the correct amount of resources to your ML application to handle request loads while minimizing cost. Ray Serve allows you to adjust the

---

2 Under the hood, Ray Serve serializes the user-provided FastAPI app object. Then, when each deployment replica runs, Ray Serve deserializes and runs the FastAPI app the same way it would be run in a typical web server. At runtime, there will be an independent FastAPI server running in each Ray Serve replica.

resources dedicated to a deployment in two ways: by tuning the number of *replicas* of the deployment and tuning the resources allocated to each replica. By default, a deployment consists of a single replica that uses a single CPU, but these parameters can be adjusted in the `@serve.deployment` decorator (or using the corresponding `deployment.options` API).

Let's modify the `SentimentClassifier` example to scale out to multiple replicas and adjust the resource allocation so that each replica uses two CPUs instead of one (in practice, you would want to profile and understand your model to set this parameter correctly). We'll also add a print statement to log the process ID of the process handling each request to show that the requests are now load balanced across two replicas:

```python
app = FastAPI()


@serve.deployment(num_replicas=2, ray_actor_options={"num_cpus": 2})
@serve.ingress(app)
class SentimentAnalysis:
    def __init__(self):
        self._classifier = pipeline("sentiment-analysis")

    @app.get("/")
    def classify(self, input_text: str) -> str:
        import os
        print("from process:", os.getpid())
        return self._classifier(input_text)[0]["label"]


scaled_deployment = SentimentAnalysis.bind()
```

Running this new version of our classifier with `serve run app:scaled_deployment` and querying it using `requests` as we did previously, you should see that there are now two copies of the model handling requests! We could easily scale up to tens or hundreds of replicas just by tweaking `num_replicas` in the same way: Ray enables scaling to hundreds of machines and thousands of processes in a single cluster.

In this example we scaled to a static number of replicas with each replica consuming two full CPUs, but Serve also supports more expressive resource allocation policies. For example:

- Enabling a deployment to use GPUs simply requires setting `num_gpus` instead of `num_cpus`. Serve supports the same resource types as Ray Core, so deployments can also use TPUs or other custom resources.

- Resources can be *fractional*, allowing replicas to be efficiently bin-packed. For example, if a single replica doesn't saturate a full GPU, you can allocate `num_gpus=0.5` to it and multiplex with another model.

- For applications with varying request load, a deployment can be configured to dynamically autoscale the number of replicas based on the number of requests currently in flight.

For more details about resource allocation options, refer to the latest Ray Serve documentation (*https://oreil.ly/zuynD*).

Request Batching

Many machine learning models can be efficiently *vectorized*, meaning that multiple computations can be run in parallel more efficiently than running them sequentially. This is especially beneficial when running models on GPUs that are purpose-built for efficiently performing many computations in parallel. In the context of online inference this offers a path for optimization: serving multiple requests (possibly from different sources) in parallel can drastically improve the throughput of the system (and therefore save cost).

Two high-level strategies take advantage of request batching: client-side batching and server-side batching. In *client-side batching*, the server accepts multiple inputs in a single request, and clients include logic to send them in batches instead of one at a time. This is useful in situations where a single client is frequently sending many inference requests. *Server-side batching*, in contrast, enables the server to batch multiple requests without requiring any modification on the client. This can also be used to batch requests across multiple clients, which enables efficient batching even in situations with many clients that send relatively few requests each.

Ray Serve offers a built-in utility for server-side batching, the `@serve.batch` decorator, that requires just a few code changes. This batching support uses Python's `asyncio` capabilities to enqueue multiple requests into a single function call. The function should take in a list of inputs and return the corresponding list of outputs.

Once again, let's revisit the sentiment classifier from earlier and this time modify it to perform server-side batching. The underlying Hugging Face `pipeline` supports vectorized inference; all we need to do is pass a list of inputs, and it will return the corresponding list of outputs. We'll split the call to the classifier into a new method, `classify_batched`, that will take a list of input texts as input, perform inference across them, and return the outputs in a formatted list. `classify_batched` will use the `@serve.batch` decorator to automatically perform batching. The behavior can be configured using the `max_batch_size` and `batch_timeout_wait_s` parameters. Here we'll set the max batch size to 10 and wait for up to 100 ms:

```
app = FastAPI()


@serve.deployment
@serve.ingress(app)
```

```
class SentimentAnalysis:
    def __init__(self):
        self._classifier = pipeline("sentiment-analysis")

    @serve.batch(max_batch_size=10, batch_wait_timeout_s=0.1)
    async def classify_batched(self, batched_inputs):
        print("Got batch size:", len(batched_inputs))
        results = self._classifier(batched_inputs)
        return [result["label"] for result in results]

    @app.get("/")
    async def classify(self, input_text: str) -> str:
        return await self.classify_batched(input_text)


batched_deployment = SentimentAnalysis.bind()
```

Notice that both the `classify` and `classify_batched` methods now use Python's `async` and `await` syntax, meaning that many of these calls can run concurrently in the same process.

To test this behavior, we'll use the `serve.run` Python API to send requests using the Python-native handle to our deployment:

```
import ray
from ray import serve
from app import batched_deployment

handle = serve.run(batched_deployment)   ❶
ray.get([handle.classify.remote("sample text") for _ in range(10)])
```

❶ Get a handle to the deployment so we can send requests in parallel.

The handle returned by `serve.run` can be used to send multiple requests in parallel: here, we send 10 requests in parallel and wait for them all to return. Without batching, each request would be handled sequentially, but because we enabled batching, we should see the requests handled all at once (evidenced by batch size printed in the `classify_batched` method). Running on a CPU, this might be marginally faster than running sequentially, but running the same handler on a GPU we would observe a significant speedup for the batched version.

Multimodel Inference Graphs

Up until now, we've been deploying and querying a single Serve deployment wrapping one ML model. As described earlier, ML models often are not useful in isolation: many applications require multiple models to be composed together and for business logic to be intertwined with machine learning. The real power of Ray Serve is its ability to compose multiple models along with regular Python logic into a single application. This is possible by instantiating many different deployments and passing a reference between them. Each of these deployments can use all of the features we've discussed up to this point: they can be independently scaled, perform request batching, and use flexible resource allocations.

This section illustrates common multimodel serving patterns but doesn't actually contain any ML models yet. The focus is on the core capabilities that Serve provides.

Core feature: binding multiple deployments

All types of multimodel inference graphs in Ray Serve center around the ability to pass a reference to one deployment into the constructor of another. To do this, we use another feature of the .bind() API: a bound deployment can be passed to another call to .bind(), and this will resolve to a "handle" to the deployment at runtime. This enables deployments to be deployed and instantiated independently and then call each other at runtime. Here is the most basic example of a multideployment Serve application:

```
@serve.deployment
class DownstreamModel:
    def __call__(self, inp: str):
        return "Hi from downstream model!"


@serve.deployment
class Driver:
    def __init__(self, downstream):
        self._d = downstream

    async def __call__(self, *args) -> str:
        return await self._d.remote()


downstream = DownstreamModel.bind()
driver = Driver.bind(downstream)
```

In this example, the downstream model is passed into the "driver" deployment. Then at runtime the driver deployment calls into the downstream model. The driver could take any number of models passed in, and the downstream model could even take other downstream models of its own.

Pattern 1: Pipelining

The first common multimodel pattern among ML applications is "pipelining": calling multiple models in sequence, where the input of one model depends on the output of the previous. Image processing, for example, often consists of a pipeline with multiple stages of transformations such as cropping, segmentation, and object recognition or optical character recognition (OCR). Each of these models may have different properties, with some of them being lightweight transformations that can run on a CPU and others being heavyweight deep learning models that run on a GPU.

Such pipelines can easily be expressed using Serve's API. Each stage of the pipeline is defined as an independent deployment, and each deployment is passed into a top-level "pipeline driver." In the following example, we pass two deployments into a top-level driver, and the driver calls them in sequence. Note that many requests to the driver could be happening concurrently; therefore, it is possible to efficiently saturate all stages of the pipeline:

```python
@serve.deployment
class DownstreamModel:
    def __init__(self, my_val: str):
        self._my_val = my_val

    def __call__(self, inp: str):
        return inp + "|" + self._my_val


@serve.deployment
class PipelineDriver:
    def __init__(self, model1, model2):
        self._m1 = model1
        self._m2 = model2

    async def __call__(self, *args) -> str:
        intermediate = self._m1.remote("input")
        final = self._m2.remote(intermediate)
        return await final


m1 = DownstreamModel.bind("val1")
m2 = DownstreamModel.bind("val2")
pipeline_driver = PipelineDriver.bind(m1, m2)
```

To test this example, you can once again use the `serve run` API. Sending a test request to the pipeline returns `"'input|val1|val2'"` as output: each downstream "model" appended its own value to construct the final result. In practice, each of these deployments could be wrapping its own ML model, and a single request may flow across many physical nodes in a cluster.

Pattern 2: Broadcasting

In addition to sequentially chaining models together, it's often useful to broadcast an input or intermediate result to multiple models in parallel. This could be to perform "ensembling," or combining the results of multiple independent models into a single result, or used in a situation where different models may perform better on different inputs. Often the results of the models need to be combined in some way into a final result: either simply concatenated or maybe a single result chosen from the lot.

This is expressed very similarly to the pipelining example: a number of downstream models are passed into a top-level driver. In this case, it's important that we call the models in parallel: waiting for the result of each before calling the next would dramatically increase the overall latency of the system:

```python
@serve.deployment
class DownstreamModel:
    def __init__(self, my_val: str):
        self._my_val = my_val

    def __call__(self):
        return self._my_val


@serve.deployment
class BroadcastDriver:
    def __init__(self, model1, model2):
        self._m1 = model1
        self._m2 = model2

    async def __call__(self, *args) -> str:
        output1, output2 = self._m1.remote(), self._m2.remote()
        return [await output1, await output2]


m1 = DownstreamModel.bind("val1")
m2 = DownstreamModel.bind("val2")
broadcast_driver = BroadcastDriver.bind(m1, m2)
```

Testing this endpoint after running it once again with `serve run` returns `'["val1", "val2"]'`, the combined output of the two models called in parallel.

Pattern 3: Conditional logic

Finally, while many ML applications fit roughly into one of the preceding patterns, often having static control flow can be very limiting. Take, for instance, the example of building a service to extract license plate numbers from user-uploaded images. In this case, we'll likely need to build an image processing pipeline as discussed, but we also don't simply want to feed any image into the pipeline blindly. If the user uploads something other than a car or an image that is low quality, we likely want to short circuit, avoid calling into the heavyweight and expensive pipeline, and provide a useful error message. Similarly, in a product recommendation use case we may want to select a downstream model based on user input or the result of an intermediate model. Each of these examples requires embedding custom logic alongside our ML models.

We can accomplish this trivially using Serve's multimodel API because our computation graph is defined as ordinary Python logic rather than as a statically defined graph. For instance, in the next example, we use a simple random number generator

(RNG) to decide which of two downstream models to call into. In a real-world example, the RNG could be replaced with business logic, a database query, or the result of an intermediate model:

```python
@serve.deployment
class DownstreamModel:
    def __init__(self, my_val: str):
        self._my_val = my_val

    def __call__(self):
        return self._my_val


@serve.deployment
class ConditionalDriver:
    def __init__(self, model1, model2):
        self._m1 = model1
        self._m2 = model2

    async def __call__(self, *args) -> str:
        import random
        if random.random() > 0.5:
            return await self._m1.remote()
        else:
            return await self._m2.remote()


m1 = DownstreamModel.bind("val1")
m2 = DownstreamModel.bind("val2")
conditional_driver = ConditionalDriver.bind(m1, m2)
```

Each call to this endpoint returns either "val1" or "val2" with 50/50 probability.

End-to-End Example: Building an NLP-Powered API

In this section, we'll use Ray Serve to build an end-to-end natural language processing (NLP) pipeline hosted for online inference. Our goal will be to provide a Wikipedia summarization endpoint that will leverage multiple NLP models and some custom logic to provide a succinct summary of the most relevant Wikipedia page for a given search term.

This task will bring together many of the concepts and features we've discussed:

- We'll be combining custom business logic along with multiple ML models.
- The inference graph will consist of all three multimodel patterns: pipelining, broadcasting, and conditional logic.
- Each model will be hosted as a separate Serve deployment so they can be independently scaled and given their own resource allocation.

- One of the models will leverage vectorized computation via batching.
- The API will be defined using Ray Serve's `FastAPI` for input parsing and defining our output schema.

Our online inference pipeline will be structured as shown in Figure 8-2:

1. The user will provide a keyword search term.

2. We'll fetch the content for the most relevant Wikipedia article for the search term.

3. A sentiment analysis model will be applied to the article. Anything with a "negative" sentiment will be rejected, and we'll return early.

4. The article content will be broadcast to summarizer and named entity recognition models.

5. We'll return a composed result based on the summarizer and named entity recognition outputs.

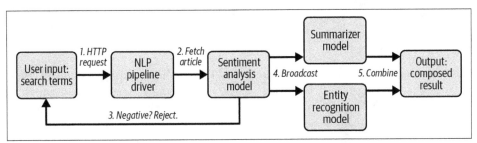

Figure 8-2. The architecture for an NLP pipeline to summarize Wikipedia articles

This pipeline will be exposed over HTTP and return the results in a structured format. By the end of this section, we'll have the pipeline running from end to end locally and ready to scale up on a cluster. Let's get started!

Before we dive into the code, you'll need the following Python packages installed locally:

```
pip install "ray[serve]==2.2.0" "transformers==4.21.2"
pip install "requests==2.28.1" "wikipedia==1.4.0"
```

Additionally, in this section we'll assume that all the code samples are available locally in a file called *app.py* so we can run the deployments using `serve run` from the same directory.[3]

---

3 We've created this *app.py* file for you in the book's GitHub repository (*https://oreil.ly/E0Zzg*). After cloning the repo and installing all the dependencies, you should be able to run `serve run app:<deployment_name>` directly from the *notebook* directory for each deployment we're referencing in a `serve run` call in this chapter.

Fetching Content and Preprocessing

The first step is to fetch the most relevant page from Wikipedia given a user-provided search term. For this, we will leverage the Wikipedia package on PyPI to do the heavy lifting. We'll first search for the term and then select the top result and return its page content. If no results are found, we'll return None—this edge case will be handled later when we define the API:

```
from typing import Optional

import wikipedia


def fetch_wikipedia_page(search_term: str) -> Optional[str]:
    results = wikipedia.search(search_term)
    # If no results, return to caller.
    if len(results) == 0:
        return None

    # Get the page for the top result.
    return wikipedia.page(results[0]).content
```

NLP Models

Next, we need to define the ML models that will do the heavy lifting of our API. We'll be using the Hugging Face Transformers library (*https://huggingface.co*) as it provides convenient APIs to pretrained state-of-the-art ML models so we can focus on the serving logic.

The first model we'll use is a sentiment classifier, the same one we used in the preceding examples. The deployment for this model will take advantage of vectorized computations using Serve's batching API:

```
from ray import serve
from transformers import pipeline
from typing import List


@serve.deployment
class SentimentAnalysis:
    def __init__(self):
        self._classifier = pipeline("sentiment-analysis")

    @serve.batch(max_batch_size=10, batch_wait_timeout_s=0.1)
    async def is_positive_batched(self, inputs: List[str]) -> List[bool]:
        results = self._classifier(inputs, truncation=True)
        return [result["label"] == "POSITIVE" for result in results]

    async def __call__(self, input_text: str) -> bool:
        return await self.is_positive_batched(input_text)
```

We'll also use a text summarization model to provide a succinct summary for the selected article. This model takes an optional max_length argument to cap the length of the summary. Because we know this is the most computationally expensive of the models, we set num_replicas=2; that way, if we have many requests coming in at the same time, it can keep up with the throughput of the other models. In practice, we may need more replicas to keep up with the input load, but we could know that only from profiling and monitoring:

```
@serve.deployment(num_replicas=2)
class Summarizer:
    def __init__(self, max_length: Optional[int] = None):
        self._summarizer = pipeline("summarization")
        self._max_length = max_length

    def __call__(self, input_text: str) -> str:
        result = self._summarizer(
            input_text, max_length=self._max_length, truncation=True)
        return result[0]["summary_text"]
```

The final model in our pipeline will be a named entity recognition model: this will attempt to extract named entities from the text. Each result will have a confidence score, so we can set a threshold to accept only results above a certain threshold. We may also want to cap the total number of entities returned. The request handler for this deployment calls the model and then uses some basic business logic to enforce the provided confidence threshold and limit the number of entities:

```
@serve.deployment
class EntityRecognition:
    def __init__(self, threshold: float = 0.90, max_entities: int = 10):
        self._entity_recognition = pipeline("ner")
        self._threshold = threshold
        self._max_entities = max_entities

    def __call__(self, input_text: str) -> List[str]:
        final_results = []
        for result in self._entity_recognition(input_text):
            if result["score"] > self._threshold:
                final_results.append(result["word"])
            if len(final_results) == self._max_entities:
                break

        return final_results
```

HTTP Handling and Driver Logic

With the input preprocessing and ML models defined, we're ready to define the HTTP API and driver logic. First, we define the schema of the response that we'll return from the API using Pydantic (*https://oreil.ly/BM7rt*). The response includes whether the request was successful and a status message in addition to our summary and named entities. This will allow us to return a helpful response in error conditions such as when no result is found or the sentiment analysis comes back as negative:

```
from pydantic import BaseModel


class Response(BaseModel):
    success: bool
    message: str = ""
    summary: str = ""
    named_entities: List[str] = []
```

Next, we need to define the actual control flow logic that will run in the driver deployment. The driver itself will not do any of the actual heavy lifting; instead, it will call into our three downstream model deployments and interpret their results. It will also house the FastAPI app definition, parsing the input and returning the correct Response model based on the results of the pipeline:

```
from fastapi import FastAPI

app = FastAPI()


@serve.deployment
@serve.ingress(app)
class NLPPipelineDriver:
    def __init__(self, sentiment_analysis, summarizer, entity_recognition):
        self._sentiment_analysis = sentiment_analysis
        self._summarizer = summarizer
        self._entity_recognition = entity_recognition

    @app.get("/", response_model=Response)
    async def summarize_article(self, search_term: str) -> Response:
        # Fetch the top page content for the search term if found.
        page_content = fetch_wikipedia_page(search_term)
        if page_content is None:
            return Response(success=False, message="No pages found.")

        # Conditionally continue based on the sentiment analysis.
        is_positive = await self._sentiment_analysis.remote(page_content)
        if not is_positive:
            return Response(success=False, message="Only positivitiy allowed!")

        # Query the summarizer and named entity recognition models in parallel.
        summary_result = self._summarizer.remote(page_content)
        entities_result = self._entity_recognition.remote(page_content)
        return Response(
            success=True,
            summary=await summary_result,
            named_entities=await entities_result
        )
```

Fetch the page content in the main handler's body using our `fetch_wikipedia_page` logic (if no result is found, an error is returned). Then, we call into the sentiment analysis model. If this returns negative, we terminate early and return an error to avoid calling the other expensive ML models. Finally, we broadcast the article contents to both the summary and named entity recognition models in parallel. The results of the two models are stitched together into the final response, and we return success. Remember that we may have many calls to this handler running concurrently: the calls to the downstream models don't block the driver, and it could coordinate calls to many replicas of the heavyweight models.

Putting It All Together

At this point, we have defined all the core logic. All that's left is to bind the graph of deployments together and run it:

```
sentiment_analysis = SentimentAnalysis.bind()
summarizer = Summarizer.bind()
entity_recognition = EntityRecognition.bind(threshold=0.95, max_entities=5)
nlp_pipeline_driver = NLPPipelineDriver.bind(
    sentiment_analysis, summarizer, entity_recognition)
```

First, we need to instantiate each of the deployments with any relevant input arguments. For example, here we pass a threshold and limit for the entity recognition model. The most important piece we pass is a reference to each of the three models into the driver so it can coordinate the computation. Now that we've defined the full NLP pipeline, we can run it using `serve run`:[4]

```
serve run app:nlp_pipeline_driver
```

This will deploy each of the four deployments locally and make the driver available at `http://localhost:8000`. We can query the pipeline using the `requests` to see it in action. First, let's try querying for an entry on Ray Serve:

```
import requests


print(requests.get(
    "http://localhost:8000/", params={"search_term": "rayserve"}
).text)
'{"success":false,"message":"No pages found.",
  "summary":"","named_entities":[]}'
```

---

[4] The models we use in this example are quite large, so be warned that it will likely take several minutes to download them the first time you run this example.

Unfortunately, this page doesn't exist yet! The first chunk of validation business logic kicks in and returns a "No pages found" message. Let's try looking for something more common:

```
print(requests.get(
    "http://localhost:8000/", params={"search_term": "war"}
).text)

'{"success":false,"message":"Only positivitiy allowed!,
  "summary":"","named_entities":[]}'
```

Maybe we were just interested in learning about history, but this article was a bit too negative for our sentiment classifier. Let's try something more neutral this time— what about science?

```
print(requests.get(
    "http://localhost:8000/", params={"search_term": "physicist"}
).text)

'{"success":true,"message":"","summary":" Physics is the natural science that
studies matter, its fundamental constituents, its motion and behavior through
space and time, and the related entities of energy and force . During the
Scientific Revolution in the 17th century these natural sciences emerged as
unique research endeavors in their own right . Physics intersects with many
interdisciplinary areas of research, such as biophysics and quantum chemistry .
","named_entities":["Scientific","Revolution", "Ancient","Greek","Egyptians"]}'
```

This example successfully ran through the full pipeline: the API responded with a cogent summary of the article and a list of relevant named entities.

To recap, in this section we built an online NLP API using Ray Serve. This inference graph consisted of multiple ML models in addition to custom business logic and dynamic control flow. Each model can be independently scaled and have its own resource allocation, and we can exploit vectorized computations using server-side batching. Because we were able to test the API locally, the next step would be to deploy to production. Ray Serve makes it easy to deploy on Kubernetes or other cloud provider offerings using the Ray Cluster launcher, and we could easily scale up to handle many users by tweaking the resource allocations for our deployments.

Summary

This chapter introduced Ray Serve, a Ray-native library for building online inference APIs. Ray Serve is focused on solving the unique challenges of serving machine learning models in production, offering functionality to efficiently scale models and allocate resources as well as compose multiple models along with business logic. Additionally, like all of Ray, Serve is designed to be a general-purpose solution that avoids vendor lock-in.

Although we walked through an end-to-end example of a multimodel pipeline, this chapter has covered only a small portion of Ray Serve's functionality and best practices for real-world applications. For more detail and examples, read the Ray Serve documentation (*https://oreil.ly/-fg0u*).

## CHAPTER 9

Ray Clusters

Richard Liaw

So far we have focused on teaching you the basics of Ray for building machine learning applications. You know how to parallelize your Python code with Ray Core and run reinforcement learning experiments with RLlib. You've also seen how to preprocess data with Ray Datasets, tune hyperparameters with Ray Tune, and train models with Ray Train. But one of the key features that Ray brings is the ability to scale out seamlessly onto multiple machines. Outside a lab environment or a big tech company, it may be difficult set up multiple machines and join them into a single Ray Cluster. This chapter is all about how to do that.[1]

Cloud technology has commoditized access to cheap machines for anyone. But it is often quite difficult to figure out the right APIs to handle the cloud provider tools. The Ray team has provided a couple of tools that abstract the complexity away. There are three primary ways of launching or deploying a Ray Cluster. You can do so manually, via a Kubernetes operator, or via the cluster launcher CLI tool.

In the first part of this chapter we'll cover these three methods in detail.[2] We only briefly explain manual cluster creation and the cluster launcher CLI, and we spend most of our time explaining how to use the Kubernetes operator. After that, we'll cover how to run Ray Clusters on the cloud and how to autoscale them up and down.

---

1 Ray itself is not opinionated about how you set up your cluster. In fact, you have many options, many of which are described in this chapter. Apart from the open source solutions we're describing here, there are also fully managed commercial solutions available, such as those offered by Anyscale or Domino Data Lab.

2 While this chapter technically has an accompanying notebook (*https://oreil.ly/eGru2*), the material presented here is not well-suited for development in an interactive Python session. We recommend that you work through these examples on the command line. No matter where you decide to work, make sure to have Ray installed with `pip install "ray==2.2.0"`.

Manually Creating a Ray Cluster

Let's start with the most basic way of creating a Ray Cluster. To build a Ray Cluster manually we assume that you have a list of machines that can communicate with each other and have Ray installed on them.[3]

To start with, you can choose any machine to be the head node. On this node, run the following command:

```
ray start --head --port=6379
```

This command will print out the IP address of the Ray GCS server that was started, namely, the local node IP address plus the port number you specified:[4]

```
...
Next steps
To connect to this Ray runtime from another node, run
  ray start --address='<head-address>:6379'

If connection fails, check your firewall settings and network configuration.
```

You need this `<head-address>` to connect your other nodes to the cluster, so make sure to copy it. If you omit the `--port` argument, Ray will use a random port.

Next, we can connect every other node in your cluster to the head node by running a single command on each node:

```
ray start --address=<head-address>
```

Make sure to pass the correct `<head-address>`, which should look something like `123.45.67.89:6379`. Running this command, you should see output of the following form:

```
--------------------
Ray runtime started.
--------------------

To terminate the Ray runtime, run
  ray stop
```

If you wish to specify that a machine has 10 CPUs and 1 GPU, you can do this with the flags `--num-cpus=10` and `--num-gpus=1`. If you see `Ray runtime started.`, then

---

3 Depending on your setup or work situation, this might not be a realistic assumption for you. Don't worry, we'll cover ways to create Ray Clusters that don't require you to have any machines running. In any case, knowing the steps involved for manual Ray Cluster creation is useful to fall back on.

4 If you already have remote Redis instances, you can use them by specifying the environment variable `RAY_REDIS_ADDRESS=ip1:port1,ip2:port2....` Ray will use the first address as primary and the rest as shards.

the node successfully connected to the head node at the --address. You should now be able to connect to the cluster with ray.init(address='auto').

 If the head node and the new node you want to connect are on a separate subnetwork with Network Address Translation (NAT), you can't use the <head-address> printed by the command starting the head node as --address. In this case, you need to find the address that will reach the head node from the new node. If the head node has a domain address like compute04.berkeley.edu, you can use that in place of an IP address and rely on the DNS.

If you see Unable to connect to GCS at ..., it means the head node is inaccessible at the given --address. This could be for several reasons. For example, maybe the head node is not actually running, a different version of Ray is running at the specified address, the specified address is wrong, or firewall settings are preventing access.

If the connection fails, to check whether each port can be reached from a node, you can use a tool such as nmap or nc. Here's an example of how to run a check with both tools in a successful case:[5]

```
$ nmap -sV --reason -p $PORT $HEAD_ADDRESS
Nmap scan report for compute04.berkeley.edu (123.456.78.910)
Host is up, received echo-reply ttl 60 (0.00087s latency).
rDNS record for 123.456.78.910: compute04.berkeley.edu
PORT     STATE SERVICE REASON        VERSION
6379/tcp open  redis?  syn-ack
Service detection performed. Please report any incorrect
  results at https://nmap.org/submit/ .
$ nc -vv -z $HEAD_ADDRESS $PORT
Connection to compute04.berkeley.edu 6379 port [tcp/...] succeeded!
```

If your node cannot access the port and IP address specified, you might see:

```
$ nmap -sV --reason -p $PORT $HEAD_ADDRESS
Nmap scan report for compute04.berkeley.edu (123.456.78.910)
Host is up (0.0011s latency).
rDNS record for 123.456.78.910: compute04.berkeley.edu
PORT     STATE  SERVICE REASON        VERSION
6379/tcp closed redis    reset ttl 60
Service detection performed. Please report any incorrect
  results at https://nmap.org/submit/ .
$ nc -vv -z $HEAD_ADDRESS $PORT
nc: connect to compute04.berkeley.edu port 6379 (tcp) failed: Connection refused
```

---

5 If you want to learn more about the specific flags used in the upcoming examples, we suggest reviewing the official reference guide (*https://nmap.org/book/man.html*).

Now, if you want to stop the Ray processes on any node, simply run `ray stop`. That's the manual way of creating a Ray Cluster. Let's move on to discussing the deployment of your Ray Clusters with the popular Kubernetes orchestration framework.

Deployment on Kubernetes

Kubernetes is an industry-standard platform for cluster resource management. It allows software teams to seamlessly deploy, manage, and scale their business applications in a wide variety of production environments. It was initially developed by Google, but many organizations have now adopted Kubernetes as their cluster resource management solution.

The community-maintained KubeRay project (*https://oreil.ly/LwUPr*) is the standard way of deploying and managing Ray Clusters on Kubernetes. The KubeRay operator helps deploy and manage Ray Clusters on top of Kubernetes (Figure 9-1). Clusters are defined as a custom `RayCluster` resource and managed by a fault-tolerant Ray controller. The operator automates provisioning, management, autoscaling, and operations of Ray Clusters deployed to Kubernetes. The main features of this operator are:

- Management of first-class `RayCluster` via a custom resource.
- Support for heterogeneous worker types in a single Ray Cluster.
- Built-in monitoring via Prometheus.
- Use of `PodTemplate` to create Ray pods.
- Updated status based on the running pods.
- Automatically populate environment variables in the containers.
- Automatically prefix your container command with the Ray start command.
- Automatically adding the volumeMount at */dev/shm* for shared memory.
- Use of `ScaleStrategy` to remove specific nodes in specific groups.

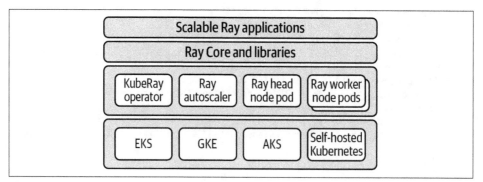

Figure 9-1. An overview of KubeRay

Setting Up Your First KubeRay Cluster

You can deploy the operator by cloning the KubeRay repository (*https://oreil.ly/a8MlJ*) and calling the following command:

```
export KUBERAY_VERSION=v0.3.0

kubectl create -k "github.com/ray-project/kuberay/manifests/\
cluster-scope-resources?ref=${KUBERAY_VERSION}&timeout=90s"

kubectl apply -k "github.com/ray-project/kuberay/manifests/\
base?ref=${KUBERAY_VERSION}&timeout=90s"
```

You can verify that the operator has been deployed using this command:

```
kubectl -n ray-system get pods
```

When deployed, the operator will watch for Kubernetes events (create/delete/update) for the `raycluster` resource updates. Upon these events, the operator can create a cluster consisting of a head pod and multiple worker pods, delete a cluster, or update the cluster by adding or removing worker pods. Now let's deploy a new Ray Cluster using a provided default cluster configuration (we'll get to this YAML file later):

```
wget "https://raw.githubusercontent.com/ray-project/kuberay/\
${KUBERAY_VERSION}/ray-operator/config/samples/ray-cluster.complete.yaml"

kubectl create -f ray-cluster.complete.yaml
```

The KubeRay operator configures a Kubernetes service targeting the Ray head pod. To identify the service, run:

```
kubectl get service --selector=ray.io/cluster=raycluster-complete
```

The output of this command should resemble the following structure:

```
NAME                            TYPE        CLUSTER-IP      EXTERNAL-IP
raycluster-complete-head-svc    ClusterIP   xx.xx.xxx.xx    <none>
    PORT(S)                     AGE
    6379/TCP,8265/TCP,10001/TCP 6m10s
```

The three ports indicated in the output correspond to the following services of the Ray head pod:

6379
:   The Ray head's GCS service. Ray worker pods connect to this service when joining the cluster.

8265
:   Exposes the Ray Dashboard and the Ray Job Submission service.

10001
:   Exposes the Ray Client server.

You should note that the Docker images we're using are quite large and can take a while to download. Also, even if you see the expected output from kubectl get service, that doesn't mean your cluster is ready to use yet. You should look at the pod status and make sure they are all actually in "Running" state.

Interacting with the KubeRay Cluster

You might be wondering why we spend so much time on Kubernetes, since you're most likely just interested in learning how to run Ray scripts on it. That's understandable, and we'll get to that in a moment.

First, let's use the following Python script as the desired script to run on the cluster. We'll name it *script.py* (for simplicity), and the script will connect to the Ray Cluster and run a couple standard Ray commands:

```python
import ray
ray.init(address="auto")
print(ray.cluster_resources())


@ray.remote
def test():
    return 12



ray.get([test.remote() for i in range(12)])
```

There are three primary ways to run this script: using kubectl exec, Ray Job Submission, or Ray Client. We'll cover them in the following sections.

Running Ray programs with kubectl

To start with, you can directly interact with the head pod via kubectl exec. Use this command to get a Python interpreter on the head pod:

```
kubectl exec `kubectl get pods -o custom-columns=POD:metadata.name |\
    grep raycluster-complete-head` -it -c ray-head -- python
```

With this Python terminal, you can connect and run your own Ray application:

```python
import ray
ray.init(address="auto")
...
```

There are other ways of interacting with these services without kubectl, but they will require some networking setup. The easiest route, and the one we'll take in what follows, is to use port-forwarding.

Using the Ray Job Submission server

You can run scripts on the cluster by using the Ray Job Submission server. You can use the server to send a script or a bundle of dependencies and run custom scripts with that set of dependencies. To start, you'll need to port-forward the job submission server port:

```
kubectl port-forward service/raycluster-complete-head-svc 8265:8265
```

Now, submit the script by setting the RAY_ADDRESS variable to the job server submission endpoint and using the Ray Job Submission CLI:

```
export RAY_ADDRESS="http://localhost:8265"

ray job submit --working-dir=. -- python script.py
```

You'll see an output that looks like:

```
Job submission server address: http://127.0.0.1:8265
2022-05-20 23:35:36,066 INFO dashboard_sdk.py:276
 -- Uploading package gcs://_ray_pkg_533a957683abeba8.zip.
2022-05-20 23:35:36,067 INFO packaging.py:416
 -- Creating a file package for local directory '.'.

-------------------------------------------------------
Job 'raysubmit_U5hfr1rqJZWwJmLP' submitted successfully
-------------------------------------------------------

Next steps
  Query the logs of the job:
    ray job logs raysubmit_U5hfr1rqJZWwJmLP
  Query the status of the job:
    ray job status raysubmit_U5hfr1rqJZWwJmLP
  Request the job to be stopped:
    ray job stop raysubmit_U5hfr1rqJZWwJmLP

Tailing logs until the job exits (disable with --no-wait):
{'memory': 47157884109.0, 'object_store_memory': 2147483648.0,
 'CPU': 16.0, 'node:127.0.0.1': 1.0}

-----------------------------------------
Job 'raysubmit_U5hfr1rqJZWwJmLP' succeeded
-----------------------------------------
```

You can use `--no-wait` to run the job in the background.

Ray Client

To connect to the cluster via Ray Client from your local machine, first make sure the local Ray installation and Python minor version match the Ray and Python versions running in the Ray Cluster. To do that, you can run `ray --version` and `python --version` on both instances. In practice, you will be using a container, in which case you can simply make sure you run everything in the same container. Also, if the versions don't match, you will see a warning message informing you of the issue.

Next, run the following command:

```
kubectl port-forward service/raycluster-complete-head-svc 10001:10001
```

This command will block. The local port 10001 will now be forwarded to the Ray head's Ray Client server.

To run a Ray workload on your remote Ray Cluster, open a local Python shell and start a Ray Client connection:

```
import ray
ray.init(address="ray://localhost:10001")
print(ray.cluster_resources())


@ray.remote
def test():
    return 12


ray.get([test.remote() for i in range(12)])
```

With this method, you can just run the Ray program directly on your laptop (instead of needing to ship the code over via `kubectl` or job submission).

Exposing KubeRay

In the previous examples, we used port-forwarding as a simple way to access the Ray head's services. For production use cases, you may want to consider other means of exposing these services. The following notes are generic to services running on Kubernetes.

By default, the Ray service is accessible from anywhere *within* the Kubernetes cluster where the Ray operator is running. For example, to use the Ray Client from a pod in the same Kubernetes namespace as the Ray Cluster, use `ray.init("ray://raycluster-complete-head-svc:10001")`.

To connect from another Kubernetes namespace, use `ray.init("ray://raycluster-complete-head-svc.default.svc.cluster.local:10001")`. (If the Ray Cluster is a nondefault namespace, use the namespace in place of `default`.)

If you are trying to access the service from outside the cluster, use an ingress controller. Any standard ingress controller should work with Ray Client and Ray Dashboard. Pick a solution compatible with your networking and security requirements—further guidance is beyond the scope of this book.

Configuring KubeRay

Let's take a closer look at the configuration for a Ray Cluster running on Kubernetes. The example file *kuberay/ray-operator/config/samples/ray-cluster.complete.yaml* is a good reference. Here is a condensed view of a Ray Cluster config's most salient features:

```yaml
apiVersion: ray.io/v1alpha1
kind: RayCluster
metadata:
  name: raycluster-complete
spec:
  headGroupSpec:
    rayStartParams:
      port: '6379'
      num-cpus: '1'
      ...
    template: # Pod template
        metadata: # Pod metadata
        spec: # Pod spec
            containers:
            - name: ray-head
              image: rayproject/ray:1.12.1
              resources:
                limits:
                  cpu: "1"
                  memory: "1024Mi"
                requests:
                  cpu: "1"
                  memory: "1024Mi"
              ports:
              - containerPort: 6379
                name: gcs
              - containerPort: 8265
                name: dashboard
              - containerPort: 10001
                name: client
              env:
                - name: "RAY_LOG_TO_STDERR"
                  value: "1"
              volumeMounts:
                - mountPath: /tmp/ray
                  name: ray-logs
            volumes:
            - name: ray-logs
              emptyDir: {}
  workerGroupSpecs:
  - groupName: small-group
    replicas: 2
    rayStartParams:
        ...
    template: # Pod template
```

```
    . . .
- groupName: medium-group
    . . .
```

 It's ideal, when possible, to size each Ray pod such that it takes up the entire Kubernetes node on which it is scheduled. In other words, it's best to run one large Ray pod per Kubernetes node; running multiple Ray pods on one Kubernetes node introduces unnecessary overhead. However, running multiple Ray pods on one Kubernetes node makes sense in some situations, such as if:

- Many users are running Ray Clusters on a Kubernetes cluster with limited compute resources.

- You or your organization is not directly managing Kubernetes nodes (e.g., when deploying on GKE Autopilot).

Some of the primary configuration values that you may use are:

headGroupSpec *and* workerGroupSpecs
A Ray Cluster consists of a head pod and a number of worker pods. The head pod's configuration is specified under headGroupSpec. Configuration for worker pods is specified under workerGroupSpecs. There may be multiple worker groups, each group with its own configuration template. The replicas field of a workerGroup specifies the number of worker pods of each group to keep in the cluster.

rayStartParams
This is a string-string map of arguments to the Ray pod's ray start entry point. For the full list of arguments, refer to the documentation for ray start (*https://oreil.ly/O5gEs*). We make special note of the num-cpus and num-gpus field arguments:

num-cpus
This field tells the Ray Scheduler how many CPUs are available to the Ray pod. The CPU count can be autodetected from the Kubernetes resource limits specified in the group spec's pod template. It is sometimes useful to override this autodetected value. For example, setting num-cpus:"0" will prevent Ray workloads with nonzero CPU requirements from being scheduled on the head node.

num-gpus
This specifies the number of GPUs available to the Ray pod. At the time of writing, this field is *not* detected from the group spec's pod template. Thus, num-gpus must be set explicitly for GPU workloads.

template

This is where the bulk of the `headGroup` or `workerGroup`'s configuration goes. The `template` is a Kubernetes Pod template that determines the configuration for the pods in the group.

resources

It's important to specify container CPU and memory requests and limits for each group spec. For GPU workloads, you may also wish to specify GPU limits, e.g., `nvidia.com/gpu: 1` if using an Nvidia GPU device plug-in.

nodeSelector *and* tolerations

You can control the scheduling of a worker group's Ray pods by setting the `nodeSelector` and `tolerations` fields of the pod spec. Specifically, these fields determine on which Kubernetes nodes the pods may be scheduled. Note that the KubeRay operator operates at the level of pods—KubeRay is agnostic to the setup of the underlying Kubernetes nodes. Kubernetes node configuration is left to your Kubernetes cluster's admins.

Ray container images

It's important to specify the images used by your cluster's Ray containers. The head and workers of the clusters should all use the same Ray version. In most cases, it makes sense to use the exact same container image for the head and all workers of a given Ray Cluster. To specify custom dependencies for your cluster, you should build an image based on one of the official `rayproject/ray` images.

Volume mounts

Volume mounts can be used to preserve logs or other application data originating in your Ray containers. (See "Configuring Logging for KubeRay" on page 189.)

Container environment variables

Container environment variables may be used to modify Ray's behavior. For example, `RAY_LOG_TO_STDERR` will redirect logs to STDERR rather than writing them to the container's filesystem.

Configuring Logging for KubeRay

Ray Cluster processes typically write logs to the directory */tmp/ray/session_latest/logs* in the pod. These logs are also visible in the Ray Dashboard. To persist Ray logs beyond the lifetime of a pod, you may use one of the following techniques:

Aggregate logs from the container's filesystem

For this strategy, mount an empty-dir volume with `mountPath` `/tmp/ray/` in the Ray container (see the preceding example configuration). You can mount the log volume into a sidecar container running a log aggregation tool such as Promtail (*https://oreil.ly/LyEGy*).

Container STDERR logging

An alternative is to redirect logging to STDERR. To do this, set the environment variable `RAY_LOG_TO_STDERR=1` on all Ray containers. In terms of Kubernetes configuration, that means adding an entry to the `env` field of the Ray container in each Ray `groupSpec`:

```
env:
  ...
  - name: "RAY_LOG_TO_STDERR"
    value: "1"
  ...
```

You may then use a Kubernetes logging tool geared toward aggregation from the STDERR and STDOUT streams.

Using the Ray Cluster Launcher

The goal of the Ray Cluster Launcher is to make it easy to deploy a Ray Cluster on any cloud. Here's what it will do for you:

- Provision a new instance/machine using the cloud provider's SDK.
- Execute shell commands to set up Ray with the provided options.
- Optionally run any custom, user-defined setup commands. This can be useful for setting environment variables and installing packages.[6]
- Initialize the Ray Cluster for you.
- Deploy an autoscaler process.

We will walk you through the details of autoscaling in "Autoscaling" on page 194. For now, let's focus on using the cluster launcher to deploy a Ray Cluster. To do so, you need to provide a cluster configuration file.

Configuring Your Ray Cluster

To run your Ray Cluster, you must specify the resource requirements in a cluster configuration file.

Here's our "scaffold" cluster specification. This is just about the minimum you'll need to specify to launch your cluster. For more information about cluster YAML files, see a large example here (let's call it *cluster.yaml*):

```
# An unique identifier for the head node and workers of this cluster.
cluster_name: minimal
```

---

6 To dynamically set up environments after the cluster has been deployed, you can use a runtime environment.

```
# The maximum number of workers nodes to launch in addition to the head
# node. min_workers default to 0.
max_workers: 1

# Cloud provider-specific configuration.
provider:
    type: aws
    region: us-west-2
    availability_zone: us-west-2a

# How Ray will authenticate with newly launched nodes.
auth:
    ssh_user: ubuntu
```

Using the Cluster Launcher CLI

Now that you have a cluster configuration file, you can use the Cluster Launcher CLI to deploy the specified cluster:

```
ray up cluster.yaml
```

This single line of code will take care of everything done via the manual cluster setup. It will interact with the cloud provider to provision the head node and start the appropriate Ray services or processes on that node.

This single line of code will not automatically start all specified nodes. In fact, it will start only a single "head" node, and run `ray start --head ...` on that head node. A Ray autoscaling process will then use the provided cluster configuration to start the worker nodes as a background thread after the head node has started.

Interacting with a Ray Cluster

After you start a cluster, you'll often want to interact with it through a variety of actions:

- Run a script on the cluster
- Move files, logs, and artifacts off the cluster
- SSH onto the nodes to inspect machine details

There is a CLI for interacting with clusters launched by the Ray Cluster Launcher. If you have an existing script (like a *script.py*, from earlier), you can run the script on the cluster via `ray job submit` after you've port-forwarded the Job Submission endpoint:

```
# Run in one terminal:
ray attach cluster.yaml -p 8265
```

```
# Run in a separate terminal:
export RAY_ADDRESS=http://localhost:8265
ray job submit --working-dir=. -- python script.py
```

`--working-dir` will move your local files onto the cluster, and python `train.py` will be run on a shell on the cluster.

Let's say after you run this script, you generate artifacts, like a *results.log* file that you want to inspect. Use `ray rsync-down` to move the file back:

```
ray rsync-down cluster.yaml /path/on/cluster/results.log ./results.log
```

Working with Cloud Clusters

This section demonstrates how to deploy Ray Clusters on AWS and other cloud providers.

AWS

First, install boto (`pip install boto3`) and configure your AWS credentials in `$HOME/.aws/credentials`, as described in the boto docs (*https://oreil.ly/WnU8N*).

Once boto is configured to manage resources on your AWS account, you should be ready to launch your cluster. The provided *example-full.yaml* cluster config file (*https://oreil.ly/rywrB*) will create a small cluster with an m5.large head node (on-demand) configured to autoscale up to two m5.large spot instance workers (*https://oreil.ly/fPFar*).

Test that it works by running the following commands from your local machine:

```
# Create or update the cluster. When the command finishes, it will print
# out the command that can be used to SSH into the cluster head node.
$ ray up ray/python/ray/autoscaler/aws/example-full.yaml

# Get a remote screen on the head node.
$ ray attach ray/python/ray/autoscaler/aws/example-full.yaml
# Try running a Ray program with 'ray.init(address="auto")'.

# Tear down the cluster.
$ ray down ray/python/ray/autoscaler/aws/example-full.yaml
```

Using Other Cloud Providers

Ray Clusters can be deployed on most major clouds, including GCP and Azure. Here is a template to get started for Google Cloud:

```
# A unique identifier for the head node and workers of this cluster.
cluster_name: minimal

# The maximum number of worker nodes to launch in addition to the head
# node. min_workers default to 0.
max_workers: 1

# Cloud-provider specific configuration.
provider:
    type: gcp
    region: us-west1
    availability_zone: us-west1-a
    project_id: null # Globally unique project id

# How Ray will authenticate with newly launched nodes.
auth:
    ssh_user: ubuntu
```

Here is a template to get started for Azure:

```
# An unique identifier for the head node and workers of this cluster.
cluster_name: minimal

# The maximum number of workers nodes to launch in addition to the head
# node. min_workers default to 0.
max_workers: 1

# Cloud-provider specific configuration.
provider:
    type: azure
    location: westus2
    resource_group: ray-cluster

# How Ray will authenticate with newly launched nodes.
auth:
    ssh_user: ubuntu
    # You must specify paths to matching private and public key pair files.
    # Use `ssh-keygen -t rsa -b 4096` to generate a new ssh key pair.
    ssh_private_key: ~/.ssh/id_rsa
    # Changes to this should match what is specified in file_mounts.
    ssh_public_key: ~/.ssh/id_rsa.pub
```

You can read more about this on the Ray documentation (*https://oreil.ly/2Eog5*).

Autoscaling

Ray is designed to support highly elastic workloads that are most efficient on an autoscaling cluster. At a high level, the autoscaler attempts to launch and terminate nodes to ensure that workloads have sufficient resources to run, while minimizing the idle resources. It does this by considering:

- User-specified hard limits (min/max workers)
- User-specified node types (nodes in a Ray Cluster do *not* have to be homogenous)
- Information from the Ray Core's scheduling layer about the current resource usage/demands of the cluster
- Programmatic autoscaling hints

The autoscaler resource demand scheduler will look at the pending tasks, actors, and placement groups, resource demands from the cluster. It will then try to add the minimum list of nodes that can fulfill these demands.

When worker nodes are idle for more than `idle_timeout_minutes`, they will be removed. The head node is never removed unless the cluster is torn down.

The autoscaler uses a simple *binpacking algorithm* to pack the user demands into the available cluster resources. The remaining unfulfilled demands are placed on the smallest list of nodes that satisfies the demand while maximizing utilization (starting from the smallest node). You can learn more about the autoscaling algorithm in the Autoscaling section of the Ray architecture whitepaper (*https://oreil.ly/u0kzS*).

Ray also provides documentation and tooling for other cluster managers such as YARN, SLURM, and LFS. You can read more about this in the Ray documentation (*https://oreil.ly/t5M9i*).

Summary

In this chapter you learned how to spin up your own Ray Clusters so that you can deploy your Ray applications on them. Besides manually setting up and shutting down clusters, we had a closer look at deploying Ray Clusters on Kubernetes using KubeRay. We also looked at the Ray Cluster Launcher in detail and discussed how to work with cloud clusters on clouds such as AWS, GCP, and Azure. Finally, we discussed how to use the Ray autoscaler to scale your Ray Clusters.

Now that you know more about scaling Ray Clusters, we'll come back to the application side of things in Chapter 10 and discuss how all the Ray ML libraries we've seen effectively come together to form the Ray AI Runtime.

## CHAPTER 10

Getting Started with the Ray AI Runtime

We've come a long way since you read about Ray AIR in Chapter 1. Besides the fundamentals of Ray Clusters and the basics of the Ray Core API, you've picked up a good understanding of all higher-level libraries of Ray that can be leveraged in AI workloads, namely, Ray RLlib, Tune, Train, Datasets, and Serve in the chapters leading up to this one. The main reason we deferred a deeper discussion of Ray AIR until now is that it's so much easier to think about its concepts and compute complex examples if you know its building blocks.

In this chapter we'll introduce you to the core concepts of Ray AIR and how you can use it to build and deploy common workflows. We'll build an AIR application that leverages many of Ray's data science libraries that you already know about. We will also tell you when and why to use AIR and give you a brief overview of its technical underpinnings. An in-depth discussion of the relationship of AIR with other systems, such as integrations and key differences, will be tackled in Chapter 11 when we talk about Ray's ecosystem as it relates to AIR.

Why Use AIR?

Running ML workloads with Ray has been a constant evolution over the last couple of years. Ray RLlib and Tune were the first libraries built on top of Ray Core. Components like Ray Train, Serve, and more recently Ray Datasets followed shortly after. The addition of Ray AIR as an umbrella for all other Ray ML libraries is the result of active discussions with and feedback from the ML community. Ray, as a Python-native tool with good GPU support and stateful primitives (Ray actors) for complex ML workloads, is a natural candidate for building a runtime like AIR.

Ray AIR is a unified toolkit for your ML workloads that offers many third-party integrations for model training or accessing custom data sources. In the spirit of the other ML libraries built on top of Ray Core, AIR hides lower-level abstractions and provides an intuitive API that was inspired by common patterns from tools such as scikit-learn.

At its core, Ray AIR was built for both data scientists and ML engineers alike. As a data scientist, you can use it to build and scale your end-to-end experiments or individual subtasks such as preprocessing, training, tuning, scoring, or serving of ML models. As an ML engineer, you can go so far as to build a custom ML platform on top of AIR or simply leverage its unified API to integrate it with other libraries from your ecosystem. And Ray always gives you the flexibility to drop down and delve into the lower-level Ray Core API.

As part of the Ray ecosystem, AIR can leverage all its benefits, which includes a seamless transition from experimentation on a laptop to production workflows on a cluster. You often see data science teams "hand over" their ML code to teams responsible for production systems. In practice this can be expensive and time-consuming, as this process often involves modifying or even rewriting parts of the code. As we will see, Ray AIR helps you with this transition because AIR takes care of concerns such as scalability, reliability, and robustness for you.

Ray AIR already has a respectable number of integrations today, but it's also fully extensible. And as we will show you in the next section, its unified API provides a smooth workflow that allows you to drop-in-replace many of its components. For instance, you can use the same interface to define an XGBoost or PyTorch Trainer with AIR, which makes experimentation with various ML models convenient.

At the same time, by choosing AIR you can avoid the problem of working with several (distributed) systems and writing glue code for them that's difficult to deal with. Teams working with many moving parts often experience rapid deprecation of integrations and a high maintenance burden. These issues can lead to *migration fatigue*, a reluctance to adopt new ideas due to the anticipated complexity of system changes.

As with every chapter, you can follow the code examples in the accompanying Jupyter notebook (*https://oreil.ly/ZrC5L*).

Key AIR Concepts by Example

AIR's design philosophy is to provide you with the ability to *tackle your ML workloads in a single script, run by a single system*. Let's begin with AIR and its critical concepts by walking through an extended usage example. Here's what we're going to do:

1. Load the breast cancer data set that you've already seen in Chapter 7 as a Ray Dataset and use AIR to preprocess it.

2. Define an XGBoost model for training a classifier on this data.

3. Set up a so-called Tuner for our training procedure to tune its hyperparameters.

4. Store checkpoints of trained models.

5. Run batch prediction using AIR.

6. Deploy our predictor as a service with AIR.

You tackle these steps by building scalable pipelines with the AIR API. To follow along this example, make sure to install the following requirements:

```
pip install "ray[air]"==2.2.0" "xgboost-ray>=0.1.10" "xgboost>=1.6.2"
pip install "numpy>=1.19.5" "pandas>=1.3.5" "pyarrow>=6.0.1" "aiorwlock==1.3.0"
```

Figure 10-1 summarizes the steps we're going to take in the following example, alongside the AIR components we'll use.

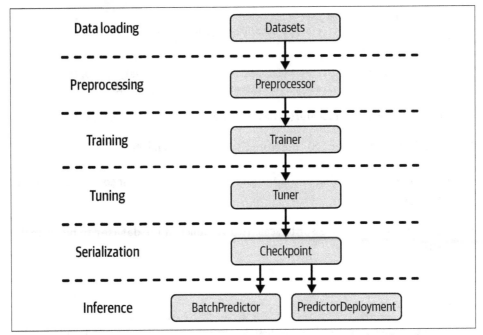

Figure 10-1. From data loading to inference with AIR as the single distributed system

Ray Datasets and Preprocessors

The standard way to load data in Ray AIR is with Ray Datasets. AIR Preprocessors are used to transform input data into features for ML experiments. We've already briefly touched on preprocessors in Chapter 7 but have not discussed them in the context of AIR yet.

Since Ray AIR Preprocessors operate on Datasets and leverage the Ray ecosystem, they allow you to scale your preprocessing steps efficiently. During training an AIR Preprocessor is *fitted* to the specified training data and can then later be used for both training and serving.[1] AIR comes packaged with many common preprocessors that cover many use cases. If you don't find the one you need, you can easily define a custom preprocessor on your own.

In our example, we want to read a CSV file from an S3 bucket into a columnar dataset first, using the `read_csv` utility. Then we split our dataset into a training and a test dataset and define an AIR Preprocessor, `StandardScaler`, which normalizes all specified columns of our dataset to have a mean of 0 and a variance of 1. Note that just specifying a preprocessor does not transform the data just yet. Here is how you implement this:

```
import ray
from ray.data.preprocessors import StandardScaler


dataset = ray.data.read_csv(
    "s3://anonymous@air-example-data/breast_cancer.csv"
) ❶

train_dataset, valid_dataset = dataset.train_test_split(test_size=0.2)
test_dataset = valid_dataset.drop_columns(cols=["target"]) ❷

preprocessor = StandardScaler(columns=["mean radius", "mean texture"]) ❸
```

❶ Load the breast cancer CSV file from S3 using Ray Datasets.

❷ After defining a training and a test dataset, we drop the `target` column on the test data.

❸ Define an AIR Preprocessor to scale two variables of the `dataset` to be normally distributed.

---

1 This gives you parity between your training and serving pipelines, which makes working with AIR convenient because you don't have to reimplement pipelines for different use cases.

Note that for simplicity we're using the test dataset as a validation dataset in future training as well, hence the naming convention.

Before moving on to the training step in AIR workflows, let's look at the different types of AIR Preprocessors that are available to you (Table 10-1). If you want to know more about all available preprocessors, you can consult the user guide on this topic (*https://oreil.ly/WcV6W*). In this book we're using preprocessors only for feature scaling, but the other types of Ray AIR Preprocessors can be very useful as well.

Table 10-1. Ray AIR Preprocessors

Preprocessor type	Examples
Feature scalers	MaxAbsScaler, MinMaxScaler, Normalizer, PowerTransformer, StandardScaler
Generic preprocessors	BatchMapper, Chain, Concatenator, SimpleImputer
Categorical encoders	Categorizer, LabelEncoder, OneHotEncoder
Text encoders	Tokenizer, FeatureHasher

Trainers

Once you have your training and test datasets ready and your preprocessors defined, you can move on to specifying a Trainer that runs an ML algorithm on your data. Trainers from the Ray Train package were introduced in Chapter 7; they provide a consistent wrapper for training frameworks such as TensorFlow, PyTorch, or XGBoost. In this example we'll focus on the latter, but it's important to note that all other framework integrations work exactly the same way in terms of the Ray AIR API.

Let's define a so-called XGBoostTrainer, one of the many specific Trainer implementations that come with Ray AIR. Defining such a trainer requires you to specify these arguments:

- An AIR ScalingConfig that describes how you want to scale out training on your Ray Cluster
- A label_column that specifies which column of your dataset is used as a *label* in supervised learning with XGBoost
- A datasets argument with at least a train key and an optional valid key to specify the training and validation datasets, respectively
- An AIR preprocessor to compute the features of your ML model
- Framework-specific parameters (e.g., the number of boosting rounds in XGBoost), as well as a common set of parameters called params visualized in Figure 10-2:

```
from ray.air.config import ScalingConfig
from ray.train.xgboost import XGBoostTrainer
```

```
trainer = XGBoostTrainer(
    scaling_config=ScalingConfig(   ❶
        num_workers=2,
        use_gpu=False,
    ),
    label_column="target",
    num_boost_round=20,   ❷
    params={
        "objective": "binary:logistic",
        "eval_metric": ["logloss", "error"],
    },
    datasets={"train": train_dataset, "valid": valid_dataset},   ❸
    preprocessor=preprocessor,   ❹
)
result = trainer.fit()   ❺
print(result.metrics)
```

❶ Every `Trainer` comes with a scaling configuration. Here we're using two Ray workers and no GPU.

❷ `XGBoostTrainers` need specific configuration, as well as a training `objective` and evaluation metrics to track.

❸ The `Trainer` specifies the datasets it's supposed to operate on.[2]

❹ In the same way, you can provide AIR Preprocessors that the `Trainer` should use.

❺ After everything is defined, a simple `fit` call is enough to start the training procedure.

Trainers provide scalable ML training that operates on AIR Datasets and preprocessors. On top of that, they're also built to integrate well with Ray Tune for HPO, as we'll see next.

To summarize this section, Figure 10-2 shows how AIR Trainers fit ML models on Ray Datasets given AIR Preprocessors and a scaling configuration.

---

2 Technically speaking, not every trainer needs to specify a `datasets` argument. You can also use framework-specific data loaders, though we can't show you any examples here.

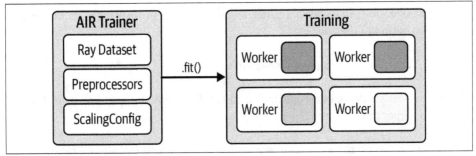

Figure 10-2. AIR Trainers operate on Ray Datasets and use AIR Preprocessors and scaling configurations

Tuners and Checkpoints

Tuners, introduced with Ray 2.0 as part of AIR, offer scalable hyperparameter tuning through Ray Tune. Tuners work seamlessly with AIR Trainers, but also support arbitrary training functions. In our example, instead of calling fit() on your `trainer` instance from the previous section, you can pass your `trainer` into a Tuner. To do so, a Tuner needs to be instantiated with a parameter space to search over, a so-called `TuneConfig`. This config has all Tune-specific configurations like the metric you want to optimize and an optional `RunConfig` that lets you configure runtime-specific aspects such as the log verbosity of your Tune run.

Continuing with the `XGBoostTrainer` we defined earlier, here's how you wrap that `trainer` instance in a Tuner to calibrate the `max_depth` parameter of your XGBoost model:

```
from ray import tune

param_space = {"params": {"max_depth": tune.randint(1, 9)}}
metric = "train-logloss"

from ray.tune.tuner import Tuner, TuneConfig
from ray.air.config import RunConfig

tuner = Tuner(
    trainer,  ❶
    param_space=param_space,  ❷
    run_config=RunConfig(verbose=1),
    tune_config=TuneConfig(num_samples=2, metric=metric, mode="min"),  ❸
)
result_grid = tuner.fit()  ❹

best_result = result_grid.get_best_result()
print("Best Result:", best_result)
```

❶ Initialize your Tuner with a Trainer instance, which in turn specifies the scaling configuration of the run.

❷ Your Tuner also takes a `param_space` to search over.

❸ It also needs a dedicated `TuneConfig` to tell Tune how to optimize your Trainer, given its parameter space.

❹ Tuner runs are started the same way as Trainers, namely, by calling `.fit()`.

Whenever you run AIR Trainers or Tuners, they generate framework-specific checkpoints. You can use these checkpoints to load models for usage across several AIR libraries, such as Tune, Train, or Serve. You can get a checkpoint by accessing the result of a `.fit()` call on either a Trainer or a Tuner. In our example, that means you can simply access a `checkpoint` on the `best_result` object, or any other entry from the `result_grid` like this:

```
checkpoint = best_result.checkpoint
print(checkpoint)
```

The other main way to work with checkpoints is by creating one from an existing, framework-specific model. Every ML framework supported by AIR can be used to do this, but since it's easiest to define a simple model with it, we're going to show you how this looks for a sequential TensorFlow Keras model:

```
from ray.train.tensorflow import TensorflowCheckpoint
import tensorflow as tf

model = tf.keras.Sequential([
    tf.keras.layers.InputLayer(input_shape=(1,)),
    tf.keras.layers.Dense(1)
])

keras_checkpoint = TensorflowCheckpoint.from_model(model)
```

Having checkpoints is great because they're AIR's native model exchange format. You can also use them to pick up trained models at a later stage, without having to worry about custom ways to store and load the models in question. Figure 10-3 schematically shows how AIR Tuners work with AIR Trainers.

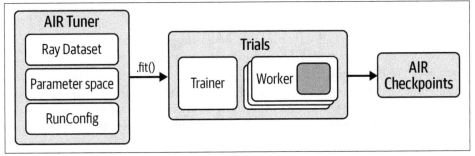

Figure 10-3. An AIR Tuner calibrates the hyperparameters of AIR Trainers

Batch Predictors

Once you have trained a model through AIR, that is, by fitting either a `Trainer` or a `Tuner`, you can use the resulting AIR Checkpoint for prediction on batches of data in Python. To do that you create a `BatchPredictor` from your Checkpoint and then use its `predict` method on your Dataset. In our case we need to use the framework-specific class of the predictor, namely, `XGBoostPredictor`, to tell AIR how to load the `checkpoint` correctly:

```
from ray.train.batch_predictor import BatchPredictor
from ray.train.xgboost import XGBoostPredictor

checkpoint = best_result.checkpoint
batch_predictor = BatchPredictor.from_checkpoint(checkpoint, XGBoostPredictor) ❶

predicted_probabilities = batch_predictor.predict(test_dataset) ❷
predicted_probabilities.show()
```

❶ Load an XGBoost model from a checkpoint into a `BatchPredictor` object.

❷ Run batch inference on our test dataset to get predicted probabilities.

This can be visualized in Figure 10-4.

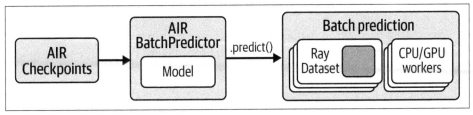

Figure 10-4. Using AIR `BatchPredictors` from AIR Checkpoints to run batch inference on AIR Datasets

Deployments

Instead of using a `BatchPredictor` and interacting with the model in question directly, you can leverage Ray Serve to deploy an inference service that you can query over HTTP. You do that by using the `PredictorDeployment` class and `deploy` it using our `checkpoint`. The only slightly tricky part about this is that our model operates on dataframes, which we can't directly send over HTTP. That means we need to explicitly tell our prediction service how to pick up and transform the *payload* we define and create a dataframe from it. We do this by specifying an *adapter* for our deployment:[3]

```
from ray import serve
from fastapi import Request
import pandas as pd
from ray.serve import PredictorDeployment


async def adapter(request: Request):    ❶
    payload = await request.json()
    return pd.DataFrame.from_dict(payload)


serve.start(detached=True)
deployment = PredictorDeployment.options(name="XGBoostService")    ❷

deployment.deploy(    ❸
    XGBoostPredictor,
    checkpoint,
    http_adapter=adapter
)

print(deployment.url)
```

❶ An adapter takes an HTTP request object and returns data in a format accepted by our model.

❷ After starting Serve we can create a deployment for our model.

❸ To actually `deploy` the deployment object we need to pass in the model `check point`, the `adapter` function, and the `XGBoostPredictor` class for correct model loading.

---

3 If you run the following example from a Jupyter notebook, you do not have to worry about it blocking the notebook—it will run just fine. Starting a server like this is often implemented as a blocking call, but `PredictorDeployment` isn't.

To test this deployment, let's create some sample input from our test data that we can throw at our service. For simplicity, we take the first item of our test dataset and convert it to a Python dictionary so that the ubiquitous Requests library can post a request to our deployment URL with it:

```
import requests

first_item = test_dataset.take(1)
sample_input = dict(first_item[0])

result = requests.post(    ❶
    deployment.url,
    json=[sample_input]
)
print(result.json())

serve.shutdown()    ❷
```

❶ Posts our sample_input to *deployment.url* with requests.

❷ After you're finished using the service, you can safely shut down Ray Serve.

Figure 10-5 summarizes how AIR deployments with the PredictorDeployment class work.

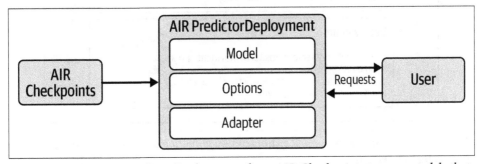

Figure 10-5. Creating PredictorDeployments from AIR Checkpoints to serve models that users can interact with

Figure 10-6 gives you a quick visual overview of all the components and concepts involved in Ray AIR, including pseudocode for all the main AIR components we've covered in this chapter.

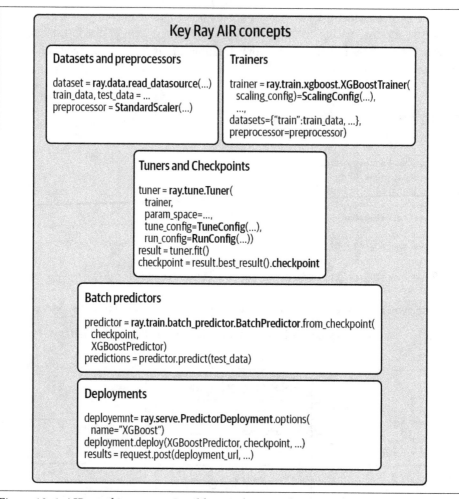

Figure 10-6. AIR combines many Ray libraries by providing a unified API for common data science workloads

It's important to stress again that we've been using *a single Python script* for this example and a single distributed system in Ray AIR to do all the heavy lifting. In fact, you can use this example script and scale it out to a large cluster that uses CPUs for preprocessing and GPUs for training and separately configure the deployment simply by modifying the parameters of the scaling configuration and similar options in that script. This isn't as easy or common as it may seem, and it is not unusual for data scientists to have to use multiple frameworks (e.g., one for data loading and processing, one for training, and one for serving).

You can also use Ray AIR with RLlib, but the integration is still in its early stages. For instance, to integrate RLlib with AIR Trainers, you'd use the `RLTrainer` that allows you to pass in all arguments that you'd pass to a standard RLlib algorithm. After training, you can store the resulting RL model in an AIR Checkpoint, just as with any other AIR Trainer. To deploy your trained RL model, you can use Serve's `PredictorDeployment` class by passing your checkpoint along with the `RLPredictor` class.

This API might be subject to change, but you can see an example of how this works in the AIR documentation (*https://oreil.ly/gB-wg*).

Workloads That Are Suited for AIR

Now that we've seen examples of AIR and its fundamental concepts, let's zoom out a little and discuss in principle which kinds of workloads you can run with it. We've tackled all of these workloads already throughout the book, but it's good to recap them systematically. As the name suggests, AIR is built to capture common tasks in AI projects. These tasks can be roughly classified in the following way:

Stateless computation
Tasks like preprocessing data or computing model predictions on a batch of data are stateless.[4] Stateless workloads can be computed independently in parallel. If you recall our treatment of Ray tasks from Chapter 2, stateless computation is exactly what they were built for. AIR primarily uses Ray tasks for stateless workloads.[5] Many *big data processing* tools fall into this category.

Stateful computation
In contrast, model training and hyperparameter tuning are stateful operations, as they update the model state during their respective training procedure. Updating stateful workers in such *distributed training* is a difficult topic that Ray handles for you. AIR uses Ray actors for stateful computations.

Composite workloads
Combining stateless and stateful computation, for instance by first processing features and then training a model, is quite common in AI workloads. In fact, it's rare for end-to-end projects to exclusively use one or the other. Running such advanced composite workloads in a distributed fashion can be described as *big*

---

4 Of course, the model used for inference has to be loaded first, but since its parameters don't change during prediction, trained models can be considered static data in this case. We sometimes refer to this situation as *soft state*.

5 Sometimes AIR uses Ray actors for stateless tasks for performance reasons, such as caching models in batch inference.

data training, and AIR is built to handle both the stateless and stateful parts efficiently.

Online serving

Lastly, AIR is built to handle scalable online serving of (multiple) models. The transition from the previous three workloads to serving is frictionless by design, as you still operate within the same AIR ecosystem.

Figure 10-7 illustrates the typical stateless tasks of Ray AIR.

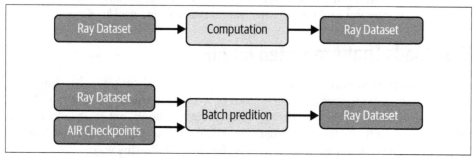

Figure 10-7. Stateless AIR tasks

These four tasks map to Ray's libraries straightforwardly. For instance, in this chapter we've discussed several ways in which Ray Datasets are used for stateless computation. You could run batch inference on a given Dataset by passing it into a `BatchPredictor` loaded from an AIR Checkpoint. Or you could preprocess a Dataset to produce features for later training.[6]

Likewise, there are three AIR libraries dedicated to stateful computations, namely, Train, Tune, and RLlib. As we've seen, both Train and RLlib integrate seamlessly with Tune in AIR by passing the respective `Trainer` objects into a `Tuner`.

When it comes to advanced composite workloads, Ray AIR and its combined usage of both tasks and actors really shines. For instance, some ML training procedures need to perform complex data processing tasks during training. Others may require shuffling the training dataset before each epoch. Since Ray AIR's training libraries (based on actors) can seamlessly leverage data processing operations (mostly based on tasks), even the most complex use cases can be reflected in AIR.

Also, since you can use any AIR Checkpoint with Ray Serve, AIR makes it easy to switch from training to serving workloads, using the same infrastructure. We've seen how you can use a `PredictorDeployment` to host a model behind an HTTP endpoint, which is optimized for low latency and high throughput. By deploying AIR, you can

---

6 Note that preprocessors *can* be stateful, but we haven't discussed any examples of that scenario here.

scale your prediction services to multiple replicas and use Ray's autoscaling features to adjust your cluster according to inbound traffic.[7]

You can use these types of workloads in different scenarios, too. For instance, you can use AIR to replace and scale out a single component of an existing pipeline. Or you can create your own end-to-end machine learning apps with AIR, as we've indicated in this chapter. Lastly, you can also use AIR to build your own AI platform, a topic that we'll look at in Chapter 11.

Figure 10-8 summarizes how these four types of AI workloads are covered by AIR as part of the Ray ecosystem.

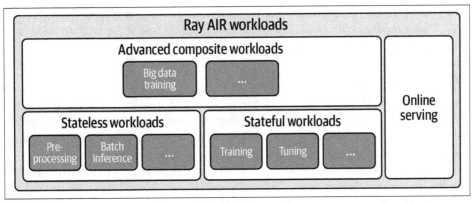

Figure 10-8. The four types of AI workloads AIR enables you to run on Ray Clusters

Next, we'll discuss several aspects of each of these four workload types of AIR in more detail. Specifically, we will investigate how Ray executes such workloads internally. Also, we're going to dive a little deeper into the technical aspects behind Ray AIR, such as how it manages memory or handles failures. We can give you only a brief overview of these topics but will provide links to more advanced material as we go.

AIR Workload Execution

Let's have a closer look at the execution model of AIR.

Stateless execution

Ray Datasets use Ray tasks or actors to execute transformations. Tasks are preferred since they allow for easier and more flexible scheduling. The Datasets library uses a scheduling strategy that evenly balances tasks and their output across your cluster.

---

7 On top of multiple replicas for single models, AIR also supports deployment of multiple models. This allows you to compose multiple models or run A/B testing.

Actors are used if a transformation has state or needs an expensive setup, like loading large model checkpoints. In this case, loading large models in an actor once to reuse it for inference tasks can benefit overall performance. When Ray Datasets is using actors, these actors are created first, and the necessary data (in our example the loaded model) is transferred to them before the transformation in question gets executed.

In general, datasets are stored in Ray object store memory, while large datasets are spilled to disk. But for stateless transformations there is often no need to keep intermediate results in memory. Using *pipelining* on Datasets, as we've shown in Chapter 6, data can instead be streamed to and from storage to increase performance.[8] The idea is to load only the fraction of the data currently needed to execute a transformation. This can drastically reduce the memory footprint of the transformation and often speed up the overall execution.

Stateful execution

Ray Train and RLlib spawn actors for their distributed training workers. As demonstrated multiple times, both libraries also integrate seamlessly with Tune. In Chapter 5 we detailed how Tune launches Trials, which in essence are groups of actors executing a certain workload. If you use Train or RLlib with Tune, that in turn means that a tree of actors gets created, namely, an actor for each Tune Trial, and subactors for the parallel training workers requested by Train or RLlib.

In terms of workload execution, this naturally creates an inner and an outer layer. Each subactor in a Tune Trial has full autonomy over its workload, as requested in the respective Train or RLlib training run you specified. This represents the inner execution layer. On the outer layer, Tune needs to monitor the status of individual trials, which it does by periodically reporting metrics to the Trial driver. Figure 10-9 illustrates this nested creation and execution of Ray actors for this scenario.

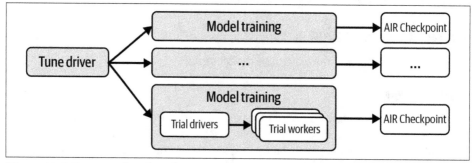

Figure 10-9. Running distributed training on AIR with Tune

---

8 All crucial AIR components such as `Trainer` or `BatchPredictor` support this pipelining feature.

Composite workload execution

Composite workloads leverage both task- and actor-based computation simultaneously. This can lead to interesting resource allocation challenges. Trial actors need to reserve their resources upfront, but stateless tasks don't. The problem you can run into is that all available resources might get reserved for your training actors with none left for data loading tasks.

AIR prevents this by allowing Tune to reserve a maximum of 80% of a node's CPU. You can tune this parameter, but this is a sensible default that ensures basic resource availability for stateless computations. In the common scenario in which your training operations leverage GPUs and your data processing steps don't, this becomes a nonissue.

Online serving execution

For online serving Ray Serve manages a pool of stateless actors to serve your requests. Some actors listen for incoming requests and call other actors to perform the predictions. Requests are automatically load-balanced using a round-robin algorithm to the pool of actors hosting the models. Load metrics are sent to the Serve component to perform autoscaling.

AIR Memory Management

In this section we take a bit of a deep dive into the specific memory management techniques of AIR. We'll discuss to what extent the Ray object store is used by AIR. You can skip this section if you find it too technical. The upshot is that Ray employs smart techniques that will ensure your data and compute are properly distributed and scheduled.

When you load data using Ray Datasets, you already know that internally these Datasets are partitioned into blocks of data in your cluster. A block is simply a collection of Ray objects. Choosing the right block size is difficult and presents a trade-off between the overhead of having to manage too many small blocks and risking out-of-memory (OOM) exceptions due to blocks that are too large. AIR takes a pragmatic approach and tries to distribute in such a way that blocks don't exceed 512 MB. In case this can't be ensured, a warning will be issued. Should a block not fit into memory, AIR will spill your data to local disk.

Your stateful workloads will use the Ray object store to varying degrees. For instance, RLlib uses Ray objects to broadcast model weights to individual rollout workers and for experience data collection. Tune uses it to set up Trials by sending and retrieving AIR Checkpoints. For technical reasons actors risk running into OOM issues if too much memory is required relative to the allocated resources.[9] If you know your memory requirements in advance, you can adapt the `memory` in your `ScalingConfig` accordingly, or simply ask for additional `cpu` resources.

In composite workloads stateful actors (e.g., for training) have to access data created by stateless tasks (e.g., for preprocessing), which makes memory allocation more challenging. Let's look at two scenarios:

- If the actors responsible for training have enough space (in the object store) to fit all training data in memory, the situation is simple. First the preprocessing steps run, and then all data blocks are downloaded to the respective nodes. Training actors then simply iterate data that's kept in memory.

- Otherwise, data processing needs *pipelined execution*, which means that data will be processed by tasks on the fly and will be downloaded on demand by training Actors afterward. If the respective training actor is co-located on the node that did the processing, data will be retrieved from shared memory.

AIR Failure Model

AIR offers fault tolerance for most stateless computations through *lineage reconstruction*. This means Ray will reconstruct Dataset blocks if they are lost due to node failures by resubmitting the necessary tasks, enabling workloads to scale to large clusters. Note that fault tolerance does not apply to head node failures. And a crash of the Global Control Service (GCS) storing cluster metadata will kill all your jobs in the cluster.[10]

Jobs involving stateful computations primarily rely on checkpoint-based fault tolerance. Tune will restart distributed trials from their last checkpoint as configured in its failure configuration. With a configured checkpoint interval, this means that Tune can run trials effectively on clusters consisting of "spot instances." In addition, it is possible to resume entire Tune experiments from the experiment-wide checkpoint in case of whole-cluster failure.

Composite workloads inherit the fault-tolerance strategies of both stateless and stateful workloads, retaining the best of both worlds. This means that lineage reconstruction applies to the stateless portion of the workload, and application-level checkpointing still applies to the overall computation.

---

9 Stateful workloads use Python's heap memory, which is not managed by Ray.

10 GCS can be deployed in *high availability* (HA) mode to prevent this, but that is typically beneficial only for online serving workloads.

Autoscaling AIR Workloads

AIR libraries can run on autoscaling Ray Clusters that we introduced in Chapter 9. For stateless workloads, Ray will autoscale automatically if there are queued tasks (or queued Dataset compute actors). For stateful workloads, Ray will autoscale up if there are pending placement groups (i.e., Tune trials) not yet scheduled in the cluster. Ray will autoscale down when nodes are idle. A node is considered idle when there is no resource usage on the node and also no Ray objects in memory or spilled on disk on the node. Since most AIR libraries leverage objects, this means that nodes may be kept if they are holding objects referenced by workers on other nodes (e.g., Dataset block used by another trial).

You should be aware that autoscaling may result in less than ideal data balancing in the cluster because nodes that are started earlier naturally run more tasks over their lifetime. Consider limiting (e.g., starting with a certain minimum cluster size) or disabling autoscaling to optimize the efficiency of data-intensive workloads.

Summary

In this chapter you've seen how all the Ray libraries we've introduced come together to form the Ray AI Runtime. You've learned about all the key concepts that allow you to build scalable ML projects, from experimentation to production. In particular, you've seen how Ray Datasets are used for stateless computations such as feature preprocessing, and how Ray Train, Tune, and RLlib are used for stateful computations such as model training. Seamlessly combining these types of computations in complex AI workloads and scaling them out to large clusters is a key strength of AIR. Deploying your AIR projects comes essentially for free, as AIR fully integrates with Ray Serve as well.

In Chapter 11 we'll show you how Ray, and particularly AIR, fits into the broader landscape of related tools. Knowing the rich set of integrations and extensions of Ray's ecosystem will help you understand how to leverage Ray in your own projects.

## CHAPTER 11

Ray's Ecosystem and Beyond

Over the course of this book, you've seen many examples of Ray's ecosystem. Now it's time to take a more systematic approach and show you the full extent of integrations currently available for Ray. We do so by discussing this ecosystem as seen from Ray AIR so that we can discuss it in the context of a representative AIR workflow.

Clearly, we can't give you concrete code examples for a majority of the libraries in Ray's ecosystem. Instead, we have to be content with giving you another Ray AIR example showcasing some integrations and discussing what others are available and how to use them. Where appropriate, we'll point you to more advanced resources to deepen your understanding.

Now that you know much more about Ray and its libraries, this chapter is also the right place to compare what Ray offers to *similar* systems. As you've seen, Ray's ecosystem is quite complex, can be seen from different angles, and is used for different purposes. That means many aspects of Ray can be compared to other tools in the market.

We'll also comment on how to integrate Ray into more complex workflows in existing ML platforms. To wrap things up, we'll give you an idea how to continue your journey of *learning Ray* after finishing this book.

 The notebook for this chapter is available on GitHub (*https://oreil.ly/mUrmi*).

A Growing Ecosystem

To give you a glimpse of Ray's ecosystem by means of a concrete example,[1] we're going to show you how to use Ray AIR with data and models from the PyTorch ecosystem, how to log your hyperparameter tuning runs to MLflow, and how to deploy your trained models with Ray's Gradio integration. Along the way we give you an overview and discuss usage patterns of other noteworthy integrations at each respective stage.

To follow the code examples in this chapter, make sure to install the following dependencies in your Python environment:

```
pip install "ray[air, serve]==2.2.0" "gradio==3.5.0" "requests==2.28.1"
pip install "mlflow==1.30.0" "torch==1.12.1" "torchvision==0.13.1"
```

We're going to load and transform a dataset using utilities from the PyTorch framework and then convert this data into a Ray Dataset to work with it in Ray AIR. We then define a standard PyTorch model and a simple training loop that we can leverage in Ray Train. Next, we wrap this `TorchTrainer` in a Tuner and log trial results to MLflow using the `MLflowLogger` that ships with Ray Tune. Finally, we're going to serve our trained model using Gradio running on Ray Serve.

In other words, the example we're discussing takes common Python data science libraries that you might already use and wraps them in an AIR workflow by leveraging Ray's ecosystem integrations. The focus is more on these integrations and how they interface with AIR and less on the concrete use case.

Data Loading and Processing

In Chapter 6 you learned about the basics of Ray Datasets, how to create them from common Python data structures, how to load Parquet files from storage systems like S3, and how to use Ray's Dask on Ray integration to interface with Dask.

To give you yet another example of Ray Dataset's capabilities, let's see how you can work with image data loaded through PyTorch's `torchvision` extension. The idea is simple. We're going to load the common CIFAR-10 dataset available in PyTorch through the `torchvision.datasets` package and then make it a Ray Dataset. Specifically, we're going to define a function called `load_cifar` that returns the CIFAR-10 data for training or testing:

---

[1] You can find the current list of integrations to the AIR ecosystems in the Ray documentation (*https://oreil.ly/S7_eb*). More generally, you find a list of integrations for Ray on the Ray Ecosystem page (*https://oreil.ly/Wiqi1*). On the latter, you find many more integrations than the ones we discuss here, such as ClassyVision, Intel Analytics Zoo, John Snow Labs' NLU, Ludwig AI, PyCaret, and SpaCy.

```
from torchvision import transforms, datasets


def load_cifar(train: bool):
    transform = transforms.Compose([  ❶
        transforms.ToTensor(),
        transforms.Normalize((0.5, 0.5, 0.5), (0.5, 0.5, 0.5))
    ])

    return datasets.CIFAR10(  ❷
        root="./data",
        download=True,
        train=train,  ❸
        transform=transform
    )
```

❶ Uses a PyTorch transform to return normalized Tensor data.

❷ Loads the CIFAR-10 dataset using the `datasets` module of the `torchvision` package.

❸ Makes it so that the `loader` function returns either training or testing data.

Note that so far we haven't touched any Ray library, and you could have used any other dataset or transform from PyTorch in the same way. To get Ray Datasets for use with AIR, we're going to supply our `load_cifar` data loader functions to the `from_torch` utility from Ray AIR:

```
from ray.data import from_torch


train_dataset = from_torch(load_cifar(train=True))
test_dataset = from_torch(load_cifar(train=False))
```

The CIFAR-10 dataset is used for image classification tasks; it consists of 32-pixel square images and comes with labels of a total of 10 categories. So far we've loaded this dataset only in the form provided by PyTorch, but we still need to transform it to use it with an AIR Trainer. You do this by creating an `image` and a `label` column that we can then reference in a Trainer. The best way to do so is by *mapping batches* of train and test data to a dictionary of NumPy arrays with precisely these two columns:

```
import numpy as np


def to_labeled_image(batch):  ❶
    return {
        "image": np.array([image.numpy() for image, _ in batch]),
        "label": np.array([label for _, label in batch]),
    }
```

```
train_dataset = train_dataset.map_batches(to_labeled_image)  ❷
test_dataset = test_dataset.map_batches(to_labeled_image)
```

❶ Transforms each `batch` of data by returning an `image` and a `label` NumPy array.

❷ Applies `map_batches` to transform our initial datasets.

Before we move on to model training, Table 11-1 shows the supported input formats of the Ray Datasets library.[2]

Table 11-1. The Ray Datasets ecosystem

Integration	Type	Description
Text, binary, image files, CSV, JSON	Basic data formats	Supporting such basic formats should not strictly speaking be considered an *integration*, but it's worth knowing that Ray Datasets can load and store these formats.
NumPy, Pandas, Arrow, Parquet, Python objects	Advanced data formats	Ray Datasets supports working with common ML data libraries such as NumPy and Pandas but can also read custom Python objects or read Parquet files.
Spark, Dask, MARS, Modin	Advanced third-party integrations	Ray interoperates with more complex data processing systems by means of community integrations, such as Spark on Ray (RayDP), Dask on Ray, MARS on Ray, or Pandas on Ray (Modin).

We'll talk about the relationship of Ray with systems such as Dask or Spark in more detail in "Distributed Python Frameworks" on page 227.

Model Training

Having properly shaped our CIFAR-10 to train and test data using Ray Datasets, we can now define a classifier to train our data on. As this is likely the most natural scenario, we're going to define a PyTorch model to define an AIR Trainer here. But it's worth reminding you of what you learned in Chapter 7: you could just as easily switch frameworks at this point and work with Keras, Hugging Face, scikit-learn, or any other library supported by AIR.

We will proceed in three steps: define a PyTorch model, specify the training loop that AIR should run using this model, and define an AIR Trainer that we can fit on our training data. To start with, let's define a simple convolutional neural network with max pooling and rectified linear (`relu`) activations with PyTorch that's built to operate on our CIFAR-10 dataset. If you know PyTorch, the following definition of

---

2 You can see the continually updated list of supported formats in the Ray Datasets documentation (*https://oreil.ly/7pmuc*). The supported *output* formats for Datasets largely overlap with the input formats.

the neural network Net should be straightforward. If you don't, it suffices to know that to define a `torch.nn.Module` the only thing you need to provide is the definition of a `forward` pass of your neural net:

```python
import torch
import torch.nn as nn
import torch.nn.functional as F


class Net(nn.Module):
    def __init__(self):
        super().__init__()
        self.conv1 = nn.Conv2d(3, 6, 5)
        self.pool = nn.MaxPool2d(2, 2)
        self.conv2 = nn.Conv2d(6, 16, 5)
        self.fc1 = nn.Linear(16 * 5 * 5, 120)
        self.fc2 = nn.Linear(120, 84)
        self.fc3 = nn.Linear(84, 10)

    def forward(self, x):
        x = self.pool(F.relu(self.conv1(x)))
        x = self.pool(F.relu(self.conv2(x)))
        x = torch.flatten(x, 1)
        x = F.relu(self.fc1(x))
        x = F.relu(self.fc2(x))
        x = self.fc3(x)
        return x
```

You already know that to define an AIR `TorchTrainer` for our `Net` you need a training dataset, a scaling, and an optional run configuration.[3] You also need to tell AIR what each worker should do when calling `fit`, by defining an explicit training loop that grants you maximal flexibility for your training process. The training function takes a `config` dictionary that we can use to specify properties at runtime.

The training loop we're using here is just what you would expect: we simply load the model and the data on each worker and then train on batches of data for a specified number of epochs (while reporting the training progress). That's a fairly standard training loop, but there are a couple of crucial spots at which you have to be careful:

- To load the model on a worker, use the `prepare_model` utility from `ray.train.torch` on our `Net()`.

- To access the data shard available to the worker, access `get_dataset_shard` on your current `ray.air.session`. For training, we use the `"train"` key of that shard and transform it to batches of the right size using `iter_torch_batches`.

---

3 To convert any PyTorch model to Ray AIR, follow the user guide on this topic (*https://oreil.ly/k2QKV*).

- To pass information about the training metrics you're interested in, use `session.report` from AIR.

Here's the full definition of our PyTorch training loop for each worker:

```
from ray import train
from ray.air import session, Checkpoint


def train_loop(config):
    model = train.torch.prepare_model(Net())    ❶
    loss_fct = nn.CrossEntropyLoss()
    optimizer = torch.optim.SGD(model.parameters(), lr=0.001, momentum=0.9)

    train_batches = session.get_dataset_shard("train").iter_torch_batches(    ❷
        batch_size=config["batch_size"],
    )

    for epoch in range(config["epochs"]):
        running_loss = 0.0
        for i, data in enumerate(train_batches):
            inputs, labels = data["image"], data["label"]    ❸

            optimizer.zero_grad()    ❹
            forward_outputs = model(inputs)
            loss = loss_fct(forward_outputs, labels)
            loss.backward()
            optimizer.step()

            running_loss += loss.item()    ❺
            if i % 1000 == 0:
                print(f"[{epoch + 1}, {i + 1:4d}] loss: "
                    f"{running_loss / 1000:.3f}")
                running_loss = 0.0

        session.report(    ❻
            dict(running_loss=running_loss),
            checkpoint=Checkpoint.from_dict(
                dict(model=model.module.state_dict())
            ),
        )
```

❶ The training loop defines the model, loss, and optimizer used first. Note the use of `prepare_model` here.

❷ Load the train dataset *shard* on this worker and create an iterator containing batches of data from it.

❸ As per our earlier definition, our `data` is a Pandas DataFrame that has an "image" and a "label" column.

❹ Compute the forward and backward pass in the training loop as we would with any PyTorch model.

❺ Keep track of a running loss term for each 1,000 training batches.

❻ Lastly, `report` this loss using our AIR `session` by passing a `Checkpoint` with the current model state.

The definition of this function might feel a bit long, given that we're doing a fairly standard training procedure. While it certainly would be possible to create a simple wrapper for PyTorch models in such cases, defining your own training loop gives you full customizability to tackle more complex scenarios. We pass the `training_loop` to the `train_loop_per_worker` argument of our AIR trainer and specify the configuration for this loop by passing a dictionary with the necessary keys to the `train_loop_config`.

To make things more interesting and to showcase another Ray integration, we will log the results of our `TorchTrainer` training run to `MLflow` by passing a callback to our `RunConfig`, namely, an `MLflowLoggerCallback`:

```
from ray.train.torch import TorchTrainer
from ray.air.config import ScalingConfig, RunConfig
from ray.air.callbacks.mlflow import MLflowLoggerCallback


trainer = TorchTrainer(
    train_loop_per_worker=train_loop,
    train_loop_config={"batch_size": 10, "epochs": 5},
    datasets={"train": train_dataset},
    scaling_config=ScalingConfig(num_workers=2),
    run_config=RunConfig(callbacks=[
        MLflowLoggerCallback(experiment_name="torch_trainer")
    ])

)
result = trainer.fit()
```

You could also use other third-party logging libraries, such as *Weights & Biases* or *CometML*, by passing similar callbacks to your AIR Trainer or Tuner.[4]

---

4 For instance, using the `WandbLoggerCallback` you not only can log training results to Weights & Biases but also automatically upload your checkpoints, as demonstrated in this Ray tutorial (*https://oreil.ly/2jWOj*).

Table 11-2 summarizes all ML training-related integrations of Ray, which span both Ray Train and RLlib.

Table 11-2. The Ray Train and RLlib ecosystem

Integration	Type
TensorFlow, PyTorch, XGBoost, LightGBM, Horovod	Train integrations maintained by the Ray Team
scikit-learn, Hugging Face, Lightning	Train integrations maintained by the community
TensorFlow, PyTorch, OpenAI gym	RLlib integrations maintained by the Ray Team
JAX, Unity	RLlib integrations maintained by the Ray Team

We distinguish between community-sponsored integrations and ones that are maintained by the Ray team itself. Most integrations we've talked about in this book were native integrations, but due to the collaborative nature of open source software, you often feel no difference in maturity between native and third-party integrations.

To wrap up the training-related integrations of AIR, Table 11-3 offers a bird's-eye view at Tune's ecosystem.

Table 11-3. The Ray Tune ecosystem

Integration	Type
Optuna, Hyperopt, Ax, BayesOpt, BOHB, Dragonfly, FLAML, HEBO, Nevergrad, SigOpt, skopt, ZOOpt	Hyperparameter optimization library
TensorBoard, MLflow, Weights & Biases, CometML	Logging and experimentation management

Model Serving

Gradio is a popular way for practitioners to demo their ML models, and it provides many simple primitives to create graphical user interface elements simply by describing them through the `gradio` library in Python. As you will see, defining and deploying Gradio interfaces is straightforward, but it's even easier to then wrap them in a so-called `GradioServer` from Ray Serve, which allows you to scale any Gradio app on a Ray Cluster.

To showcase how to run a Gradio app with Ray Serve on the model we just trained, let's first store the `result` of our training procedure to disk. We do this by writing the respective AIR Checkpoint to a local folder of our choice so that we can restore this model *from checkpoint* in another script:

```
CHECKPOINT_PATH = "torch_checkpoint"
result.checkpoint.to_directory(CHECKPOINT_PATH)
```

Next, let's create a file called *gradio_demo.py* next to the `"torch_checkpoint"` path for simplicity. In this script, let's load our PyTorch model again by first restoring the

TorchCheckpoint and then using this checkpoint and our `Net()` definition to create a TorchPredictor that we can use for inference:

```
# gradio_demo.py
from ray.train.torch import TorchCheckpoint, TorchPredictor

CHECKPOINT_PATH = "torch_checkpoint"
checkpoint = TorchCheckpoint.from_directory(CHECKPOINT_PATH)
predictor = TorchPredictor.from_checkpoint(
    checkpoint=checkpoint,
    model=Net()
)
```

Note that this requires you to import, or otherwise make available, the definition of `Net` in the *gradio_demo.py* script.[5]

Next, we have to define the Gradio `Interface`, which we define to take images as input and produce labels as output. Additionally, we have to specify how an input `Image` has to be transformed to produce a `Label`. By default, Gradio represents images as NumPy arrays, so we can ensure that this array has the right shape and data type and then pass it to our `predictor`. As this `predictor`, namely, our TorchPredictor, produces a probability distribution, we take the `argmax` of its prediction to get an integer result that we can use as a label. Put the following code into your *gradio_demo.py* Python script:

```
from ray.serve.gradio_integrations import GradioServer
import gradio as gr
import numpy as np


def predict(payload):      ❶
    payload = np.array(payload, dtype=np.float32)
    array = payload.reshape((1, 3, 32, 32))
    return np.argmax(predictor.predict(array))


demo = gr.Interface(      ❷
    fn=predict,
    inputs=gr.Image(),
    outputs=gr.Label(num_top_classes=10)
)

app = GradioServer.options(      ❸
    num_replicas=2,
    ray_actor_options={"num_cpus": 2}
).bind(demo)
```

---

5 For simplicity, we duplicated the definition of `Net` in *gradio_demo.py* on GitHub.

❶ The predict function maps Gradio inputs to outputs by leveraging our predictor.

❷ The Gradio interface has one input (an image), one output (a label for 1 of 10 categories of the CIFAR-10 dataset), and a function fn to connect the two.

❸ We bind the Gradio demo to a Ray Serve GradioServer object that gets deployed on two replicas with two CPUs each as resources.

To run this application, you can now simply type the following command into a shell:[6]

```
serve run gradio_demo:app
```

This command spins up our Serve-backed Gradio demo that you can access on localhost:8000. You can upload or drag and drop images into the respective input field and request predictions that you see in the output field of the app.[7]

It's important to note that this example is really just a thin wrapper around Gradio and would work with any other Gradio app of your choice. In fact, if you called demo.launch() instead of defining the Serve app in your script, you could simply launch this as a regular Gradio app with *python gradio_demo.py*.

The other noteworthy detail that's easy to overlook is that we fed our predictor a NumPy array. If you check the definition of the data format we used for training, you'll recall that predictor is expected to work on Ray Dataset instances. The predictor instance is also smart enough to infer that a single NumPy input must be the "image" portion of the full input (we don't need a "label" to run inference).

To wrap up this section, review Table 11-4, which lists Serve's current integrations.

Table 11-4. The Ray Serve ecosystem

Library	Description
Serving frameworks and applications	FastAPI, Flask, Streamlit, Gradio
Explainability and observability	Arize, Seldon Alibi, WhyLabs

---

6 When using the Gradio integration, Ray Serve will automatically run a Gradio app under the hood. The Gradio app is instrumented to access the type hints on each Serve deployment. When the user submits a request, the Gradio app displays the output of each deployment using a Gradio Block that matches the output type.

7 The application expects images of the right size, as we didn't want to make preprocessing in predict more involved than necessary. You can use the image data provided in the repository of this book (*https://oreil.ly/ 7JS-l*) or simply search for CIFAR-10 images online to test the app yourself.

Building Custom Integrations

Before explaining the relationship of Ray with other complex software frameworks in a bit more detail, let's talk about how to build your own integrations for Ray AIR. Since AIR is designed for extensibility, you can find suitable interfaces for all the tasks you want to build custom integrations for.

For example, let's say you want to read data from Snowflake, train a JAX model on it, and log your tuning results to Neptune.[8] At the time of this writing, there are no such integrations available, but it's likely this will change in the future. We didn't pick these integrations (Snowflake, JAX, Neptune) to showcase any preference; they just happen to be interesting tools from the ecosystem. In any case, it's worth knowing how to build such integrations.

To load data from Snowflake into a Ray Dataset, you have to create a new `Data source`. You define a `Datasource` by specifying how to set it up (`create_reader`), how to write to the source (`do_write`), and what happens on successful and failed write attempts (`on_write_complete` and `on_write_failed`). Given a concrete `Snow flakeDatasource` implementation, you could then read your data into a Ray `Dataset`:

```
from ray.data import read_datasource, datasource


class SnowflakeDatasource(datasource.Datasource):
    pass


dataset = read_datasource(SnowflakeDatasource(), ...)
```

Next, let's say you have an interesting JAX model that you want to scale out using Ray Train's capabilities. Specifically, let's assume you want to run data-parallel training of the model, that is, to train this single model on several data shards in parallel. For this purpose, Ray comes with a so-called `DataParallelTrainer`. To define one, you have to create a `train_loop_per_worker` for your training framework and define how JAX should be handled by Train internally.[9] With a `JaxTrainer` implementation, you can leverage the same `Trainer` interface that we've used in all AIR examples:

```
from ray.train.data_parallel_trainer import DataParallelTrainer


class JaxTrainer(DataParallelTrainer):
```

---

8 In this chapter we're going to assume that you know about these different tools from the ecosystem. If you don't, for this section it's enough to understand that Snowflake is a database solution that you might want to integrate with, JAX is an ML framework, and Neptune can be used for experiment tracking.

9 To be precise, you have to define a `Backend` for JAX, together with a `BackendConfig`. Your `DataParallel Trainer` then has to be initialized with this backend and your training loop.

```
    pass


trainer = JaxTrainer(
    ...,
    scaling_config=ScalingConfig(...),
    datasets=dict(train=dataset),
)
```

Finally, to use Neptune for logging and visualizing your Tune Trials, you can define a LoggerCallback that gets passed into the run configuration of your Tuner. To define one, you need to specify how to create the logger (setup), what's supposed to happen at the beginning and end of a trials (log_trial_start and log_trial_end), and how to log your results (log_trial_result). If you've implemented such a class, for example, NeptuneCallback, you can use it the same way we used the MLflowLogger Callback in "Model Training" on page 218:

```
from ray.tune import logger, tuner
from ray.air.config import RunConfig


class NeptuneCallback(logger.LoggerCallback):
    pass


tuner = tuner.Tuner(
    trainer,
    run_config=RunConfig(callbacks=[NeptuneCallback()])
)
```

While building integrations is not always as difficult as initially perceived, third-party software is a moving target and maintaining integrations can be challenging. Still, you are now aware of three of the most common integration scenarios for new AIR components, and maybe you feel inclined to work on a community-sponsored integration of your favorite tool.

An Overview of Ray's Integrations

Let's summarize all the integrations mentioned in this chapter (and throughout the book) in one concise diagram. In Figure 11-1 we list all integrations available at the time of writing.

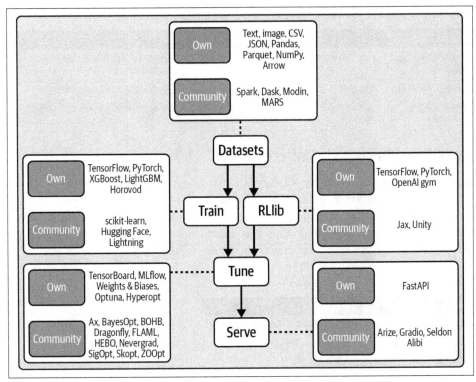

Figure 11-1. The Ray AIR ecosystem summarized

Ray and Other Systems

We've not made any direct comparisons with other systems up to this point, for the simple reason that it makes little sense to compare Ray to something if you don't have a good grasp of what Ray is yet. As Ray is quite flexible and comes with a lot of components, it can be compared to different types of tools in the broader ML ecosystem.

Let's start with a comparison of the more obvious candidates, namely, Python-based frameworks for cluster computing.

Distributed Python Frameworks

If you consider frameworks for distributed computing that offer full Python support and don't lock you into any cloud offering, the current "big three" are Dask, Spark, and Ray. While there are certain technical and context-dependent performance differences between these frameworks, it's best to compare them in terms of the workloads you want to run on them. Table 11-5 compares the most common workload types.

Table 11-5. Comparing workload type support of Ray, Dask, and Spark

Workload type	Dask	Spark	Ray
Structured data processing	First-class support	First-class support	Supported via Ray Datasets and integrations, but not first class
Low-level parallelism	First-class support via tasks	None	First-class support via tasks and actors
Deep learning workloads	Supported, but not first class	Supported, but not first class	First-class support via several ML libraries

Ray AIR and the Broader ML Ecosystem

Ray AIR focuses primarily on *AI compute*, for instance by providing any kind of distributed training via Ray Train, but it's not built to cover every aspect of an AI workload. For instance, AIR chooses to integrate with tracking and monitoring tools for ML experiments, as well as with data storage solutions, rather than providing native solutions. Table 11-6 identifies the ecosystem's complementary components.

Table 11-6. Complementary ecosystem components

Category	Examples
ML tracking and observability	MLflow, Weights & Biases, Arize, etc.
Training frameworks	PyTorch, TensorFlow, Lightning, JAX, etc.
ML feature stores	Feast, Tecton, etc.

On the other side of the spectrum, you can find categories of tools for which Ray AIR can be considered an alternative. For instance, there are many framework-specific toolkits such as TorchX or TFX that tie in tightly with their respective frameworks. In contrast, AIR is framework-agnostic, thereby preventing vendor lock-in, and offers similar tooling.[10]

It's also interesting to briefly touch on how Ray AIR compares to specific cloud offerings. Some major cloud services offer comprehensive toolkits to tackle ML workloads in Python. To name just one, AWS Sagemaker is a great all-in-one package that allows you to connect well with your AWS ecosystem. AIR does not aim to replace tools like SageMaker. Instead, it aims to provide alternatives for compute-intensive components like training, evaluation, and serving.[11]

AIR also represents a valid alternative to ML workflow frameworks such as KubeFlow or Flyte. In contrast to many container-based solutions, AIR offers an intuitive,

---

10 This represents a clear trade-off, as framework-specific tools are highly customized and offer many benefits.

11 Anyscale itself provides a managed service with enterprise features to support building ML applications on top of Ray.

high-level Python API and offers native support for distributed data. Table 11-7 summarizes these alternatives.

Table 11-7. Alternative ecosystem components

Category	Examples
Framework-specific toolkits	TorchX, TFX, etc.
ML workflow frameworks	KubeFlow, Flyte, FBLearner FLow

Sometimes the situation is not as clear-cut, and Ray AIR can be seen or used as both an alternative or a complementary component in the ML ecosystem.

For instance, as open source systems, Ray and AIR in particular can be used within hosted ML platforms such as SageMaker, but you can also build your own ML Platforms with it.[12] Also, as mentioned, AIR can't always compete with dedicated big data processing systems like Spark or Dask, but often Ray Datasets can be enough to suit your processing needs.

As we mentioned in Chapter 10, it is central to AIR's design philosophy to have the ability to express your ML workloads in a single script and execute it on Ray as a single distributed system. Since Ray handles all the task placement and execution on your cluster for you under the hood, there's usually no need to explicitly orchestrate your workloads (or stitch together many complex distributed systems). Of course, this philosophy should not be taken too literally—sometimes you need multiple systems or to split up tasks into several stages. On the other hand, dedicated workflow orchestration tools like Argo or AirFlow can be very useful when used in a complementary fashion.[13] For instance, you might want to run Ray as a step in the Lightning MLOps framework. Table 11-8 provides an overview of components that can be used alongside AIR or for which AIR can be an alternative.

Table 11-8. Ecosystem components that AIR can complement or substitute

Category	Examples
ML platforms	SageMaker, Azure ML, Vertex AI, Databricks
Data processing systems	Spark, Dask
Workflow orchestrators	Argo, AirFlow, Metaflow
MLOps frameworks	ZenML, Lightning

---

12 We'll give you a rough sketch for how to do this in the next section.

13 Ray has a library called *Ray Workflows*, which is currently in alpha. Compared to tools such as AirFlow, Workflows is more low-level but allows you to run durable application workflows natively on Ray. You can find more information about Workflows in the Ray documentation (*https://oreil.ly/XUT7y*).

In case you already have an ML platform, such as Vertex or SageMaker, you can use any subset of Ray AIR to augment your system.[14] In other words, AIR can complement existing ML platforms by integrating with existing pipeline or workflow orchestrators, storage, and tracking services, without requiring a replacement of your entire ML platform.

How to Integrate AIR into Your ML Platform

Now that you have a deeper understanding of the relationship of Ray, and AIR in particular, to other ecosystem components, let's summarize what it takes to build your own ML platform and integrate Ray with other ecosystem components.

The core of your ML system build with AIR consists of a set of Ray Clusters, each responsible for different jobs. For instance, one cluster might run preprocessing, train a PyTorch model, and run inference; another one might simply pick up previously trained models for batch inference and model serving, and so on. You can leverage the Ray Autoscaler to fulfill your scaling needs and could deploy the whole system on Kubernetes with KubeRay. You can then augment this core system with other components as you see fit, for example:

- You might want to add other compute steps to your setup, such as running data-intensive preprocessing tasks with Spark.
- You can use a workflow orchestrator such as AirFlow, Oozie, or SageMaker Pipelines to schedule and create your Ray Clusters and run Ray AIR apps and services. Each AIR app can be part of a larger orchestrated workflow, for instance by tying into a Spark ETL job from the first bullet point.[15]
- You can also create your Ray AIR clusters for interactive use with Jupyter notebooks, for instance hosted by Google Colab or Databricks Notebooks.
- If you need access to a feature store such as Feast or Tecton, Ray Train, Datasets, and Serve have an integration for such tools.[16]
- For experiment tracking or metric stores, Ray Train and Tune provide integration with tools such as MLflow and Weights & Biases.
- You can also retrieve and store your data and models from external storage solutions like S3, as shown.

---

14 We use the term *ML platform* in the broadest sense possible, namely, to signify any system that is responsible for running end-to-end ML workloads.

15 Orchestration of task graphs can be handled entirely within Ray AIR. External workflow orchestrators will integrate nicely but are needed only if running non-Ray steps.

16 The Ray team has built a demo (*https://oreil.ly/Pi3Xf*) of a reference architecture that showcases the Feast integration.

Figure 11-2 puts all the pieces together in one concise diagram.

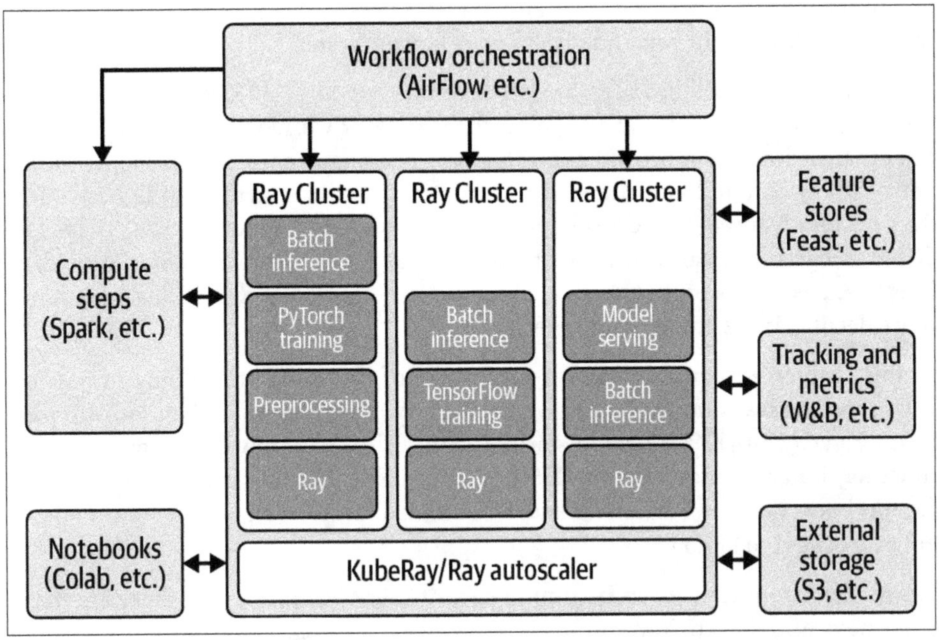

Figure 11-2. Building your own ML platform with Ray's AI Runtime and other components from the ML ecosystem

Where to Go from Here?

We've come a long way from an overview of Ray in Chapter 1 to the discussion of its ecosystem in this one. But as this is an introductory book, we've just touched the proverbial tip of the iceberg of Ray's capabilities. While you should now have a good grasp of the basics of Ray Core and how Ray Clusters work and know when to use AIR and its constituent libraries Datasets, Train, RLlib, Tune and Serve, there's still so much more to learn about each aspect.

To start with, the extensive user guides of Ray Core (*https://oreil.ly/cX6vj*) will give you a much deeper understanding about Ray tasks, actors, and objects; their placement on cluster nodes; and how to handle dependencies for your applications. In particular, you will find interesting patterns and anti-patterns to design your Ray Core programs well and avoid common pitfalls. To learn more about the inner workings of Ray, we recommend reading some of the advanced papers on Ray, such as its architecture whitepaper (*https://oreil.ly/lfW_h*).

An interesting topic we skipped entirely is Ray's tooling around *observability*. The official Ray Observability documentation (*https://oreil.ly/xDWtK*) is a good starting point for this topic. You can learn how to debug and profile your Ray applications there, log information from your Ray Clusters, monitor their behavior, and export important metrics there. You will also find an introduction to the *Ray dashboard* there,[17] which can help you understand your Ray programs.

The focus of this book has been to introduce the core ideas of Ray to ML practitioners and give you practical starting points to tackle your workloads with Ray. However, a topic that deserves more attention than the one chapter we could include in this book is how to build, scale, and maintain Ray Clusters. Currently, the best introduction to advanced Ray Cluster topics is the Ray documentation (*https://oreil.ly/ SGa9w*). There you can learn how to deploy clusters on all major cloud providers, how to scale clusters on Kubernetes, and how to submit Ray jobs to a cluster, in much more detail than we could cover here.

In this chapter we could mention the majority of Ray integrations only in passing. If you want to learn more about Ray's third-party integrations, Ray's Ecosystem page (*https://oreil.ly/5wqYZ*) is a good starting point. Also, it's important to mention that more Ray libraries (*https://oreil.ly/Yt5hX*) are available that simply didn't make the cut for this book, like Ray Workflows and a distributed, drop-in replacement for Python's `multiprocessing` library.

Lastly, if you're interested in becoming part of the Ray community, there are many good ways of doing so. You can join the Ray Slack (*https://oreil.ly/a83QM*) to get in touch with Ray developers and other community members, or join Ray's discussion forum (*https://discuss.ray.io*) to get your questions answered. If you want to help develop Ray, whether contributing to the documentation, adding a new use case, or helping the open source community with new features or bug fixes, you should check out the official contributor guide to Ray (*https://oreil.ly/6AgiE*).

Summary

In this chapter you learned more about Ray's ecosystem, as seen from its AI Runtime. You've seen the full extent of available integrations of Ray AIR libraries and an example of training and serving an ML model using three different integrations: PyTorch for data loading and training, MLflow for logging, and Gradio for serving your model. You should now be able to go out there and run your own AIR experiments, together with all the tools you're already using or intend to use in the future. We've also discussed Ray's limits, how it compares to various related systems, and how you can use Ray with other tools to augment or build out your own ML platforms.

---

17 At the time of this writing, the dashboard is being overhauled. The look and functionality might change drastically, so we didn't include descriptions or screenshots here.

This wraps up this chapter and the book. We hope it piqued your interest in Ray and helped you start your journey with it. The introduction of AIR brought many new features to the Ray ecosystem, and there's certainly more on the road map to be excited about. There's no doubt that you can now dive into any advanced Ray material—maybe you already have an idea about building your first own Ray app.

Index

Symbols

@ray.remote decorator, 27, 36
@serve.batch decorator, 165
@serve.deployment decorator, 19, 161
    tuning replicas and resource allocation for a
    deployment, 164

A

abstractions
    law of leaky abstractions, 2
    provided by Ray, 4
action distribution, 78, 81
action space (RL), 66, 87
    defining for policy server in RLlib environ-
    ment, 92
    parametric action spaces in RLlib, 99
actions (RL), 66
    computing in Python RLlib API, 78
    passed to steps in multi-agent environment,
    88
    probabilities of taking each action, 78
    simplifying assumptions about, 66
actors, 33
    controller actor for Ray Serve deployments,
    161
    converting Simulation class to actor, 62
    GCS storing location of, 39
    mapping data with, support by Datasets, 127
    Ray AIR usage combined with tasks for
    advanced composite workloads, 208
    Ray Datasets, using in distributed batch
    inference, 147
    in Ray Serve deployment, 160
    Ray patterns and anti-patterns for, 47

stateful, accessing data from stateless tasks
    in composite workloads, 212
    use for transformations with state, 210
adapter function, 204
AdvancedEnv, 96
agents (RL), 66, 69
    working with multiple agents, 85-90
        mapping agents to policies, 86, 89
aggregations, support by Ray Datasets, 122, 125
AI (see artificial intelligence)
AI Runtime (see Ray AIR)
"AI and Compute", 3
Airflow, 137
Algorithm class, 75, 82
    accessing all Algorithm instances on work-
    ers, 79
    providing with a curriculum in RLlib, 95
    training in multi-agent environment, 89
AlgorithmConfig class, 75, 82
    methods for categories of common algo-
    rithm properties, 82
AlphaFold, 3
Amazon Web Services (AWS), 192
analyses (Tune), 104, 106, 107
    getting in training of Keras model, 118
Apache Airflow, 137
Apache Arrow, 10
    distributed, use in Ray Datasets, 122
    Plasma project, 37
Apache Hadoop, 121
Apache Spark, 121, 227
API Reference for RLlib algorithms, 83
architecture (Ray)
    overview of components, 40

whitepaper, 38
Arrow for Python, installing, 10
artificial intelligence (AI)
  Ray AIR, 195
  Ray AIR focus on AI compute, 228
  recent developments in, 3
  types of AI workloads AIR enables Ray
    Clusters to run, 209
asynchronous execution, 28
  running dependent tasks asynchronously
    and in parallel, 33
asyncio capabilities (Python), 165, 166
Atari environments (gym), 73
autoscaling
  cluster, 194
  of Ray AIR workloads, 213
  of Ray Serve replicas, 165
  support by Ray Clusters, 5
await syntax (Python), 166
AWS (Amazon Web Services), 192
Azure, 193

B
backends, 20
BaseEnv class, 85
base_model, 79
batch inference, 208
  distributed, using Ray Train, 147
  example in Ray documentation, 124
  using Datasets, 127
batch normalization layers, 143
batch predictors, 203, 208
batch_timeout_wait, 165
Bayesian optimization, 108
bayesian-optimization library, 108
BayesOptSearch, 109
behavior cloning, 98
bias, 110, 114
big data processing tools, 207
big data training, 208
.bind API, instantiating copy of deployment,
  162
binding multiple deployments, 167
binpacking algorithm, 194
blocking, 30
  Datasets operations, 127
blocks
  blocks_per_window parameter, ds.window
    function, 129

in Datasets, 122
  and repartitioning, 125
broadcasting, 168
  in NLP-powered API example, 171

C
callbacks
  configuring for Ray Tune, 111
  LoggerCallback to pass to Tuner run config,
    226
  MLFlowLoggerCallback, 221
  particularly useful methods on, 113
  TuneReportCallback as custom Keras call-
    back, 117
  using to monitor training in Ray Train, 156
cartpole-ppo tuned example, 14
CartPole-v1 environment, 14
categorical variables, 116
chat bots, 157
checkpoints
  Checkpoint class provided by Ray Train,
    141
  checkpoint property of Ray Train Trainers,
    148
  creating from existing, framework-specific
    model, 202
  creating RL algorithm checkpoints, 77
  creation by Ray Tune, 113
  creation by Ray Tune for RLlib, 74
  creation by rllib command, 74
  evaluating trained algorithm from, 15
  exporting trained model as Checkpoint in
    Ray Train, 147
  generated by Ray AIR Trainers or Tuners,
    202
  Ray AIR
    creating batch predictor from, 203
    deploying PredictorDeployment, 204
    Tuners and checkpoints, 201
  reporting model checkpoint, 146
  stateful computations relying on
    checkpoint-based fault tolerance, 212
CIFAR-10 dataset, 216
Clarke's third law, 32
classes
  converting Python classes to actors, 34
  tasks and actors working as distributed ver-
    sions of, 24
classifier, training copies in parallel, 130-133

classify method, 166
classify_batched method, 165
CLI (command-line interface)
    RLlib CLI, running, 73-74
    using Ray Cluster Launcher CLI to deploy
        cluster, 191
client-side batching, 165
clients
    defining policy client in RLlib environment,
        92
    PolicyClient, 90
    Ray Client, 185
cloud computing, 179
    working with cloud clusters, 192-194
        AWS, 192
        other cloud providers, 193
clusters (Ray), 6, 179
    (see also Ray Clusters)
    basic components, 6
    defining ScalingConfig for, 152
    head node processes for cluster manage-
        ment, 39
    starting a local cluster, 24
Codex, 3
columnar format (Arrow), 126
communication in Ray Clusters, 39
composite workloads, 207
    execution of, 211
    fault-tolerance strategies, 212
    Ray AIR usage of actors and tasks for, 208
    stateful actors accessing data from stateless
        tasks, 212
compute_actions method, 78
compute_single_action method, 78
computing over Datasets, 126
concurrent trials (Ray Tune), 111
conditional logic, 169
config argument (tune.run), 115
container images, 189
containers, 186
    environment variables, 189
    KubeRay operations on, 182
    specifying resources for, 189
continuous action space (RL), 66
continuous parameters, 102
controller actor, 161
core layer (Ray), 5
    (see also Ray Core)
CPUs

allocating two per replica in Ray Serve, 164
    specifying for machines in Ray Cluster, 180
cpu_intensive_preprocessing function, 128
CSV files
    reading from S3 bucket into columnar data-
        set, 198
    writing to/reading back from in Ray Data-
        sets, 123
curriculum learning, applying with RLlib, 95-97
CurriculumEnv, 96

D

Dask, 20, 227
    built-in support for Python datetime utilit-
        ies, 143
    Dask on Ray, 216
        example, 135
        using to train PyTorch neural network,
            142
data formats
    flexibility within Datasets, 126
    serialization formats supported by Datasets,
        124
data parallelism, 140
data processing, 9, 121
    (see also Ray Data; Ray Datasets)
    external library integrations with Ray Data-
        sets, 134
    Spark and Dask engines for, 20
    using Ray Datasets library, 10
data science, 8
    Ray AIR and data science workflow, 8
data scientists, 1
    uses of Ray AIR, 196
data shards, 130
    get_data_shard utility, 146
    iterating over with iter_torch_batches, 146
data-parallel training, 144
DataFrames, 126
    converting predictor service payload to, 204
    Dask, 135
        df.compute calls, 136
    Dask on Ray, 142
    external processing systems for, 134
DataParallel (PyTorch), 144
DataParallelTrainer, 225
DatasetPipeline, 12
    creation using ds.repeat function, 130, 132
    Datasets conversion to, 129

Datasets (Ray), 10, 121
    (see also Ray Datasets)
    contents of a Dataset, 122
    creating a Dataset, 123
    transforming datasets, 11
datasets argument (XGBoostTrainer in AIR),
    199
datasets dictionary (Ray Train Trainers), 147
deep learning
    defining model for, 143
    training in, 127
deep learning frameworks, RLlib working with,
    70
Deep Q-Learning, 61, 78
Deep Q-Networks (DQN), 61
    using DQNConfig to define DQN algo-
        rithm, 73
Deepmind's AlphaFold, 3
Dense layers, 80, 117
dependencies
    handling for tasks, 31
    installing for Ray, 7
    ownership versus, 38
    resolution by Raylet scheduler, 37
    resolution for tasks, 40
    task, dynamic execution dealing with, 4
deployment.options API, 164
deployments
    Ray Clusters, 179
    Ray Clusters on Kubernetes, 182-190
    in Ray AIR, 204
        with PredictorDeployment, 205
    in Ray Serve, 160
        binding multiple deployments, 167
        converting Python class to deployment,
            161
        tuning replicas and resources allocated
            to, 164
design philosophy (Ray AIR), 197
design principles (Ray), 4
deterministic environment (in RL), 67
dictionaries
    config dictionary to pass to trainer as
        train_loop_config, 151
    datasets dictionary, Ray Train Trainers, 147
    Python, creating Dataset with schema from,
        126
difficulty, 96
    setting task difficulty, 96

discount_factor, 102
discrete action space (RL), 66, 72
Discrete class, 51
distributed batch inference (Ray Train), 147
distributed computing
    difficulties of, 3
    Ray AI providing universal interface for, 25
    Ray as glue code for distributed workloads,
        4
    Ray Core capabilities, 23
    Ray framework for, 6
distributed model training, 207
    basics, 139-141
    training ML model using Ray Datasets,
        130-133
distributed object transfer, 39
distributed Python frameworks, 227
distributed scheduler, 39
dones, 54
    game considered done, 53
    in RL, 66
        gym.Env having done condition, 72
        in multi-agent environment, 88
        is_done helper to work with multiple
            agents, 87
DQN (see Deep Q-Networks)
DQNConfig object, 75
    multi_agent method, 89
driver, 6, 39
driver deployment, 167
    defining control flow logic for, 174
Dropout rate, 117, 118
ds.repeat function, 130, 132
dynamic execution, 4

E
ecosystem (Ray), 5, 20, 215-233
    building custom integrations, 225-226
    data loading and preprocessing, 216
    distributed Python frameworks, 227
    growth of, 216
    integrating Ray AIR into ML platforms, 230
    model serving, 222-225
    model training, 218-222
    Ray AIR and broader ML ecosystem, 228
    Ray and other systems, 227
    where to go from here, 231
ensembling, 168
entity recognition model, 173

Environment class, 52
    methods implemented for, 53
    using to play 2D maze game, 54
environment method (AlgorithmConfig), 82
environments (in RL), 66
    building a gym environment, 71
    deterministic environment, 67
    environment configuration for RLlib experiments, 84
    specifying for DQNConfig using Python RLlib API, 75
    using gym environment with RLlib, 73-74
    working with RLlib environments, 85-93
        overview of RLlib environments, 85
        policy servers and clients, 90-93
        using multiple agents, 86-90
episodes (in RL), 61, 66
    randomly rolled out in multi-agent environment, 89
epochs
    number of, 146
    train_one_epoch function, 149
    workers in, core logic needed to train on batch of data, 145
estimating arrival times, 158
evaluate command (rllib), 15, 74
evaluating RLlib models in Python API, 77
evaluation results for trained RL algorithm, 15
example command (rllib), 15
experiences (in RL), 66
ExperimentAnalysis object, 107
exploiting or exploring environment in RL, 66, 78
exploration method (AlgorithmConfig), 82
ExternalEnv, 85

F

failures
    in distributed computing, 5
    handling by Ray Datasets, 123
    Ray AIR failure model, 212
FastAPI framework, 163
    parsing input_text query parameter, 163
    Ray Serve's FastAPI for input parsing and output schema, 171
fault tolerance and ownership, 37
feature engineering, 9
featurization

building features using load-dataset function in Ray Train, 142
    in distributed batch inference, 147
fetch_wikipedia_page driver logic, 175
filter function, 11
filtering data, 122
    filter operations in Ray Datasets, 125
fit method (Trainer), 148, 151
fitting to training data, AIR preprocessor, 198
flat_map function, 11
flexibility (Ray), 4, 46
flexible distributed Python for machine learning, 2
fractional resources, 111, 164
frameworks
    framework specification for RLlib algorithms, 79
    third-party training frameworks, 141
functional programming in Ray Datasets, 11
functions
    converting Python function to Ray task, 27
    tasks and actions as distributed versions of, 24
futures, 28, 31
    resolved by ray.get in follow_up_task, 32

G

GCS (Global Control Service), 39
GCS server (Ray)
    failures of, 212
    printing out IP address of, 180
    Unable to connect to GCS at …, 181
get function, 29, 35
get_best_config function, 106
GitHub repository for this book, xvi
Global Control Service (GCS), 39
Global Interpreter Lock (GIL), 27
Google Cloud, 193
GPT-2 model, 18
GPUs
    allocating to Ray Serve deployments, 164
    expense of running online inference services, 159
    specifying for machines in Ray Cluster, 180
    use_gpu flag, 151
gpu_intensive_inference, 128
gradient boosted decision tree frameworks, 148
Gradio, 222-225
greedily choosing an action, 79

grid search, 17, 108
groupby, 122, 125
gRPC, 39
gym library, 71
    building a gym environment, 71
    installing, 13
gym.Env, 73
    VectorEnv wrapper for, 85
GymEnvironment class
    defining multi-agent version of, 86
    implementing a gym.Env, 72
        using with RLlib, 73
gymnasium library, 73

H

Hadoop, 121
head (in deep learning), 80
head node, 6, 39, 180
    address of, NAT and, 181
    connecting every other node in Ray Cluster
        to, 180
head pod, 183, 184
heterogeneity (Ray), 4
hidden units, 118
hierarchy of agents, 85
high availability mode (GCS), 212
HPO (see hyperparameter optimization)
HPO tools, Ray Tune supporting algorithms
    from, 20
HTTP API and driver logic, defining for NLP-
    powered API, 173
HTTP endpoint wrapping an ML model, defin-
    ing, 161-163
HTTP requests, defining logic to handle, 162
HTTP, inference service queryable over, 204
Hugging Face models in Python, 18
Hugging Face pipeline supporting vectorized
    inference, 165
Hugging Face Transformers library, 161, 172
Hyperopt and Optuna integrations (Ray Tune),
    108
HyperOptSearch algorithm, 118
hyperparameter optimization (HPO), 16,
    101-119
    introduction to Ray Tune, 105-115
    machine learning with Ray Tune, 115-119
    Ray AIR Trainers integration with Ray Tune
        for, 200
    Ray Train integration with Ray Tune, 154

tuning hyperparameters, 102-105
    building random search example with
        Ray, 102-104
    difficulty of, 104
hyperparameter tuning, 9
    using Ray Tune, 16
hyperparameters, 102
    depending on other hyperparameters, 114
    specifying ranges for XGBoostTrainer, 154
    TrainingWorker, 132

I

image processing, 167
imitation learning, 98
inference, 127
    multimodel inference graphs, 166-170
    vectorized, 128
        Hugging Face pipeline supporting, 165
init function, 7
installing Ray, 7
integrations, custom, 225-226
integrations, Ray, overview of, 226-231
intermediate scores, 109
ipython interpreter, 7
items, retrieving from database, 25
iter_torch_batches function, 146

J

JAX, 225
jobs, 6
JSON-serializable output (HTTP request), 162
JsonLoggerCallback, 156
Jupyter notebooks, 7

K

Keras, 20, 79
    tuning Keras models in Ray Tune, 116
key-value pairs produced in map phase of Map-
    Reduce, 41
key-value store (GCS), 39
kubectl, running Ray programs with, 184
KubeRay project, 182
Kubernetes, 8, 41, 176
    Ray Cluster deployment on, 182-190
        configuring KubeRay, 187-188
        configuring logging for KubeRay, 189
        interacting with the KubeRay cluster,
            184-186

KubeRay operator, 182
setting up first KubeRay cluster, 183

L

label_column argument (XGBoostTrainer in AIR), 199
lambda functions, 126
latency
ML services online and applications, 158
online inference and, 157
law of leaky abstractions, 2
layers in Ray, 5
leasing worker processes to task owners, 39
libraries (Ray), 5
data science libraries, 8
dedicated libraries for machine learning steps, 9
model training, 12
LightGBM, 148
LightGBMTrainer, 148
lineage reconstruction, 212
list comprehensions, 26
loading data, 216
in distributed batch inference, 147
loading model in Ray Train, 142
training and validation data for training workers, 146
load_dataset function (Ray Train), 142, 146
local clusters, 6
LoggerCallback interface, 156
logging
configuring for KubeRay, 189
trial results to MLFlow, 216
using Neptune for, 226
loss, 146

M

machine learning (ML)
basic pipelines, Ray Train components used in, 141
broadcasting to multiple models in parallel, 168
building ML pipeline using Ray Datasets, 136-138
conditional logic for control flow, 169
data science processes involved in, 9
distributed training of ML models, 130
flexible distributed Python for, 2
integrating Ray AIR into ML platforms, 230

models are compute intensive, 158
models not useful in isolation, 159
multiple models in NLP-powered API example, 170
online inference interacting with ML models, 157
performance for, Ray Datasets, 121
Ray AIR and broader ML ecosystem, 228
Ray AIR as umbrella for all other Ray ML libraries, 195
Ray AIR uses by ML engineers, 196
recent developments in, 3
reinforcement learning, 50
tackling workloads with single script run by single system, 197
training-serving skew in deployments, 153
using Ray Tune, 115-119
tuning Keras models, 116
using RLlib with Tune, 115
machine learning frameworks, Ray Train Trainers integration with, 148
map function, 11
performing custom transformations on Datasets, 126
mapping, 122
Datasets support for, using Ray actors, 127
mapping model across whole dataset, 147
mapping batches, 217
MapReduce
example using Ray, 41-47
mapping and shuffling document data, 43
reducing word count, 45
running MapReduce on distributed corpus of documents, 42
MARL (multi-agent reinforcement learning) problem
RLlib support for, 90
training, 89
max_batch_size, 165
max_depth parameter (XGBoost model), 201
maze problem, setting up, 50-55
memory
AIR memory management, 211
distributed, 39
efficient usage by Ray Datasets, 123
Raylet object store managing shared memory pool, 37
specifying for trials in Ray Tune, 111

metrics
    configuring for report in Ray Tune, 111
    getting best hyperparameters found, 106
    optimizing in BayesOptSearch, 109
    passing RLlib metrics to Ray Tune, 115
    passing to Ray Tune scheduler, 110
migration fatigue, 196
min, 125
MinMaxScaler, 154
ML (see machine learning)
ML platforms, 230
    hosted, use of Ray and AIR in, 229
    integrating Ray AIR into, 230
MLFlow, 156, 221
MLFlowLogger, 216
MLFLowLoggerCallback, 156, 221
MNIST data, 116
mode
    getting best hyperparameters found, 106
    passing to Ray Tune scheduler, 110
    specifying for trials in Ray Tune, 112
model parallelism, 140
model serving, 9, 222-225
    using Ray Serve, 18
model training, 9, 218-222
    distributed model training basics, 139-141
    example, training copies of a classifier in
        parallel using Datasets, 130-133
    parallelizing with Ray, 64
    Ray libraries for, 12
        Ray RLlib, 12
    training reinforcement model, 59-62
model.state_value_head.summary method, 80
models
    accessing state in Python RLlib API, 78
    checkpoints as Ray AIR native model
        exchange, 202
    customizing for RLlib experiments, 80
    in Deep-Q learning used in DQN, 79
    defining deep learning model, 143
    distributed training of ML models, 130
    NLP, 172
    in Ray Train Checkpoints, 147
    state_action_table of policy, 66
    tuning Keras models in Ray Tune, 116
Moore's law, 3
MultiAgentEnv, 85
    defining with two agents, 86
multimodel inference graphs, 166-170

broadcasting pattern, 168
conditional logic pattern, 169
core Ray Serve feature, binding multiple
    deployments, 167
in NLP-powered API example, 170
pipelining pattern, 167
multiple agents (RL), 66
multi_agent method (AlgorithmConfig), 82

N
NAT (Network Address Translation), 181
natural language processing (NLP), 170
nc tool, 181
Neptune, 225, 226
Network Address Translation (NAT), 181
neural networks, 78
    in Deep Q-Networks (DQN), 61
    defining and training in Ray Train, 141
    FarePredictor PyTorch network, 143
    parallelizing computations to speed up
        training, 140
New York City taxi trips, predicting big tips in
    (example), 141
NLP (natural language processing), 170
NLP-powered API, building (example),
    170-176
    architecture for NLP pipeline to summarize
        Wikipedia articles, 171
    fetching content and preprocessing, 172
    HTTP handling and driver logic, 173
    NLP models, 172
    putting it all together, 175-176
nmap tool, 181
nodes
    checking whether each port can be reached
        from, 181
    connecting to head node in Ray Cluster, 180
    stopping Ray processes on, 182
    unable to access port and IP address speci-
        fied, 181
nonblocking calls, using Ray wait function for,
    30
numpy.square optimized implementation, 126
num_gpus, 164
num_replicas, 164, 173

O
object references, 32
    remote Ray tasks returning, 28

object store, 24
    component of Raylets, 36
    putting database in, 30
    putting policy into, 63
    using with put and get, 29
objective, 103
    converting to Ray task, 103
    stopping Ray Tune objective analysis, 114
objective functions, 16, 103
    defining, 105
    defining to compute intermediate scores,
        109
    Keras objective function in Tune, 117
objects
    distributed object transfer, 39
    equality with tasks and actors in Ray Core,
        35
    Ray tasks as primary means of creating, 28
    sharing between driver and workers or
        between workers, 29
    spilling and recovery in Ray Datasets, 123
observability, 231
observation space (RL), 66, 87
    defining for policy server in RLlib environ-
        ment, 92
    in gym environment, 72
observations (in RL), 52
    computing actions for given observations,
        78
    in multi-agent environment, 88
    taken in by DQN model, 80
    transforming to form expected by model, 81
offline data
    Python API for in RLlib, 99
    working with, 97
offline_data method (AlgorithmConfig), 82
online inference, 157-159
    building services with Ray Serve, 160
        (see also Ray Serve)
    differences in serving ML models, 158-159
        compute intensive ML models, 158
        ML models not useful in isolation, 159
    pipeline in NLP-powered API example, 171
    use cases, 157
online serving, 208
online serving execution, 211
OpenAI
    Codex, 3
    'AI and Compute", 3

ownership, 37
    dependencies versus, 38
ownership table, 37

P
Pandas DataFrames, 126
Pandas on Ray, 20
parallel execution of dependent tasks, 33
parallelization
    data-parallel training, 144
    parallelizing code, Ray Train, 141
parametric action spaces, 99
Parquet data, 124, 126
    Dataset transformations on, 128
partitioning, 122
    blocks and repartitioning in Datasets, 125
payload (predictor service), 204
performance, measuring for Ray task, 28
pipelined execution, 212
pipelines
    building ML pipeline using Ray Datasets,
        136-138
    Dataset, 127-130
    DatasetPipeline, 12
    online inference, 171
pipelining
    multimodel pattern in ML applications, 167
    using on Ray Datasets, 210
Plasma, 37
pods
    head and worker pods on KubeRay cluster,
        183
    interacting with KubeRay cluster head pod,
        184
    Ray Cluster, configuring on KubeRay, 188
PodTemplate, 182
policies (RL), 66
    accessing state of in Python RLlib API, 78
    in multi-agent environment
        mapping agents to policies, 89
    in multi-agent RL environments, 86
    working with policy servers and clients in
        RLlib environment, 90-93
        defining a client, 92
        defining a server, 91
Policy class, 56
    replacement in future RLlib release, 79
    state_action_table, 57
    updating values in state_action_table, 59

PolicyClient, 92
PolicyServerInput object, 91
PredictorDeployment class, 204
predictors, 141, 224
    batch, 203
.predict_pipelined function, 147
prepare_model function, 146
preprocessing, 216
    content in NLP-powered API example, 172
    in distributed batch inference, 147
    using load_dataset function in Ray Train,
        142
    using Ray Train, 153
preprocessors
    built into Ray Train, 153
    choosing between for Ray Train integration
        with Ray Tune, 154
    provided by Ray Train, 141
    Ray AIR, 198
        different types available, 199
        specifying for XGBoostTrainer, 199
    in Ray Train Checkpoints, 147
probabilities of taking actions, 78
Prometheus, 182
Proximal Policy Optimization (PPO) algo-
    rithm, 14
put function, 28, 35
    placing data into distributed object store, 29
Pydantic, 173
PyGame, installing, 14
Python
    datetime utilities, Dask support for, 143
    distributed computing frameworks, 227
    Global Interpreter Lock, 27
    Ray for data science community, 2
    RLlib API (see RLlib Python API)
    use for data science, 1
    versions and support for Ray, 7
    Zen of, 43
Python-first frameworks, 2
PyTorch, 70, 79
    backing Ray RLlib and Train libraries, 20
    DataParallel, 144
    loading and transforming dataset using, 216
    loss_function and batch_loss, 146
    migrating existing model to Ray Train, 148,
        150
    torchvision extension, 216

training PyTorch neural network using
    Dask on Ray, 142

Q

Q-Learning algorithm, 59-61, 66
Q-values, 66, 78
    (see also state-action values)
    getting for DQN models, 81

R

random number generator (RNG), 169
random.uniform sampler (numpy), 114
randomly sampling hyperparameters, 102
Ray
    about, 2
    architecture whitepaper, 28
    design principles, 4
    ecosystem, 20, 215
        (see also ecosystem)
    installing, 7
    origins of, 2
    relating to other systems, 41
Ray AIR (AI Runtime), 5, 144, 195-213
    as umbrella for current Ray data science
        libraries, 10
    and data science workflow, 8
    Datasets and preprocessors, 198
    extensibility, 196
    key AIR concepts by example, 197-207
        batch predictors, 203
        from data loading to inference with AIR,
            197
        Trainers, 199
        Tuners and checkpoints, 201
    Ray ecosystem and beyond, 215-233
        AIR and the broader ML ecosystem, 228
        building custom integrations, 225-226
        data loading and preprocessing, 216
        distributed Python frameworks, 227
        ecosystem components AIR can comple-
            ment or substitute, 229
        growing ecosystem, 216
        integrating AIR into ML platforms, 230
        model serving, 222-225
        model training, 218-222
        Ray and other systems, 227
        where to go from here, 231
    third-party integrations, 195
    uses of, 195

workloads suited for, 207-213
  AIR failure model, 212
  AIR memory management, 211
  autoscaling AIR workloads, 213
  workload execution, 209-211
Ray Client, 7
  using to connect to KubeRay cluster, 185
Ray Clusters, 6, 8, 179-194, 230
  deployment on Kubernetes, 182-190
    configuring KubeRay, 187-188
    configuring logging for KubeRay, 189
    interacting with the KubeRay cluster,
      184-186
    setting up first KubeRay cluster, 183
  manually creating, 180-182
  types of AI workloads AIR enables running
    on, 209
  using Ray Cluster Launcher, 190-192
    configuring your Ray Cluster, 190
    interacting with a Ray Cluster, 191
    using Cluster Launcher CLI, 191
  working with cloud clusters, 192-194
    AWS, 192
    Azure, 193
    Google Cloud, 193
Ray Core, 8, 23-47
  building your first distributed application,
    49-67
    building a simulation, 55-58
    building the app, 62-64
    introduction to reinforcement learning,
      49-50
    setting up simple maze problem, 50-55
  first example using Ray API, 25-35
    from classes to actors, 33
    functions and remote Ray tasks, 27-29
    handling task dependencies, 31
    using object store with put and get, 29
    using wait function for nonblocking
      calls, 30
  introduction to, 24-25
  major API methods of, 35
  simple MapReduce example with, 41-47
    mapping and shuffling document data,
      43
    reducing word count, 45
  understanding Ray system components,
    36-40
    distributed scheduling and execution, 39

head node, 39
scheduling and executing work on a
  node, 36-39
Ray Data, 121
  allowing sharing of in-memory data across
    parallel training runs, 130
  ecosystem integrations allowing better data
    processing, 134
Ray Datasets, 9, 121-138, 122-133
  basics, 123-126
    blocks and repartitioning, 125
    built-in transformations, 124
    creating a dataset, 123
    reading and writing to storage, 123
    schemas and data formats, 125
  benefits of, 121, 123
  building ML pipeline, 136-138
  computing over Datasets, 126
  data processing with, 10
  Dataset pipelines, 127-130
  ecosystem, 218
  example of capabilities, 216
  example, training copies of a classifier in
    parallel, 130-133
  external library integrations, 134-136
  loading data into Ray AIR, 198
  loading Snowflake data into, 225
  scheduling strategy, 209
  use by Ray AIR Trainers, 200
  use for stateless computation, 208
  use with Ray Train to implement complete
    ML workflow as single application, 148
  using in distributed batch inference, 147
Ray Job Submission server, 185, 191
Ray RLlib, 10, 69-99
  advanced concepts, 93-99
    applying curriculum learning, 95-97
    other advanced topics, 98
    working with offline data, 97
  configuring experiments, 82-84
    environment configuration, 84
    resource configuration, 83
    rollout worker configuration, 83
  ecosystem, 222
  getting started with, 71-81
    building a gym environment, 71
    running RLlib CLI, 73-74
    using RLlib Python API, 75
  overview, 70

reinforcement learning with, 12
using with Ray Tune, 115
working with environments, 85-93
    overview of RLlib environments, 85
    policy servers and clients, 90-93
    using multiple agents, 86-90
Ray runtime started, 180
Ray Serve, 10, 158, 160-177
    deploying inference service to query over
        HTTP, 204
    ecosystem, 224
    end-to-end example, building NLP-powered
        API, 170-176
        defining HTTP API and driver logic, 173
        fetching content and preprocessing, 172
        NLP models, 172
        putting it all together, 175-176
    GradioServer, 222
    introduction to, 160-170
        architectural overview, 160
        defining basic HTTP endpoint, 161-163
        multimodel inference graphs, 166-170
        purpose-built features for compute-
            heavy ML models, 160
        request batching, 165
        scaling and resource allocation, 163
    serving model using Gradio on, 216
Ray Serve library
    model serving with, 18
ray start --head … command, 191
ray stop command, 182
Ray Train, 10, 122, 139-156
    ecosystem, 222
    introduction to, 141-147
        distributed batch inference, 147
        distributed training with Train, 144
        example, predicting big tips in NYC taxi
            rides, 141
        Train components used in basic ML
            pipelines, 141
    loading, preprocessing, and featurization,
        142
    standard PyTorch model and training loop
        to leverage in, 216
    support for gradient boosted decision tree
        frameworks, 148
    Trainers in, 148-156
        integrating Trainers with Ray Tune, 154

        migrating to Ray Train with minimal
            code changes, 150
        preprocessing with Ray Train, 153
        scaling out Trainers, 152
        using callbacks to monitor training, 156
    using to scale out JAX model, 225
Ray Tune, 10, 101, 122
    configuring and running, 110-115
        callbacks and metrics, 111
        checkpoints, stopping, and resuming,
            113
        custom and conditional search spaces,
            114
        specifying resources, 111
    ecosystem, 222
    how it works, 106-110
        integration with other HPO frameworks,
            108
        overview of components, 106
        schedulers, 109
        search algorithms, 108
    hyperparameter tuning with, 16
    integrating Ray Train Trainers with, 154
    introduction to, 105-106
    machine learning with, 115-119
        tuning Keras models, 116
        using RLlib with Tune, 115
    MLFlowLogger shipped with, 216
    Ray AIR Trainers integration with, 200
    supporting algorithms from notable HPO
        tools, 20
    use by RLlib, 74
Ray Workflows, 229
ray.get function, 28, 36
    using object store with, 29
ray.init method, 36, 180
ray.put method, 36
ray.remote function, 28, 34, 36
ray.wait function, 36
RayCluster, 182
Raylets, 36
    scheduler, 37
reading from and writing to storage (Ray Data-
    sets), 123
read_csv utility, 198
recommendation systems, 157
    challenges around the edges, 159
recovery, 5

rectified linear unit (ReLU) activation function, 118

Redis instances, remote, using, 180

reduce phase (MapReduce), 42
  reducing word count, 45

reinforcement learning
  Q-Learning algorithm, 61
  terminology recap, 66-67
  training a model, 59-62
  using Ray RLlib, 12

relational data processing systems, integration with Ray, 134

remote function, 35

remote Ray tasks, functions and, 27-29

rendering RL environments, 72, 84
  modifying in multi-agent environment, 89

repartitioning, 125, 128

repeat function (Datasets), 132

replicas (Ray Serve), 160
  FastAPI server running in each, 163
  instantiating replica of deployment, 162
  setting for text summarization model, 173
  tuning for a deployment, 164

reporting, using Ray AIR session, 144

request batching, 159, 165

requests library, 19

requests package, 160
  using to test sentiment classifier, 162

resets (RL environments), 72

resource management
  by head node, 39
  by Raylet scheduler, 37

resources
  allocation in Ray Serve, 163
    more expressive policies, 164
  compute resources used by a Trainer, 152
  configuring for KubeRay cluster, 189
  configuring for RLlib experiments, 83
  idle, naive Dataset computation leading to, 128
  specifying for Ray Tune trials, 111
  viewing use by Ray Cluster, 24

resources method (AlgorithmConfig), 82

responses (HTTP), defining schema for, 173

ResultGrid (Tuner API), 107

results
  human-readable output of training results, 76

state and training results of RLlib DQN algorithm, 76
  training, writing to directory, 74

resuming Ray Tune runs, 113

rewards (RL), 66
  in multi-agent environment, 88

RISELab (UC Berkeley), 3

RL (see Ray RLlib; reinforcement learning)

RLlib algorithms page (Ray documentation), 70

rllib command-line tool, 13

rllib evaluate command, 74

RLlib Python API, 75
  accessing policy and model status, 78
  saving, loading, and evaluating RLlib models, 77
  training RLlib algorithms, 75-76

rllib train command, 73

RLlib Training API documentation, 84

RNG (see random number generator)

robotics, 158

rollouts (in RL), 66
  finished rollouts used to update policy, 64
  rollout worker configuration for RLlib experiments, 83
  rollouts method of Python RLlib API, 75

rollouts method (AlgorithmConfig), 82

RunConfig, 155, 201

runs (Tune), 108

Rust compiler, installing, 18

S

sampling functions (Tune), 106

saving RLlib algorithms in Python API, 77

scalability
  Ray, 5
  Ray Datasets, 123

ScaleStrategy, 182

scaling
  online inference services of ML models, 159
  in Ray Serve, 163
  scaling out Trainers in Ray Train, 152

ScalingConfig
  adapting memory in, 212
  defining for XGBoostTrainer in Ray AIR, 199
  Ray AIR Trainers, 200
  Ray Train Trainers, 147, 151
  specifying parameters of cluster nodes, 152

schedulers

Dask scheduler packaged with Ray, 135
Ray Tune, 107, 109
    combining with search algorithms, 110
scheduling and executing work on a node,
    36-37
    distributed scheduling and execution, 39
schemas, 125
    defining for HTTP responses, 173
scikit-learn, 218
    installing locally, 131
    SGDClassifier algorithm, 131
scores (HPO), 103
    formulating flexible stopping condition for,
      114
    intermediate scores, 109
    retuning as dictionary, 105
search algorithms, 104, 108
    custom, HyperOptSearch, 118
    support by Tune, 107
search example (random), building with Ray,
    102-104
search spaces, 104, 104, 106
    custom and conditional, 114
    defining with random library, 102
    defining with tune.uniform, 105
searchers (see search algorithms)
self-driving cars, 158
sentiment classifier model, 161, 171
    modifying to do server-side batching, 165
    POSITIVE and NEGATIVE output, 162
    scaling out to multiple replicas and adjust-
      ing resource allocation, 164
    testing using requests package, 162
    use in NLP-powered API example, 172
sequential TensorFlow Keras model, 202
serialization formats, 124
serve run app:scaled_deployment command,
    164
serve run CLI command, 162, 171
serve.run, 162
server-side batching, 165
"Serving RLlib Models" tutorial, 70
sessions
    Ray, 146
    Ray AIR, 144
SGDClassifier algorithm, 131
    TrainingWorker wrapper for, 132
sharding data, 130, 220
    get_data_shard utility, 146

shared pool of memory, 37
shuffle phase (MapReduce), 42
shuffling data, 42, 43
simplicity, 4
Simulation class, 56
    converting to Ray actor, 62
    implementation of, 57
SimulationActor instances, 63
simulations
    impossibility of faithfully simulating some
      physical systems, 67
Snowflake, 225
soft state, 207
sort operations (Ray Datasets), 125
sorting data, 122
Spark, 20, 121, 227
speed (Ray), 5
StandardScaler, 154, 198
state
    accessing for model and policy in Python
      RLlib API, 78
    in RL environment, 66
state transition probabilities, 67
state-action values (RL), 66, 78, 80, 102
    and state-action functions, 80
stateful computations, 33, 207
    relying on checkpoint-based fault tolerance,
      212
stateful execution, 210
stateful workloads, autoscaling, 213
stateless computations, 207
stateless execution, 209
stateless tasks of Ray AIR, 208
stateless workloads, autoscaling, 213
state_action_table (Policy example), 57
    updating values in, 59
step method, 53
steps (in RL), 66, 72
    actions passed to in multi-agent environ-
      ment, 88
stochastic gradient descent, 131
stops
    stopping Ray processes on a node, 182
    stopping Ray Tune run, 113
sum, 125
synchronous execution
    approach by distributed training algorithms,
      130
    Datasets operations, 127

systems related to Ray, 41

T

task graphs, 135
task scheduler, 36
tasks, 6
  converting objective to, 103
  execution of, 40
  handling task dependencies, 31
  modifying existing task to incorporate actor, 34
  Ray AIR usage with actors for advanced composite workloads, 208
  Ray patterns and anti-patterns for, 47
  setting difficulty for, 96
  stateless data from, accessed by stateful actors in composite workloads, 212
TaskSettableEnv, 96
TBXLoggerCallback, 156
TensorBoard, 156
TensorFlow, 70, 79
  backing Ray RLlib and Train libraries, 20
  installing, 12
TensorFlow Keras model (sequential), 202
text summarization model, 173
TorchTrainer, 146
  instantiating and working with, 151
  wrapping in a Tuner, 216
torchvision, 216
TPE (Tree-structured Parzen Estimator) searcher, 108
train command (rllib), 73
trainables, 106
  RLlib trainers passed as argument to tune.run, 115
Trainers, 141
  more on Trainers in Ray Train, 148-156
    integrating Trainers with Ray Tune, 154
    migrating to Ray Train, 150
    preprocessing with Ray Train, 153
    scaling out Trainers, 152
    Trainer classes in Ray Train sharing common interface, 148
    using callbacks to monitor training, 156
  Ray AIR
    checkpoints generated by, 202
    Tuners working with, 201, 202
  Ray Train
    datasets dictionary for, 147

ScalingConfig fo, 147
  specifying for Ray AIR, 199
  TorchTrainer, 146
training algorithms, impressive range in RLlib, 99
training frameworks
  third-party, Trainers as wrappers for, 141
training method (AlgorithmConfig), 82
training RLlib algorithms, 75-76
  in multi-agent environment, 89
training-serving skew, 153
TrainingWorker, 131
training_loop, 149
train_loop_config, 151
train_loop_per_worker function, 151
train_one_epoch helper function, 149
transformations
  columns into format used as features in ML model, 143
  custom, performing on Datasets, 126
  dataset, using Ray Datasets, 11
  Ray Datasets, 122
    built-in transformations, 124
    on Parquet data, 128
transformers package, 160
trial schedulers, 109
trials (HPO), 104, 106
  specifying resources for in Ray Tune, 111
Tune (see Ray Tune)
tune function, 17
Tune's scheduler compatibility matrix, 110
tune.report function, 110
tune.run function, 17, 106, 108
  passing RLlib arguments to, 115
tune.samle_from function, 114
TuneConfig, 201
tuned examples, 13
Tuner API, 107, 154
TuneReportCallback, 117
Tuners, 201
  AIR Tuners working with AIR Trainers, 202
tune_objective function, 105
tuples, 32

U

UC Berkeley, RISELab, 3
Unable to connect to GCS at …, 181
unions, 124

V

value function head, 80
vectorized computations, 126, 159, 165
    using Serve's batching API, 172
    vectorized inference, 128
vectorized inference, 165
video-processing pipelines, 158
volume mounts, 189

W

wait function, 36
    using for nonblocking calls, 30
weights, 102, 110
    getting for RLlib models in Python API, 79
    using random.uniform sampler from
        numpy, 114
Wikipedia articles, summarizing (see NLP-
    powered API, building)
Wikipedia package on PyPI, 172
window function, 12
windows, 129
worker nodes, 6
    scheduling and executing work on, 36
        (see also Raylets)
    system components comprising, 38
worker pods, 183
worker processes, 6
    fault tolerance and ownership, 37
    leasing to task owners, 39
workers

defining TrainingWorker to train classifier
    copy, 131
RLlib, getting policy and model weights
    from, 79
rollout, 76
rollout worker configuration for RLlib
    experiments, 83
training, loading training and validation
    data for, 146
training, specifying number of, 151
workload execution (Ray AIR), 209-211
    composite workload execution, 211
    online serving execution, 211
    stateful execution, 210
    stateless execution, 209
workload type support, Spark, Dask, and Ray,
    227

X

XGBoost, 148
XGBoostPredictor, 203, 204
XGBoostTrainer, 148
    creating and specifying hyperparameter
        ranges, 154
    defining for Ray AIR, 199
        wrapping instance with Tuner, 201

Z

Zen of Python, 43

About the Authors

Max Pumperla is a data science professor and software engineer located in Hamburg, Germany. He's an active open source contributor, maintainer of several Python packages, author of machine learning books, and speaker at international conferences. He currently works as a software engineer at Anyscale. As head of product research at Pathmind Inc. he developed reinforcement learning solutions for industrial applications at scale using Ray RLlib, Serve, and Tune. Max has been a core developer of DL4J at Skymind, helped grow and extend the Keras ecosystem, and is a Hyperopt maintainer.

Edward Oakes is a software engineer and team lead at Anyscale, where he leads the development of Ray Serve and is one of the top open source contributors to Ray. Prior to Anyscale, he was a graduate student in the EECS department at UC Berkeley.

Richard Liaw is a software engineer at Anyscale, working on open source tools for distributed machine learning. He is on leave from the PhD program at the Computer Science Department at UC Berkeley, advised by Joseph Gonzalez, Ion Stoica, and Ken Goldberg.

Colophon

The animal on the cover of *Learning Ray* is a marbled electric ray (*Torpedo marmorata*), also known as a torpedo ray. Marbled electric rays can be found in the eastern Atlantic Ocean from Africa to Norway, as well as in the Mediterranean Sea. They are bottom dwellers, preferring to live in shallow to moderately deep water in rocky reefs, seagrass beds, and muddy flats.

Marbled electric rays are mottled brown and black, camouflaging them in the muddy waters where they hide during the day. At night, the rays emerge to hunt and forage for small fish such as gobies, mullet, mackerel, and damselfish. These rays can grow up to 2 feet long, expand their jaws to swallow fish larger than their mouths, and kill with an electric charge of up to 200 volts.

Because these rays are capable of electrocution, they have few natural predators. Many of the animals on O'Reilly covers are endangered; all of them are important to the world.

The cover illustration is by Karen Montgomery, based on an antique line engraving from Lydekker's *Royal Natural History*. The cover fonts are Gilroy Semibold and Guardian Sans. The text font is Adobe Minion Pro; the heading font is Adobe Myriad Condensed; and the code font is Dalton Maag's Ubuntu Mono.

O'REILLY®

Learn from experts.
Become one yourself.

Books | Live online courses
Instant Answers | Virtual events
Videos | Interactive learning

Get started at oreilly.com.